# Wills

## A Practical Guide

### Second Edition

# Wills
## A Practical Guide

### Second Edition

Lesley King and
Peter Gausden

WS
&H

Wildy, Simmonds and Hill Publishing

© Lesley King and Peter Gausden, 2019

ISBN: 9780854902743

British Library Cataloguing in Publication Data

A catalogue record for this book is available from the British Library

The right of Lesley King and Peter Gausden to be identified as the authors of this Work has been asserted by them in accordance with sections 77 and 78 of the Copyright, Designs and Patents Act 1988.

First edition 2011

This edition published in 2019 by

Wildy, Simmonds & Hill Publishing
Wildy & Sons Ltd
Lincoln's Inn Archway
Carey Street
London WC2A 2JD
www.wildy.com


Typeset by Heather Jones, North Petherton, Somerset.
Printed in Great Britain by Ashford, Unit 600, Fareham Reach, Fareham Road, Gosport, Hampshire PO13 0FW.

# Contents

# Preface

'The wreck of the Testator's estate is already total, there can be nothing left in it for anyone', per Sir Andrew Morritt in *Perrins v Holland and others* [2010] EWCA Civ 840 at [37].

Litigation over disputed wills is sadly on the rise. The costs of such litigation can, as Sir Andrew Morritt said, easily swallow up the whole of modest to moderate estates. Just as bad as the financial waste are the irreconcilable rifts and misery that bitter family disputes can cause.

This book explains what is involved in making a will, with particular reference to avoiding those issues which often give rise to litigation. It is intended for people who know a little about making wills, but need to know more. Our hope is that it will help readers avoid costly mistakes.

The book is a concise guide to what is involved in making a will. It is not a precedent book as we assume readers will have access to a suitable bank of precedents once a decision has been made as to the provisions required. However, the text is supported by many examples of typical precedent clauses which we hope will be useful as illustrations of the points made in the text.

We have provided a description of the law and practice of will making and described what wills can do – and also what they cannot; for example, there is a section describing property that people often believe can be left by will but which, in fact, cannot.

This is a practical book and the focus is on avoiding problems and on best practice.

To that end we have included sections on testamentary capacity and related issues, particularly those involving the elderly, which may affect the validity of the will.

There are also sections on aspects of will making which often cause problems for practitioners, including gifts for the care of pets, gifts to employees, gifts of business interests, mutual (as distinguished from mirror) wills, testamentary options, burial and other requests and dealing with property overseas.

We deal briefly with the inheritance tax implications of will planning and drafting along with common strategies for dealing with family wealth by making best use of exemptions and reliefs, the transferable nil rate band and the residence nil rate band. There are illustrative case studies of tax-efficient wills appropriate for testators with common will making problems. Clearly, in a book of this size it would be foolish to attempt to deal with sophisticated tax-saving schemes for the super-rich and we have not done so.

The book also deals with the problems caused if the existence of a will is uncertain and so there is a helpful section on storing and locating a will.

As anyone who deals with will drafting on a regular basis will know, taking instructions is where things can all go wrong. We have therefore included a chapter considering practical issues when taking instructions (and also at execution).

The final chapter offers tips on avoiding common drafting pitfalls.

In any parts of the text where we use the masculine pronoun, this of course also includes the feminine.

The law is stated as at 31 May 2019.

*Lesley King*
*Peter Gausden*

# 1 Wills and Other Death Dispositions

## 1.1 Why make a will?

The most obvious reason for a person to make a will is to avoid any questions of inheritance being decided by the rules of intestacy (see para 1.4), which may apply in a general and impersonal fashion. However, a practitioner advising a client might also consider the following:

(a) A will is a flexible instrument which permits the person making it (the testator) to make more varied and complex provision for the testator's family and dependants (e.g. by way of a will trust) than that which is offered under the intestacy rules. So even though the intestacy rules may ultimately benefit the same people that the testator wants to name in the will, the testator can determine the terms and conditions upon which they inherit. Chapters 13–15 look at the types of dispositive provisions typically found in wills.

(b) Testators may select their own executors and trustees to carry out the terms of their wills, whereas, on an intestacy, the choice of administrators to do a similar job is determined by the court under rule 22 of the Non-Contentious Probate Rules 1987 (NCPR 1987) (as amended). The appointment of executors and trustees is considered further in Chapter 11.

(c) A will may incorporate additional powers for its executors and trustees to facilitate the administration of the estate and satisfy further demands of the testator. This may be of particular relevance if, for example, the will sets up a trust for children or the estate comprises a business which needs to be managed or sold during the administration. Such additional powers can also be to the advantage of the beneficiaries. The provision of powers for executors and trustees is considered further in Chapters 18 and 19.

(d) A will may appoint a guardian for the testator's minor children. This can be an important issue for those with young children. The appointment of guardians is considered in Chapter 12.

(e) There may be tax advantages in a carefully drafted will, particularly if tax planning through a will is considered in conjunction with wider lifetime tax and financial planning. The larger the estate, the more likely it is that this will be a significant issue (see, further, Chapter 17, which considers the planning of a tax-efficient will).

(f)    A will may offer an opportunity to plan for future care fees or for a disabled beneficiary in cases where conferring an absolute entitlement on a beneficiary might prejudice entitlement to state funding and benefits.

(g)    A will offers the testator some certainty and peace of mind. Looked at from the point of view of the beneficiaries, it is also a positive statement of generosity on the part of the testator.

Appendix 1 contains an example of a family will with a supporting commentary. This illustrates the usual layout, structure and content of a will, and serves as an introduction to some of the terms that are used in this book.

## 1.2    What wills can give away

As most people might expect, a will can generally dispose of any property which a person owns. Subject to what is said at para 1.3, a person can, by will, not just give away tangible assets, such as land and personal chattels, but also dispose of intangibles, such as contractual rights, benefits and other interests which are capable of transmission or assignment to another. Furthermore, the fact that a will does not come into effect until death means that it can dispose of all property which is owned when someone dies and not just that owned when the will was made.

However, whilst a will is an important step to ensuring that a person's last wishes are met, not everything that someone apparently 'owns' can be left by will. It is vital for anyone advising on the terms of a will to be made fully aware of the testator's property interests. Where necessary, any competing claims to ownership must be properly investigated, not just to ensure that an asset is capable of being dealt with in the will, but also to consider what impact the nature of the testator's interest might have on any prospective inheritance tax liability.

## 1.3    What wills cannot give away

It may be stating the obvious, but a will can dispose only of property that is capable of being given away by will.

Certain types of property cannot be given away by will and so pass on death according to different rules, irrespective of whether a person makes a will or not.

Such property may be divided into two categories:

(a)     property belonging to the deceased but not passing to his personal representatives (PRs);

(b)     property not belonging to the deceased but with which he has some sort of a connection.

The importance of the distinction is that in the case of the former, the property may still be taxable as part of the inheritance tax estate. However, if the property is in the latter category, it is usually not part of the taxable estate.

Anyone advising on the terms of a new will needs to find out from the testator the extent to which such interests exist before advising how property will devolve on death and to whom, including the inheritance tax consequences (if any).

### 1.3.1     Property belonging to the deceased but not passing to his personal representatives

PRs are the people who will have responsibility on death for dealing with assets belonging to the deceased which pass under the terms of his will (or intestacy, if there is no will). If appointed by will, they are called 'executors'. If appointed under the NCPR 1987 (see para 1.1 (b)), they are called 'administrators'.

A grant of representation issued by the court is usually required to confirm both the validity of the will (if there is one) and the appointment of the PRs. As such, it is recognised as the PRs' authority for dealing with the deceased's assets. So, once they have the grant, they can deal with the property passing under the will to give effect to what the will says.

However, some property does not pass by will and so does not pass to the PRs on death. It follows that a grant of representation is not required to deal with such property and someone other than the PRs will be involved. As said at para 1.3, although such property does not pass to the PRs, it will still be treated as part of the estate for inheritance tax purposes by virtue of the deceased's beneficial interest in it and so must be taken into account by anyone seeking tax planning advice.

#### Property held under a beneficial joint tenancy

If the deceased was a *beneficial joint tenant* of any property, his interest passes automatically on his death to the surviving joint tenant(s). Unless the deceased takes action before death, such an interest cannot devolve on his PRs to pass under his will or under the intestacy rules. Bank and building society accounts, shareholdings and, of course, houses and other types of land can all be held jointly.

Usually, production of a death certificate is all that is necessary for a bank, for example, to recognise the right of the survivor to the money in the account. Similarly, sending a death certificate to HM Land Registry will enable the removal of the deceased joint tenant's name from the proprietorship register if the land has a registered title. In the case of an unregistered title, a copy of the death certificate should be placed with the title deeds.

Having said this, it is very important to consider the nature of the deceased's beneficial interest in any asset which is co-owned. This is particularly true of land because although the legal estate has to be held by co-owners as joint tenants, it does not necessarily follow that the beneficial (or equitable) interest is held in the same way. How the beneficial interest is held is initially a question of what the parties have agreed or if that is not conclusive or it is disputed, it may depend on rules applied by the court. This topic is outside the scope of this book, but suffice to say that if the *beneficial* interest is held under a tenancy in common, then there *is* an interest which will pass to PRs and as such it can be given away by will.

It is important to note that a beneficial joint tenancy can easily be converted into a tenancy in common by, for example, the service of a written notice of severance on the other co-owner(s) under the provisions of section 36(2) of the Law of Property Act 1925 (LPA 1925). Doing so, therefore, creates an interest which can then be left by will to a third party rather than allowing it to pass automatically to the surviving co-owner(s) as a beneficial joint tenancy. However, a beneficial joint tenancy cannot be severed by a statement in the will itself.

It is not uncommon for co-owners of, say, the family home to be unaware of whether they hold the beneficial interest as joint tenants or tenants in common. They may have made a decision when they bought the property but have since forgotten what their legal adviser told them. It is vital for the will drafter to ascertain the nature of the beneficial ownership and, if necessary, to advise the need for severance if this is necessary to give effect to what is intended by a proposed will. Failure to do so can be negligent if it results in a purported gift of an interest as tenant in common not taking effect because property was held under a joint tenancy (see the Court of Appeal decision in *Carr-Glynn v Frearsons* [1998] 4 All ER 225).

## Nominated property

Although not commonly encountered these days, it is possible to make a statutory nomination but only in respect of deposits in friendly societies and industrial and provident societies, up to a limit of £5,000 in each case. To be effective, a nomination must be in writing, attested by one witness and made by a person who is aged 16 or over. A nomination is revoked by a subsequent marriage/civil partnership, a later nomination or if the nominee predeceases the nominator. It is not revoked by a later will. On the nominator's death, payment can be made directly to the nominee on production of a death certificate.

If no effective nomination has been made, then the deposits in question will pass to, and be dealt with by, the PRs in the normal way.

There is another type of so-called nomination used in connection with payments under certain pension schemes which operates in an entirely different way (see para 1.3.2, Pension scheme benefits).

## Donatio mortis causa

*Donatio mortis causa (DMC)* is a Latin phrase meaning 'gift because of death'. It is sometimes called a 'deathbed gift', although donors do not necessarily have to be literally on their deathbed. A *DMC* is a lifetime gift made when the donor contemplates his death happening in a particular way, such as serious surgery which he might not survive. A gift will not qualify as a *DMC* just because the donor fears death from natural causes, such as old age.

A *DMC* is different from other lifetime gifts because it is conditional on the donor's death and until then can be revoked by the donor, either expressly, or by implication if the donor survives the event, for example, the surgery, which led to the making of the *DMC*. Otherwise, the gift is complete when the death occurs, even if the death is caused by something other than that contemplated. At that moment, the *DMC* is perfected in equity retrospectively from the date it was made.

Whilst the donor's PRs may have to take steps to perfect the donee's legal title, for example, making an assent of land, the subject matter is not part of the donor's estate passing under his will or intestacy, although it is subject to inheritance tax.

## Property abroad

Land belonging to a testator situated outside the United Kingdom is immovable property and as such its devolution is likely to pass under the *lex situs,* i.e. the local law of the jurisdiction where the land is situated. While such land can be dealt with by the testator's will made under the law of England and Wales, if the provisions dealing with the disposal of the land either conflict with, or are not recognised by, the *lex situs,* then the latter will prevail (see, further, Chapter 9).

If the deceased was domiciled (or deemed domiciled for tax purposes) in the United Kingdom, his worldwide assets are subject to inheritance tax. If the deceased was domiciled elsewhere, inheritance tax is charged only on his UK assets.

## 1.3.2    Property not belonging to the deceased but with which he has some sort of a connection

Certain categories of property that might appear to belong to the deceased do not actually form part of his estate because the deceased had no beneficial interest in it. Such property will neither pass by will nor (usually) be considered as part of the estate for inheritance tax purposes. It can normally be dealt with on production of a death certificate.

### Pension scheme benefits

Many occupational pension schemes are drafted in such a way that the benefits that become payable do not form part of the member's estate on their death because the benefits are payable at the *discretion* of the trustees of the scheme. Consequently, unless paid to the deceased's estate, the amount payable is not dealt with by the deceased's PRs. Instead, the scheme administrator will pay the benefit direct to one or more beneficiaries designated by the scheme, usually within the immediate family or dependants of the member.

Apart from the fact that such benefits are not subject to inheritance tax, they provide a means of enabling payments to be made to those who might be financially dependent on the deceased member without having to wait for a grant of representation.

Most schemes ask members to indicate their wishes as to whom payment should be made, though the indication is not binding on the trustees. This is sometimes referred to as a 'nomination of a preferred recipient', but should not be confused with a statutory nomination of 'nominated property' in para 1.3.1, Nominated property.

### Trust or assigned life assurance policies

Under section 11 of the Married Women's Property Act 1882, a policy of life assurance on a person's life expressed to be for the benefit of his spouse or civil partner and/or children creates a trust in their favour. If the beneficiary is to be someone other than the spouse, civil partner or children, the policy will need to be written expressly in trust for, or assigned to, the person(s) concerned.

Either way, the person taking out the policy has no proprietary interest to leave by will, even though it is that person's life which has been assured and it is his death which triggers payment of the policy proceeds. On his death, the sum insured is payable directly to the persons named on the policy who will take either absolutely or as trustees of a continuing trust created by the policy.

Only if a policy is taken out by the deceased on his own life, but without imposing a trust or assigning the benefit, do the proceeds become payable to his estate (and potentially taxable as such).

### Other trust interests

A person may have a vested interest in possession under a trust as a life tenant. This means that person has a *right* to income from the trust property or a *right* to enjoyment of property such as a house held by the trustees. When that person dies, his interest as life tenant ends and the devolution of the property is governed by the terms of the trust. In other words, it is not something that can be dealt with in that person's will (unless, exceptionally, the trust gives the life tenant a power of appointment over the trust property which is capable of being exercised by his will).

However, the life tenant's entitlement to income, or enjoyment of the trust property, may result in the underlying trust property being treated as part of the life tenant's estate for inheritance tax purposes. This is the case even though the trust property does not pass under the life tenant's will and is not disposed of by the terms of that will (see Chapter 17).

In the case of discretionary trusts, a trust beneficiary has no entitlement to either income or capital but is merely a member of a class of beneficiaries to whom the trustees may at their discretion choose to appoint income or capital. There is clearly nothing the discretionary beneficiary can leave by will and his death has no implications for inheritance tax.

It should be noted that some trust interests *are* capable of passing by will. For example, if X is entitled to trust capital following the death of a life tenant, L, who is still alive, then X has a remainder interest under the trust (sometimes called a 'reversion'). As long as X's interest is vested when X dies and is not defeated by a condition, such as a requirement that he is alive when L dies, then X's remainder interest is an asset that can pass under X's will. So, a gift in X's will of 'all my estate to my wife' will include X's reversion under the trust if X dies while L is still alive.

### Property held in a fiduciary capacity beneficially for another

A person, Y, may be a trustee of property or a PR, either alone or with others. In one sense the property 'belongs' to Y but in another it does not. Although Y may own the legal title, Y holds the beneficial interest for a third party entitled under the trust or estate, as the case may be. Therefore, neither the legal nor beneficial interest can be disposed of by Y's will.

## 1.4  Intestacy

Reference is made earlier in this chapter to the intestacy rules and the fact that making a will can avoid them.

When a person dies without having disposed of any property by a valid will, there will be a *total intestacy*. Even if there is a will, property can still end up passing under the intestacy rules if there is a *partial intestacy*. This can happen if the will fails to dispose of the whole of the estate, for example, because a residuary beneficiary has predeceased the testator and there is no effective substitutional gift in the will. Consequently, one aim of good will drafting is to ensure this does not happen.

Appendix 2 contains an outline of how the intestacy rules apply.

# 2 Restrictions on Testamentary Freedom

## 2.1 Introduction

In Chapter 1, we see that a testator can give away by will any property which is capable of being so given. It is also the case that a testator is generally free to make dispositions of property to whomever he pleases. Unlike the situation in some overseas jurisdictions, there are no forced heirship rights applicable to England and Wales which might otherwise compel a person to leave property to a particular person (see Chapter 9).

However, this so-called testamentary freedom is to some extent eroded, firstly, by statute and, secondly, but to a less frequent extent, by what the testator may have done through the giving of some sort of enforceable promise. This chapter considers in turn:

(a)    Inheritance (Provision for Family and Dependants) Act 1975 (I(PFD)A 1975);

(b)    mutual wills;

(c)    contracts to leave property by will;

(d)    proprietary estoppel.

Circumstances in which any of these may be relevant should ideally be identified when taking instructions for a will so that any limits on its terms might be known. However, this is only possible if the testator co-operates.

## 2.2 Inheritance (Provision for Family and Dependants) Act 1975

### 2.2.1    What the Inheritance (Provision for Family and Dependants) Act 1975 does

The I(PFD)A 1975 allows certain categories of people to apply for reasonable financial provision from the estate of a deceased who has died domiciled in England and Wales. They may be disappointed because they have been left out of a will or are not inheriting on intestacy, or they may already have an entitlement under the will or intestacy but think they ought to have received more.

### 2.2.2    Time for making a claim

An applicant must apply to the court either before or no later than 6 months after the issue of the first effective grant of representation (see para 1.3.1) to the estate, although the court has a discretion to extend this time limit.

### 2.2.3    Those who can apply

The following can make a claim (section 1(1) of the I(PFD)A 1975):

(a)    a spouse or civil partner of the deceased;

(b)    a former spouse or civil partner of the deceased, but not one who has formed a subsequent marriage or civil partnership (often, the court granting the decree of divorce, dissolution or nullity will include a term barring the former spouse or civil partner from making a claim);

(c)    any person who, during the whole of the period of 2 years ending immediately before the date when the deceased died, was living: (i) in the same household as the deceased; and (ii) as the husband, wife or civil partner of the deceased (in other words, a cohabitee). The parties must be living together *as husband and wife or as civil partners* in the sense that there is a commitment to permanence with such relationship being openly acknowledged and unequivocally displayed;

(d)    a child (regardless of age or gender) of the deceased. This includes an illegitimate, adopted or legitimated child of the deceased and a child *en ventre sa mère* at the deceased's death. A child who has been adopted cannot claim as a child of his *natural* parent;

(e)    any person (not being a child of the deceased) treated by the deceased as a child of a family in which the deceased stood in a parental role (e.g. a step-child). A 'family' includes one where the deceased was the only member (apart from the applicant) and so includes a single parent family;

(f)    any person (not otherwise included in the foregoing categories) who, immediately before the death, was being maintained by the deceased either wholly or in part. A person is 'maintained' if 'the deceased, otherwise than for consideration pursuant to a commercial arrangement, was making a substantial contribution in money or money's worth towards the reasonable needs of that person' (section 1(3) of the I(PFD)A 1975). This would allow a claim by, for example, a dependent relative or a secret lover, but not an employee, such as the deceased's live-in nanny or carer, because any accommodation provided or money received from the deceased was by way of consideration paid under a commercial arrangement.

### 2.2.4    What the applicant must prove

The only ground for an application is that the disposition of the deceased's estate effected by the will or intestacy, or a combination of both, is not such as to make reasonable financial provision for the applicant. There are two standards for judging reasonable financial provision:

(a)   *the surviving spouse/civil partner standard*: this allows a surviving spouse or civil partner such financial provision as is reasonable in all the circumstances, whether or not required for maintenance (section 1(2)(a) of the I(PFD)A 1975); and

(b)   *the ordinary standard*: this applies to all other categories of applicant and allows such financial provision as it would be reasonable in all the circumstances for the applicant to receive for his *maintenance* (section 1(2)(b) of the I(PFD)A 1975).

The word 'maintenance' in the ordinary standard has been held to connote only payments which, directly or indirectly, enable the applicant in the future to discharge the cost of his daily living at whatever standard of living is appropriate to him. Claimants who can provide for their own maintenance needs will not succeed. This is often a source of disappointment to adult children who feel that their parents have unfairly deprived them of an inheritance.

### 2.2.5    What the court takes into account

Statutory guidelines assist the court in determining whether the will and/or intestacy makes reasonable financial provision for the applicant. Some matters are common guidelines to be considered for every claimant. These are in section 3(1) of the I(PFD)A 1975:

(a)   the financial resources and needs of the applicant, other applicants and beneficiaries of the estate now and in the foreseeable future;

(b)   the deceased's moral obligations towards any applicant or beneficiary;

(c)   the size and nature of the estate;

(d)   the physical or mental disability of any applicant or beneficiary;

(e)   anything else which may be relevant, such as the conduct of the applicant.

There are also additional guidelines in section 3(2) of the I(PFD)A 1975 that are particular to the category of applicant.

So, if the applicant is the surviving spouse/civil partner, the court also takes into account the applicant's age and contribution to the welfare of the family and the duration of the marriage or civil partnership. It also takes account of the provision which the applicant might reasonably have expected to receive had the marriage or civil partnership ended on divorce or dissolution rather than death, but the court is instructed not to regard such provision as setting either an upper or lower limit that might be made in the actual family provision claim.

If the applicant is a child of the deceased, or treated as a child of a family in which the deceased stood in a parental role, the court must additionally take account of the applicant's current and expected education or training requirements.

When considering all guidelines, the court takes into account the facts at the date of the hearing rather than death.

### 2.2.6    How the court makes its decision

This requires the court to determine two questions. In answering both, the common and particular guidelines in para 2.2.5 are relevant. The court must also take account of whichever of the two standards of provision applies to the application (see para 2.2.4):

(a)    The first question is whether or not the provision made for the applicant by the will/intestacy *is reasonable*. This is an objective question for the court on the facts and is not a case of asking whether or not the deceased acted reasonably.

In *Ilott v The Blue Cross* [2017] UKSC 17, the Supreme Court for the first time considered an application under the I(PFD)A 1975. The claimant was the estranged adult daughter left nothing by her mother's will; instead, the mother left her estate to charities, having clearly stated in a side letter her reasons for disinheriting her daughter. The Supreme Court highlighted the difficulty in applying the statutory guidelines and the weight given to each, particularly, as here, where the claimant was an able bodied adult child in poor financial circumstances. There is a need to balance the needs and resources of not only the applicant, but also others with a claim on the estate (in this case the charities). The trial judge, at first instance, had found that, taking everything into account, nothing was not 'reasonable provision' for the applicant and awarded the daughter a small sum. The Supreme Court found it was open for the trial judge to make the order he did on the facts as he found them and saw no reason to interfere, notwithstanding that arguments could be made either for more provision (as previously determined by the Court of Appeal), or for no provision at all. All cases have to be decided on an individual basis by the trial judge, whose verdict should not be interfered with by an appeal court unless the judge had erred in principle or law.

(b) If the court, in answering the first question, decides reasonable financial provision has not been made, it then considers the second question which is whether such provision *should* be made and if so, what form that should take (see para 2.2.7).

### 2.2.7 What orders the court can make

The court has wide powers to make orders against the 'net estate', as defined in section 25 of the I(PFD)A 1975. These include orders for periodical payments, lump sum payments or the transfer of specific property to the applicant. The 'net estate' includes not only property which has been, or could have been, disposed of by will, but also any share of joint property passing by survivorship.

There are also anti-avoidance provisions in sections 10 and 11 of the I(PFD)A 1975 which allow the court to claw back certain pre-death dispositions made for the purpose of evading the Act.

### 2.2.8 Implications of the Inheritance (Provision for Family and Dependants) Act 1975 for the testator and adviser

The obvious implication is that the testator's will, or at the very least, some of it, is at risk of being re-written by the court in the event of a successful claim, perhaps at great cost.

If it becomes evident that reasonable financial provision is not being made for someone for whom it might have been expected, then it is probably the duty of the adviser to explain the possible consequences to the testator who can then decide what, if anything, he wishes to do.

Possible options include:

(a) going ahead anyway and leaving it to the court to make an order if it sees fit, or to the parties to negotiate a settlement, if they can;

(b) making *some limited provision* for the likely applicant in the hope this will deter them from proceeding further; this might include making the applicant one of the objects of a discretionary trust, although this may not be a sufficient deterrent;

(c)    making provision as in (b) with a proviso that should the applicant seek to challenge the quantum of the legacy it will fail; this is intended to make the applicant weigh up the merits of gaining more against the risk of losing all. However, although such a proviso is valid (see *Nathan v Leonard* [2002] EWHC 1701 (Ch), [2002] WTLR 1061), it may not be sufficient to deter a claim. If the applicant goes to court, the loss of the legacy might make the claim a stronger one;

(d)    leaving a statement of the testator's reasons for making either no provision or limited provision. While such a statement is admissible as evidence of fact, its subjective nature means it is not directly relevant to the question of whether or not the provision was objectively reasonable. Such a statement carries no more weight than any other factor mentioned in the statutory guidelines (see para 2.2.5). Any statement made is best left outside the will owing to the public nature of the will itself.

## 2.3   Mutual wills

Mutual wills are wills made by two people with an agreement that neither will revoke unilaterally. Although it is not possible to make a will irrevocable, if the first party dies having carried out the agreement, equity will impose a trust over the agreed property reflecting the terms of the agreement. The survivor is free to make a new will but the will cannot affect the destination of the property subject to the trust.

The trust imposed is unusual. It 'floats' during the survivor's lifetime, crystallising on the death of the survivor and leaving the survivor free to deal with the property in the meantime (see *Birmingham v Renfrew* (1937) 57 CLR 666). This means the survivor may spend all the assets, for example on care home fees, so there is no certainty the agreed ultimate beneficiary will get anything. Hence, a mutual will is no help in protecting assets if the survivor has to go into care.

However, the survivor is not free to *give away* assets subject to the trust. Norris J in *Healey v Brown* [2002] EWHC 1405 (Ch) said that this would be a breach of fiduciary duty, which would lead to early 'crystallisation'.

Mutual wills are usually encountered in the context of a married couple or civil partners, but can equally be relevant to two testators who are not in such a relationship. A typical feature of mutual wills is that the two testators have in mind one or more common beneficiaries whom they eventually wish to benefit on the death of the survivor. Subject to that, the survivor takes an interest under the will of the first to die.

'Mutual wills' must be distinguished from so-called 'mirror wills' or 'reciprocal wills', which may outwardly look the same as mutual wills but which lack the vital agreement required to become mutual wills. The very existence of mutual wills depends on the parties making an agreement that once the wills are made, neither party can revoke their will without the consent of the other.

In *Fry v Densham-Smith* [2010] EWCA Civ 1410, the Court of Appeal reviewed previous authorities saying to prove the existence of mutual wills, the evidence has to establish:

(a) a prior agreement by the testators to make mutual wills intending their agreement to become irrevocable on the death of the first to die (the agreement can be in writing, contained in the will or oral); and

(b) the making of mutual wills pursuant to that agreement.

If the testators fail to execute mutual wills pursuant to their agreement, the agreement does not become irrevocable on the death of the first to die. To satisfy the court that, on the balance of probabilities, such an agreement had been made, the evidence required for an express agreement not to revoke the wills has to be:

(a) certain;

(b) unequivocal or clear; and

(c) satisfactory.

An agreement will not be implied simply from the fact that the testators had made similar reciprocal or mirror wills.

In *Fry v Densham-Smith* (above), the Court of Appeal found the trial judge had been entitled to find on the evidence there had been an oral mutual wills agreement so as to entitle the defendant to one half of the survivor's estate, notwithstanding that the survivor had changed her will three times after the first party to the agreement had died. A constructive trust had been imposed when the first party died and this was binding on the survivor's estate.

In *Charles and others v Fraser* [2010] EWHC 2154 (Ch), involving reciprocal wills made by two sisters with no reference to an agreement in the wills, the deputy judge was satisfied there had been such agreement through mutual promises the sisters had made to each other and reported to others. The deputy judge was critical of those involved in the drafting of the wills for apparently not establishing the sisters' intentions as to revocation, nor advising on the effect of making mutual wills and then failing to ensure that the agreement was clearly and accurately recorded in the will. He said it was the 'plain duty' of a draftsman, so instructed, to have done these things.

In the absence of clear express words as to whether wills were intended to be 'mutual' (or not, as the case may be), there is scope for dispute between those ultimately entitled under the survivor's original will and those claiming under a later one. This is what happened in *Legg & Burton v Burton* [2017] EWHC 2088 (Ch), which went to the High Court despite the value of the estate being around only £325,000. A husband (H) and wife (W) made identical wills in 2000 leaving everything to the other and on the survivor's death to the couple's two daughters (the claimants). Their wills made no reference to any agreement not to revoke. H died followed by W and between the two deaths W made 13 further wills in varying terms, the last one giving modest legacies to the daughters while residue was divided between grandchildren and the partner of one of them (the defendants). The judge acknowledged that private client lawyers do not often advise true mutual wills as 'they take away some of the testator's ability to adapt his or her will to changing circumstances'. However, he rejected the defendants' claim that H and W had not made mutual wills just because it was inherently improbable for any testator to want to make a mutual will, particularly, as in this case, where the wills were made with the benefit of legal advice and supervision. The judge found there was sufficient evidence on the balance of probabilities to establish a mutual will agreement.

These decisions reinforce the need for practitioners to explain to testators the differences between mutual wills and wills which are drafted in similar terms but can be unilaterally revoked. This is especially so if the clients wish to provide for each other and for the survivor's estate to pass to either a common beneficiary, or perhaps each party's share of the combined estate passing to different beneficiaries. Practitioners should ensure each testator considers whether the survivor is to be free to revoke his will. Clients may find the idea of mutual wills potentially attractive, but practitioners should advise on the difficulties which can arise, particularly if there is likely to be a substantial time gap between the two deaths and changed circumstances.

Above all, it is vital to record carefully any agreement, both in the will and in a separate attendance note. Indeed, if reciprocal or mirror wills are *not* intended to be mutual, then this fact should also be recorded in each will to avoid allegations to the contrary after the survivor's death.

EXAMPLE CLAUSES

*(a) Agreement for mutual wills*

> I declare that [my husband/wife/civil partner, etc] [XXXX] and I have agreed with one another to execute wills of the same date and in similar terms, and have further agreed that such respective

wills shall not hereafter be revoked or altered either during our joint lives for so long as we remain married or by the survivor of us and I, relying upon such agreement, hereby make this will in the following terms

### (b) Declaration negating mutual wills

I declare that although my husband/wife/civil partner, etc [XXXX] is making a will in similar terms to those of this will, the two wills are not intended to be mutually irrevocable and each of us is free to alter the disposition of [his] [her] estate in any way and at any time without reference to the other

Lastly, mention must be made of *Healey v Brown* [2002] EWHC 1405 (Ch), which held that if a mutual wills agreement relates to a specific disposition of land, then it is subject to section 2 of the Law of Property (Miscellaneous Provisions) Act 1989 as a contract for the disposition of an interest in land. As such, the agreement must not only be in writing, but must also be signed by both parties. In this case, the court found both wills did form a contract intended to deal with the devolution of property, formerly held jointly, on the survivor's death. However, since neither will contained *both* signatures of the two parties, it could not be enforceable as a contract for the disposal of an interest in land. Therefore, if a mutual wills agreement is likely to deal with land or an interest in land, there needs to be a separate written agreement signed by both parties. However, in *Olins v Walters* [2008] EWCA Civ 782, the court held that section 2 did not apply if the agreement related to the residue of the estate which happened to include land at the date of death. The judge in *Legg & Burton v Burton* [2017] EWHC 2088 (Ch) described the distinction as 'unprincipled' and suggested that *Healey v Brown* was not necessarily correct.

## 2.4 Contract to leave property by will

The nature of a will means it has no effect until the testator dies and until then it is freely revocable as long as the testator has the capacity to do so. The will is still revocable even though the testator may have entered into a contract with a third party not to revoke it, usually in circumstances where the existing will benefits the third party or perhaps another.

However, if the testator chooses to revoke the existing will and replace it with another, his estate may be liable for his breach of contract. Consequently, the compensation the estate may have to pay could render the terms of any new will ineffectual.

The implications of section 2 of the Law of Property (Miscellaneous Provisions) Act 1989 will also be relevant if the contract includes land (see para 2.3, final paragraph).

## 2.5    Proprietary estoppel

Like mutual wills at para 2.3, proprietary estoppel is a development of equity which has seen a few high profile cases come before the courts in recent years, culminating in the House of Lords' (as it then was) decision in *Thorner v Majors* [2009] UKHL 18.

Broadly, a proprietary estoppel arises when one person, J, acts to his detriment on the faith of a belief, which is known to and encouraged by the testator, T, that J either has been given or will be given a right to T's property (or an interest in or over it). Equity says in that situation that T cannot insist on what might otherwise be J's legal rights if to do so would be unconscionable.

In other words, suppose John is Tamzin's faithful chauffeur and housekeeper who works all hours of the day for Tamzin. There eventually comes a point where Tamzin says to John, something along the lines of 'I can't afford to keep paying you but I've made up my mind to give you the house'. Relying on that statement, John decides to continue working for Tamzin for no wages, and from time to time Tamzin repeats the encouraging words to John until she dies. Tamzin's will leaves the house and everything else to distant relatives with no provision for John.

Although Tamzin was legally free to leave her property by will in the way that she did, there is every chance that John could make a claim of proprietary estoppel. If he successfully proves sufficient detrimental reliance, the court will intervene and order provision from the estate, thereby depriving the beneficiaries named in the will.

In *Thorner v Majors* (above), the House of Lords said the main issue was the character and quality of the assurances given to the claimant which needed to be such that they were reasonably understood to be a commitment by the deceased and reasonably relied on by the claimant. The claimant must also have suffered some detriment. It should be noted, proprietary estoppel claims do not have to wait until death since the court can intervene during the promisor's lifetime and order provision is made for the promise (see, e.g. *Gillett v Holt* [2001] Ch 211).

Any part of the deceased's estate can be the subject of a proprietary estoppel claim, but the promisee will not necessarily be awarded what was promised. Proving the claim is one thing, but calculating the amount of compensation, if successful, is another. The court will award the minimum necessary to achieve an equitable result with proportionality between the expectation and the detriment.

In *Jennings v Rice* [2002] EWCA Civ 159, [2002] WTLR 367, the claimant was promised 'all this' but was only aware of the house and contents (valued at £435,000). The Court of Appeal agreed with the trial judge that to award everything (£1.2 million), or even the house and contents, would be disproportionate to the detriment suffered. The claimant was awarded £200,000 (see, also, para 21.1.11).

The Court of Appeal was involved again in *Davies and another v Davies* [2016] EWCA Civ 463. E had worked on her parents' large dairy farm for long hours at low wages over many years, in reliance on her parents' assurances the farm would one day be hers. In 2012, E's parents brought proceedings to evict E and her family from the farmhouse. E counter-claimed an interest in the farm, land and business, so beginning a bitter and long-running family dispute. Eventually, the Court of Appeal reduced the High Court award of £1.3 million to £500,000. In deciding how to satisfy the equity, the court said it must weigh the detriment suffered by the claimant in reliance on the defendant's assurances against any countervailing benefits enjoyed in consequence of that reliance. In particular, there had to be proportionality between the remedy and the detriment. That did not mean the court should abandon expectations and seek only to compensate detrimental reliance, but, if the expectation was disproportionate to the detriment, the court should satisfy the equity in a more limited way.

The difficulty for the person advising the testator is that the testator is unlikely to be aware of words or conduct which amount to the sort of assurances that may later be the basis of a proprietary estoppel claim. Even if the person advising is made aware through questioning at the instructions stage, the most that can be done is to advise the testator of the implications if a will is made which reneges on any such promises.

# 3 Testamentary Capacity and Intention

## 3.1 Introduction

If a will is to be admitted to probate, its formal validity must be established. One aspect of this is that it must meet the statutory formalities necessary for its due execution, and this is dealt with in Chapter 4. However, it is also necessary to show the testator had the ability to make a will, and it is this which is covered by this chapter.

To make a will, the testator must not only meet an age requirement (see para 3.2), but must also have the necessary testamentary capacity (see para 3.3) and testamentary intention (see para 3.4).

Testamentary capacity is concerned with the testator's ability to understand what needs to be considered when engaged in the act of making a will, while testamentary intention is to do with the testator's knowledge and approval of the terms of his particular will, so that it can be said to represent his genuine wishes. These are two different aspects of will making but are obviously connected since they both concern the mind of the testator.

Questions of capacity and intention are often problematical to deal with and are potentially a breeding ground for contentious probate claims. There are important issues here:

(a) a practitioner instructed to prepare a will for a client must try to ensure the will is in due course recognised as a valid will; this involves a consideration of steps that might be taken to lessen the risk of any challenge to the will's validity in appropriate cases; and

(b) if instructed after a death, the practitioner must know the requirements for establishing validity in order to advise on the admissibility of a will to probate and the extent to which effect can be given to its provisions.

## 3.2   Testator's age and physical capacity

Testators must be aged at least 18 at the date when they execute their will. A person who dies a minor under the age of 18 dies intestate (even if married or in a civil partnership).

There is an exception to this rule which relates to 'privileged wills'. These can be made in certain circumstances by members of the armed forces if on actual military service and also by mariners and seamen 'at sea'. A minor who enjoys privileged status can make a privileged will. They are called 'privileged wills' because they are not subject to the same formalities and can be made in an informal way, even orally (see para 4.7.1 where privileged wills are considered further).

Subject to being an adult, there are no other physical qualifications to making a will and no one is disqualified just because he may be in prison or bankrupt. Nor does it matter that testators lack the physical ability to write or read their own will (see para 4.3.3 as regards the execution arrangements if making a will for such an individual).

## 3.3   Testator's mental capacity

### 3.3.1   *Banks v Goodfellow* test

A testator's mental capacity to make a will is not necessarily the same as his capacity to make other important decisions. The traditional test applied by the courts in dealing with capacity issues for wills (testamentary capacity) is that in *Banks v Goodfellow* [1870] LR 5 QB 549.

The basic *Banks v Goodfellow* test requires the testator to understand three things:

(a)   *the nature of the act and its effects*: in other words testators must be able to appreciate they are making a will which disposes of their property when they die and until then the property remains theirs;

(b)   *the extent of the testator's property*: testators do not have to know the exact value of everything they own but must be able to appreciate the general extent of their wealth;

(c)   *the claims to which the testator ought to have regard*: the testator must be able to remember those around him who, morally speaking, might have a claim on his property. Many capacity cases are litigated on this aspect of the rule, where the allegation is that the testator was unaware of his immediate family when making the will.

A further requirement of *Banks v Goodfellow* is the testator must not have been suffering from any delusion which affected the terms of his will. In

*Kostic v Chaplin* [2007] EWHC 2298 (Ch), the court found the testator lacked capacity because he was suffering from a delusion his son and other members of his family were implicated in an international conspiracy in which he (the testator) was the victim. The testator had left his substantial estate to a political party.

So too, in *Re Ritchie* [2009] EWHC 709 (Ch), the deceased had made a will leaving her £2.5 million estate to charity disinheriting her four children. She was a difficult woman with some elements of obsessive compulsive disorder. The deceased had told her solicitor that her sons were stealing from her, that one son was violent to her, and that her daughters never came to see her or gave her help. These allegations were strenuously denied by the children. The judge found the mother's beliefs were delusions and, pronouncing against the will, accepted the deceased would not have disinherited her children if she had not suffered from these delusions.

Of course, a testator might have a delusion which has no effect on his will. If a man who has a wife and two children makes a will in which they are the only beneficiaries but at the time he is in poor mental health and is deluded into thinking he is manager of the England football team, he still passes the *Banks v Goodfellow* test. If in the same circumstances, the testator's will gives a legacy of £10,000 to the first England player to score a goal after his death, his delusion might be held to have affected his testamentary capacity but only to the extent of the legacy. The case of *In the Estate of Bohrmann* [1938] 1 All ER 271 shows the court can omit from probate part of a will affected by a delusion while allowing the rest of the will to stand. So, the legacy to the goal scorer fails, but the rest of the will takes effect.

In *Key v Key* [2010] EWHC 408 (Ch), a will was executed by a testator within a few days of his wife's death, having been married for 65 years. In his judgment, Briggs J said:

> Without in any way detracting from the continuing authority of *Banks v Goodfellow*, it must be recognised that psychiatric medicine has come a long way since 1870 in recognising an ever widening range of circumstances now regarded as sufficient at least to give rise to a risk of mental disorder, sufficient to deprive a patient of the power of rational decision making, quite distinctly from old age and infirmity. The mental shock of witnessing an injury to a loved one is an example recognised by the law, and the affective disorder which may be caused by bereavement is an example recognised by psychiatrists. The symptomatic effect of bereavement as capable of being almost identical to that associated with severe depression. Accordingly, although neither I nor counsel has found any reported case dealing with the effect of bereavement on testamentary capacity, the *Banks v Goodfellow* test must be applied so as to accommodate this, among other factors capable of impairing testamentary capacity, in a way in which, perhaps, the court would have found difficult to recognise in the 19th century.

Generally, testamentary capacity must have existed at the date of execution. However, under the rule in *Parker v Felgate* [1883] 8 PD 171, confirmed by the Court of Appeal in *Perrins v Holland and others* [2010] EWCA Civ 840, it is sufficient to show:

(a)    the testator had the required capacity at the date they gave instructions to prepare their will;

(b)    the will was prepared in accordance with those instructions;

(c)    at the time of execution, the testator was able to (and did) understand they were signing a will for which they had given instructions. It does not matter the testator could not then remember their instructions or could not have understood the will if it was read over to them.

The rule in *Parker v Felgate* was applied in *Clancy v Clancy* [2003] EWHC 1885 (Ch) where the testatrix had capacity at the time of giving instructions, but probably did not at the time of execution as she was in hospital and heavily sedated.

### 3.3.2    Mental Capacity Act 2005

The Mental Capacity Act 2005 (MCA 2005) came into force on 1 October 2007. It deals with the determination of mental capacity generally and is not specifically aimed at wills.

Section 1(2) of the MCA 2005 says a person is assumed to have capacity unless it is established he lacks capacity, and section 2(3) provides lack of capacity cannot be established just by reference to a person's age, condition or aspect of behaviour which might lead others to make unjustified assumptions about his capacity.

Section 2(1) of the MCA 2005 gives a little more guidance on the meaning of lack of capacity by saying a person lacks capacity 'in relation to a matter if at the material time he is unable to make a decision for himself in relation to the matter because of an impairment of, or a disturbance in the functioning of, the mind or brain'.

Section 3(1) of the MCA 2005 then goes on to say:

a person is unable to make a decision for himself if he is unable—

(a)    to understand the information relevant to the decision,

(b)    to retain that information,

(c)    to use or weigh that information as part of the process of making the decision, or

(d)    to communicate his decision (whether by talking, using sign language or any other means).

This makes it clear that capacity must be assessed with reference to the *particular decision or act* in question.

The general consensus of cases decided since the MCA 2005 came into force is that the statutory test has not replaced the *Banks v Goodfellow* test. The *Code of Practice*, supplemental to the MCA 2005, states that the statutory test is in line with existing common law tests but that judges may adopt the new test if they think it is appropriate. Munby J clarified the meaning of 'if they think it is appropriate' in *Local Authority X v M* [2007] EWHC 2003 (Fam). He suggested that it is only appropriate where the statutory test merely encapsulates in the language of the parliamentary draftsmen the principles expounded in earlier case law.

In *Scammel v Farmer* [2008] EWHC 1100 (Ch), [2008] WTLR 1261, a case concerned with a testatrix suffering from Alzheimer's disease, the court said the statutory test is a modern restatement of the test in *Banks v Goodfellow*.

In *Walker v Badmin* [2014] EWHC 71 (Ch), where the deceased's testamentary capacity was in dispute, the judge hearing the case distinguished two tests:

(a)   the common law test, applied in probate disputes, to decide whether or not a deceased person had capacity when executing his will; and

(b)   the statutory test, applied by the Court of Protection when deciding whether a statutory will (see para 4.7.2) should be executed on behalf of a living person who lacked capacity to execute his own will.

In most cases, applying either test produces the same result, but this is not inevitable. In addition to section 3(1) of the MCA 2005 requiring understanding of *all* the information relevant to making a decision, section 3(4) requires appreciation of the reasonably foreseeable consequences of making, or not making, that decision. By contrast, the common law test does not require a testator to understand every detail about the terms of the will, nor the collateral consequences of its dispositions. The Court of Appeal in *Simon v Byford* [2014] EWCA Civ 280, involving a testatrix who at the time was suffering from mild dementia, specifically stated that a testator is not required to understand the collateral consequences of what he says in his will as long as he meets the basic requirements of understanding in *Banks v Goodfellow*, which the Court said was the *potential* to understand and was not to be equated with a test of memory.

Questions of capacity may lead to conflict and problems for practitioners. For example, Ted is in the early stages of dementia and wants to make a will exclusively benefiting his civil partner, Pete. Ted's solicitor thinks that Ted fulfils the common law test but is close to the borderline. The solicitor can suggest to Ted that it would be helpful to get a medical opinion on Ted's current mental state from a specialist in dementia. Ted may refuse either because he does not want to subject himself to such examination or because he does not want to pay the cost (which is likely to be significant).

If the solicitor thinks that Ted is probably on the right side of the capacity line, refusing to draft the will deprives Ted of the opportunity to put his testamentary wishes into effect. The best course is probably to set out the risks of challenge after death in a letter to Ted and to make a full attendance note setting out the reasons the solicitor has for believing that the common law test is fulfilled. (For a fuller discussion of practical steps see para 3.5.)

If the solicitor believes that Ted lacks testamentary capacity, it is possible to make an application to the Court of Protection for a statutory will. The court must be satisfied that Ted lacks capacity and will then make a will in his best interests. This will involve balancing Ted's wishes and also the views of others involved in his care. Ted will not necessarily get the will he wanted.

Many people regard the common law test as outdated and in need of replacement by a test reflecting modern conditions, such as increased life expectancy and the fact that an inability to make a decision may manifest itself in ways unknown to the Victorians. However, as was recognised in *Key v Key* [2010] EWHC 408 (Ch) when concerned with capacity during the aftermath of bereavement, the courts have been willing to extend and adapt the old test to meet advances through modern psychiatric medicine in understanding how the mind works. The Law Commission is considering the adequacy of the law on testamentary capacity, along with some other issues affecting wills.

### 3.3.3    Burden of proving capacity

Traditionally, the propounder of the will (the person seeking to have it admitted to probate) had to prove capacity, and two rebuttable presumptions were applied, as follows.

(a)    *Rational will*: if a duly executed will appeared rational, capacity was presumed. If evidence was produced to rebut the presumption, the propounder then had to prove capacity.

(b)    *Continuing mental state*: if the testator generally lacked capacity (e.g. as a mental patient), it was presumed this state of affairs continued to the time of executing the will. Therefore, the propounder had to rebut the presumption by showing either that the testator had recovered by the time of execution, or that the will was made during a lucid interval.

However, in *Masterman-Lister v Brutton & Co and another* [2002] EWCA Civ 1889, the Court of Appeal cast doubt on the continued existence of this second presumption. The modern approach is to regard capacity as issue and time specific. In *A, B and C v X, Y and Z* [2012] EWHC 2400 (COP), the court found that an elderly man suffering from dementia had capacity to marry and would sometimes have capacity to make a will but often would not. The times when he lacked capacity would inevitably become more frequent. It followed, the judge said, that any will now made by X, if unaccompanied by contemporary medical evidence asserting capacity, would be seriously open to challenge.

In *Key v Key* [2010] EWHC 408 (Ch), Briggs J (as he then was) set out the rules on proving testamentary capacity as follows:

i)   While the burden starts with the propounder of a will to establish capacity, where the will is duly executed and appears rational on its face, then the court will presume capacity.

ii)   In such a case the evidential burden then shifts to the objector to raise a real doubt about capacity.

iii)   If a real doubt is raised, the evidential burden shifts back to the propounder to establish capacity nonetheless.

In this case, the testator had been suffering from mental problems resulting from sudden bereavement and so there was sufficient medical evidence to raise 'a real doubt' which the beneficiaries were unable to dispel.

### 3.3.4   Practical issues

There is an obvious necessity to ensure the testator is competent to give instructions and has the necessary mental capacity to make the will. This important issue is considered at para 3.5.

## 3.4   Testator's intention

### 3.4.1   Need for knowledge and approval of the will

The testator must have the general intention to make a will and, more specifically, to make the particular will the testator executes. Put another way, the testator must know and approve the contents of his will and, before a will is admitted to probate, the court must be satisfied on both these points. The critical time is again the date of execution of the will, though the rule in *Parker v Felgate* [1883] 8 PD 171 also applies in this context, as was confirmed by the Court of Appeal in *Perrins v Holland and others* [2010] EWCA Civ 840 (see para 3.3.1).

A person may have testamentary capacity but at the same time lack testamentary intention. For example, Gill, who clearly has capacity to make a will might say to a stranger 'write out a will for me saying anything you like and I'll sign it without reading it'. If the stranger wrote such a will and Gill signed it in that way, it could not be admitted to probate because although Gill had the capacity and a general intention to make a will, signing in ignorance of its contents means she could not possibly have had the specific intention to give effect to its terms. Similarly, Gill's specific intention is lacking if she is mistaken as to the contents of the will, as where she thinks the will says X but in fact it says Y.

Any part of the will of which the testator did not know and approve cannot be admitted to probate.

If a will is made in consequence of force, fear, fraud or undue influence as considered at paras 3.4.2 to 3.4.4, it is not regarded as the act of the testator because it lacks the testator's true knowledge and approval. Traditionally, the burden of proof is on the person alleging the irregularity and there are no presumptions to assist. This makes such allegations difficult to prove as the main witness is dead so there is usually little or no evidence.

However, in cases where there is suspicion that one of these factors exists, the will may be declared invalid if the propounder is unable to prove the will was made with knowledge and approval (see, e.g. at para 3.4.6 the case of *Gill v Woodall & Others* [2010] EWCA Civ 1430).

### 3.4.2    Force and fear

Claims of wills being induced as a result of someone having been injured or threatened with injury are rare. In *Betts v Doughty* (1879–80) LR 5 PD 26, a disappointed beneficiary in a later will was entitled to the benefit he would have received under an earlier will where the testator had been induced by threats of violence to omit the legacy from his later will. A threat need not be a physical one. A threat by a child to withdraw financial support from an elderly relative could have the effect of negating knowledge and approval.

### 3.4.3    Fraud

Fraud misleads the testator. Lord Langdale said, in *Giles v Giles* (1836) 1 Keen 685, 692, 'a legacy given to a person in a character which the legatee does not fill, and by the fraudulent assumption of which character the testator has been deceived, will not take effect'.

Fraud can include the deliberate making of false representations about the character of others to induce the testator to make or revoke gifts, or to exclude persons from a proposed will. This is known as 'fraudulent calumny' and is really a cross between pure fraud and undue influence. In *Re Edwards* [2007] EWHC 1119 (Ch), one son of the deceased, Y, alleged that the other, X, had induced their mother to change her will in X's favour by lying about Y. The testatrix was clearly frightened of X who had removed her from care against medical advice. X drank, was very aggressive and prevented other family members from visiting. When the testatrix gave instructions to her solicitor to change her will, she said that:

(a)  X was the one who looked after her (untrue);

(b)  Y wanted to put her in a home (untrue); and

(c)  Y's wife had stolen from her (untrue).

The judge found that X had exerted undue influence by fraudulent calumny against Y in order to procure a will in his favour. The order was for the will to be set aside and for an earlier will dividing the estate equally between X and Y to be proved.

Fraudulent calumny is a difficult claim to establish as it is necessary to show that the person making the untrue statement must either know that the aspersions are false or not care whether they are true or false. If a person believes that he is telling the truth about a potential beneficiary then even if what he tells the testator is objectively untrue, the will is not liable to be set aside on that ground alone. In *Kunicki v Hayward* [2016] EWHC 3199 (Ch), the judge found that the statements complained of were not false but, even if they had been, the elements of fraudulent calumny would not have been established because the person making them believed them to be true. Moreover, the statements complained of had not been responsible for the testator making a will excluding the claimant.

### 3.4.4    Undue influence

Undue influence overpowers the volition of the testator. It is permissible to persuade, but not to coerce, a testator. It may be difficult in some situations to distinguish between persuasion and undue influence, but provided the testator retained real freedom of choice, a court does not normally interfere. If, on the other hand, the testator surrendered to intolerable pressure, the court will intervene. The court is more inclined to find undue influence if the testator is physically or mentally weak or otherwise in a vulnerable situation.

In the case of lifetime gifts, undue influence is presumed in cases where the donor places trust and confidence in the donee and the transaction requires an explanation. However, undue influence is never presumed in relation to a will (see *Parfitt v Lawless* (1872) LR 2 P&D 462). It must always be proved by the person alleging it. This is no easy task as evidence is normally scant and, as explained above, persuasion is allowable. For an example of a litigant in person failing to understand the significance of the burden of proof, see *Re Devillebichot (Deceased)* [2013] EWHC 2867 (Ch). The consequences of making such a claim unsuccessfully are severe as costs are awarded against the unsuccessful claimant and may, as in *Re Devillebichot*, result in the unsuccessful party being at risk of losing his home.

### 3.4.5    Mistake

Mistakes can occur if:

(a)    testators execute a will containing words they do not know are there, or do not contain words which they believe are there;

(b)    testators mistakenly believe certain circumstances or facts exist, which affect their motives for the provisions of the will.

In both cases, the offending words are omitted from the probate of the will on the basis the testator did not know or approve them (see *Re Phelan* [1972] Fam 33).

However, if the testator intends to include words in a will and does so but is mistaken as to the legal effect of the will as a whole, or any of its provisions, the common law position is that the will, or those provisions, is/are admitted to probate (see *Collins v Elstone* (1893) P 1).

If the testator died after 31 December 1982, by section 20 of the Administration of Justice Act 1982 (AJA 1982) the court can order rectification of a will so it carries out the testator's intention, but only if the court is satisfied it fails to carry out such intention because of either: (a) clerical error; or (b) failure to understand the testator's instructions (see, further, Chapter 7). The power extends to adding words intended by the testator to the will. However, if the will does not carry out the testator's intention for a reason other than (a) or (b), section 20 does not apply.

The limitations of section 20 of the AJA 1982 are less important since the Supreme Court's ruling in *Marley v Rawlings* [2014] UKSC 2, which made it clear that the modern approach to interpretation of wills should mirror the flexible approach to interpretation of commercial and other documents. Adopting this approach effectively means a court of construction can construe the will *as if* certain words were inserted, omitted or changed in virtually any circumstances provided it is clear an error or omission has been made in the wording and it is clear what the substance of the intended wording was. (As to *Marley v Rawlings* and construction issues, see Chapter 7.)

### 3.4.6    Proving testamentary intention

Subject to what is said below, the burden of proof has traditionally fallen on the propounder of the will, but in practice there is a presumption that if a testator had the necessary capacity when executing the will, he did so with the necessary knowledge and approval of its contents. In such cases, anyone wishing to challenge must show the testator was induced to make the will (or a particular provision in it) by force, fear, fraud or undue influence, or the testator lacked the necessary knowledge and approval because of a mistake.

However, there is *no* presumption of knowledge and approval in the following situations, and if one of these applies, the burden of proof starts with the propounder:

(a)    The testator is blind or illiterate, or the will is signed by someone other than the testator on his behalf as permitted by section 9 of the Wills Act 1837 (WA 1937), for example, if the testator is too weak to sign (see para 4.3.3).

In these cases, the most satisfactory manner of dealing with the potential problem is to read the will to the testator and amend the standard form attestation clause, both to show the will was read and to explain the circumstances of the execution (see para 4.3.3). If this precaution is not taken at execution, the probate registry will want further evidence to show the testator knew and understood the contents of the will. The registry may also call for evidence if the form of the testator's signature suggests the testator may not have been able to appreciate the significance of what he was doing (as where the signature shows signs of extreme feebleness, or where there has been an abortive attempt at a signature, or the signature is incomplete). Evidence to establish knowledge and approval must inevitably be provided by the witnesses to the will or someone else who was present.

(b)    There are circumstances which 'excite the suspicion of the court' (see *Barry v Butlin* [1838] 2 Moo PC 480).

The court has always treated with suspicion a will which substantially benefits a person connected with its preparation, or a close relative of such a person. In such cases, the propounder must remove the 'suspicion' if the will is to be admitted. In *Pearce v Beverley* [2013] EWHC 2627 (Ch), the judge said the circumstances excited suspicion because the beneficiary had arranged the meeting with the will-writer and was present throughout the interview. Consequently, there was no presumption of knowledge and approval. It was for the beneficiary to establish it and, in the circumstances, she could not.

The degree of suspicion and evidence to displace it varies according to the circumstances of the case.

For example, in *Wyniczenko v Plucinska-Surowka* [2005] EWHC 2794 (Ch), the testatrix made a new will, differing from her previous one by excluding charitable bequests and a gift to her niece (who was the claimant), and leaving all her estate to the defendant. It became apparent the defendant had drafted the will for the testatrix. The involvement of the beneficiary aroused the court's suspicions. The defendant could not satisfy the court that the will reflected the testatrix's true wishes and so the will failed.

A contrasting case is *Knight v Edonya* [2009] EWHC 2181 (Ch), where the testator made a will 2 days before he died. The will appointed the claimant as one of the executors, and the claimant was given a share of residue along with the defendants in the case. The defendants did not seek to assert a positive case of lack of knowledge and approval, but nonetheless insisted that the claimant prove the will in solemn form (i.e. in open court proceedings). The evidence showed that the claimant initiated the process of drawing up the will but, crucially, she was not present, either when the testator gave instructions for the will or at the time of its actual execution. The court held none of the circumstances relied on by the defendants were such as to excite the suspicion and concern of the court. Furthermore, the court was satisfied the will truly represented the testator's testamentary intentions and he knew and approved its contents.

Recent decisions, for example, *Gill v Woodall & Others* [2010] EWCA Civ 1430, suggest the court now demands positive proof of testamentary intention from the propounder if there are *any* circumstances justifying such an approach.

Mr and Mrs Gill were a farming couple who made 'mirror' wills (see para 2.3) in 1993 leaving residue to each other, with a default provision if this gift failed to the RSPCA (a charity). Mr Gill died first. So when Mrs Gill later died, the RSPCA stood to benefit. Nothing had been left in either will to the couple's only daughter, Dr Christine Gill. She challenged her mother's will.

Mrs Gill's testamentary capacity was not in doubt, but Dr Gill claimed her mother lacked knowledge and approval of her will. The judge accepted it was suspicious for Mrs Gill to disinherit her only child in favour of a charity with which she had no previous connection and so there was no presumption of knowledge and approval. However, the trial judge considered that the evidence presented was enough to dispel his initial suspicion. The reasons included the correct procedure for the will's preparation being followed by her solicitor and the will being short and clearly worded. Since the suspicion was dispelled, the trial judge accepted Mrs Gill knew and approved her will. However, Dr Gill had also alleged undue influence. To succeed, she had to show her mother was coerced into making a will she did not really want to make. The trial judge held Mr Gill had exerted such pressure on Mrs Gill to make a will disinheriting their only child that it amounted to coercion on his part.

The matter went to the Court of Appeal, which again held the will invalid but on different grounds. The Court of Appeal found Mrs Gill had simply lacked knowledge and approval when she executed her will. Contrary to the views of the trial judge, the court said the available evidence could not justify his initial determination that Mrs Gill had the necessary testamentary intention. The exclusion of Mrs Gill's only daughter, with whom she enjoyed a close relationship, in favour of a charity with which she had no lifetime links was indeed suspicious. Having regard to the nature and weight of evidence, the trial judge had been wrong to conclude testamentary intention had been established. Since there was no knowledge and approval to begin with, there was no need for the Court of Appeal to consider undue influence.

In *Hawes v Burgess* [2013] EWCA Civ 74, the testatrix omitted her son, P, from her will. It was another case where the Court of Appeal felt the circumstances required positive proof of knowledge and approval. Various factors suggested this was lacking, including the testatrix's daughter being instrumental in making arrangements to see the solicitor and giving instructions for its contents. Crucially, she had remained in the room during the solicitor's discussion with the testatrix (contrary to the 'golden rule' – see para 3.5.2). Whilst the solicitor did keep notes, the daughter had provided incorrect information about the motive for her mother omitting P from the will. It was also noted the solicitor did not send the testatrix a draft to check and approve before she attended at the office to sign it.

## 3.5   Practical issues for the practitioner preparing the will

There is an obvious necessity to ensure that the testator is competent to give instructions and has the necessary mental capacity and intention to make the will.

Of course, in the majority of cases, the age and general health of the testator will be such that it is obvious to all concerned there is no problem. However, in cases where there might be some doubt about the capacity of the testator or a suspicion that this might be challenged in the future, certain precautions should be taken.

### 3.5.1    Use of medical expertise and views of the practitioner preparing the will

Ideally, an objective written medical opinion regarding the testator's capacity should be obtained, although many general practitioners may be reluctant to provide one, either because they do not have the time or, more likely, because they feel they do not have the level of expertise to give a view on testamentary capacity that would stand scrutiny from a court.

Unless the person providing the opinion is an expert specialising in capacity issues, he will need guidance as to the specific criteria which apply to the making of a will. For example, the letter requesting the opinion could at the very least summarise the main criteria from *Banks v Goodfellow* [1870] LR 5 QB 549 (see para 3.3.1). The point is to make clear to the practitioner exactly what he is being asked to assess. Simply asking whether the practitioner thinks the testator has capacity generally or even capacity to make a will is not likely to yield a response that carries much weight if the will is ever challenged in court.

Ideally, the person providing the opinion should also be asked to witness the will.

The practitioner making the will when attending its execution should also make, and preserve, a detailed file note of his views on the matter and observations made about the testator. This is particularly important if expert medical evidence is lacking or proves unreliable. In *Hawes v Burgess* [2013] EWCA Civ 74, the importance of the practitioner's file notes was emphasised by the Court of Appeal when saying only the clearest evidence of lack of capacity should set a will aside if an experienced solicitor had prepared the will and contemporaneously recorded his view that a testator had capacity. In that case, the solicitor's attendance note stated the testatrix was 'entirely *compos mentis*'. There was also evidence from a medical expert that in the last years of her life, the testatrix had suffered from dementia of modest severity, which could account for her omitting her son from her will, even though she might have understood she was making a will and was aware of her property. However, the expert had neither met nor examined the testatrix and the court said it should be cautious in accepting 'after the event' evidence in preference to that of the solicitor, who although not medically qualified, had formed his opinion after seeing the testatrix. Despite the weight placed on the solicitor's attendance note, it was far from being a model of good practice. It would have been better if the solicitor had set out the evidence such as statements of the testatrix which led the solicitor to conclude that she fulfilled the elements of the *Banks v Goodfellow* test.

## 3.5.2    Golden rule

The courts often refer to a so-called 'golden rule', a phrase first used by Templeman J in *Kenward v Adams* (1975) *The Times*, 29 November 1975 when referring to the duties of practitioners in doubtful capacity cases. In addition to obtaining medical approval where an elderly or ill person wants to make a will, solicitors should also ensure:

(a)    they discuss any previous will with the client and the reasons for wanting to change its terms; and

(b)    they take instructions in the absence of anyone who stands to benefit or who may have some influence over the testator.

Non-compliance with the golden rule does not mean that the will is invalid. In *Cattermole v Prisk* [2006] 1 FLR 693, it was observed:

> This 'golden rule' provides clear guidance as to how, in relevant cases, disputes can be avoided, or minimised (with the material relevant to the determination of the dispute contemporaneously recorded and preserved). The 'golden rule' is not itself a touchstone of validity and is not a substitute for the established tests of capacity and of knowledge and approval.

Similarly, in *Allen v Emery* [2005] EWHC 2389 (Ch), [2005] All ER (D) 175:

> It is undoubtedly a desirable precaution, and one which can save a great deal of trouble in the future, for a solicitor to observe the golden rule where there is the possibility of dispute as to testamentary capacity. Failure to do so, however, is not in my judgment determinative; the rule is no more than prudent guidance for a solicitor; see the observations of Peter Gibson LJ on the golden rule in the context of want of knowledge and approval in *Hoff and Others v Atherton* [2004] EWCA Civ 1554. Ultimately, capacity is a question of fact like any other which the Court must decide on the evidence as a whole.

Clearly, complying with the rule provides contemporaneous medical evidence which may assist in the avoidance of a dispute, or minimise the chance of a dispute arising. It is vital, however, that a medical practitioner or other expert asked to give an opinion on the testator's capacity is properly briefed as to the legal test for determining capacity.

The case of *Key v Key* [2010] EWHC 408 (Ch) (see para 3.3.1) shows that the ability to make rational decisions can be affected by mental disorders, such as the effects of bereavement, which might not be easily recognised by lawyers and non-medical professionals. This may make it increasingly difficult for practitioners to realise they are dealing with a case where they should follow the golden rule, particularly if the will, as in *Key v Key*, is a rational one.

In that case there were two medical experts who gave evidence. The expert appearing for the testator's two daughters was very experienced with a focus on psychiatric problems of the elderly. The expert called by the two sons was less experienced in that area but had the advantage of having examined the testator whilst he was alive. The judge was of the opinion that this advantage outweighed what might otherwise have been the greater weight attached to the daughters' expert's experience and his specialisation.

A further aspect of this case was criticism made by the trial judge of the way instructions were taken. In giving judgment, Mr Justice Briggs (as he then was), said the solicitor accepted instructions for preparation of the will, 'without taking any proper steps to satisfy himself of Mr Key's testamentary capacity, and without even making an attendance note of his meeting'. The solicitor in question had seen the testator a few months before when dealing with the dissolution of his farming partnership and so saw no reason to question his client's capacity to make a will which appeared to be a rational one. However, the judge criticised the solicitor for failing to comply with the golden rule, which 'greatly increased the difficulties to which this dispute has given rise'.

Practitioners have long been aware of the practical difficulties in complying with the golden rule. This was judicially recognised in *Wharton v Bancroft* [2011] EWHC 3250 (Ch), when the High Court acknowledged the difficulties for practitioners if trying to follow the 'golden rule' when preparing a will for an elderly or seriously ill testator. The judge's comments were prompted by criticism of a solicitor who prepared the will of a 78-year-old man who had only a matter of days to live. The solicitor had not observed the golden rule of arranging for a medical practitioner to satisfy himself of the testator's capacity and understanding before making a contemporaneous record of his findings.

Norris J considered in this particular case the solicitor had acted correctly in making his own assessment of his client's testamentary capacity and then proceeding to make the will, saying (at [110]):

> I consider the criticism of [the solicitor] for a failure to follow 'the golden rule' to be misplaced. His job was to take the will of a dying man. A solicitor so placed cannot simply conjure up a medical attendant. He must obtain his client's consent to the attendance of and examination by a doctor. He must procure the attendance of a doctor (preferably the testator's own) who is willing to accept the instruction. He must make arrangement for any relevant payment (securing his client's agreement). I do not think [the solicitor] is to be criticised for deciding to make his own assessment (accepted as correct) and to get on with the job of drawing a will …

### 3.5.3    Mirror will issues

A further practical aspect arises when couples want to make 'mirror' wills, that is wills where the wishes of both parties are effectively the same and there is a common ultimate beneficiary (see para 2.3).

It is common practice for the will drafter to send both draft wills for approval in the same envelope addressed to the couple. However, if one of the parties may be in a more domineering and influential position, as in *Gill v Woodall & Others* [2010] EWCA Civ 1430 (see para 3.4.6), it may be appropriate to send each will in a separate envelope, asking each party to confirm individually the terms of his or her will. However, whilst this might assist in dealing with any concerns over testamentary intention, it would not necessarily help if undue influence ever became an issue.

In one sense, there is no substitute to seeing each party separately and keeping detailed notes of the discussion. However, this approach may also cause ethical difficulties because if seeing one party alone prompts a change of instructions, it then becomes impossible to comply with the duty to act in the best interests of the other (whose instructions are unchanged) without breaching confidentiality.

### 3.5.4    *Larke v Nugus* letters

On 11 December 2018, the Law Society issued an updated version of a previously issued Practice Note, *Disputed wills: Guidance for practitioners*, dealing with the situation where a solicitor, who has prepared a will, is asked after the testator's death to disclose information about the circumstances surrounding its preparation or execution. Previous Law Society advice was affirmed by the Court of Appeal in *Larke v Nugus* [2000] WTLR 1033, and the Practice Note updates that earlier advice with supplementary information on disclosure and the potential liability for costs for failure to do so.

The guidance points out that a solicitor who has taken instructions for a will is a material witness as to the circumstances surrounding its preparation and execution. So, the solicitor should provide the information in advance and make available any documents in his possession that are relevant to any potential proceedings. Doing so will avoid the cost of unnecessary applications to court and limit the costs of a full hearing. Since the court has power to order attendance under section 122 of the Senior Courts Act 1981 and pre-action disclosure under Civil Procedure Rules (CPR), rule 31.16, failure to provide information promptly may result in costly litigation with the solicitor held liable in costs.

This Practice Note again highlights not only the importance of making and preserving good file notes, but also the fact the notes may need to be disclosed if the will is later contested.

The Practice Note may be viewed at:

> www.lawsociety.org.uk/support-services/advice/practice-notes/
> disputed-wills/

# 4 Requirements for Valid Execution

## 4.1 Introduction

The execution of a will is usually very easy to get right. However, things can be dealt with in such a way that even though the will may turn out to have been validly executed, difficulties arise after the testator's death in proving that it meets the necessary requirements. This not only leads to additional costs and time taken before a grant is issued, but also inevitably increases the anxiety levels of those whose expectations are dependent on the outcome.

Those involved in the preparation of a will need to know what to do to ensure a will is executed in such a way that difficulties will not arise when the will is the subject of an application for a grant. Equally, they must be able to look at a will which they did not prepare and give a view on whether its admissibility to probate might be called into question, either by the probate registrar or someone who might seek to challenge the will's validity. Often, the appearance of a will may raise doubts as to whether it has been executed correctly, in which case it is necessary to know what further investigations need to be undertaken to establish its validity.

## 4.2 A simple recipe for getting it right

The formalities for executing a will are set out in section 9 of the WA 1837 (as amended by section 17 of the AJA 1982), and this is considered in detail at paras 4.3 to 4.3.10. With the exception of a privileged will (see para 4.7.1) or a statutory will made by the court under powers in the MCA 2005 (see para 4.7.2), any will which does not comply with these requirements will be invalid and so cannot be admitted to probate.

However, assuming the testator is able and willing to read the will and give effect to it with his own signature and the will is in a conventional format with a standard attestation clause (see para 4.3.9), a valid execution can be achieved by following these steps:

(a)    the testator and two suitable witnesses (see para 4.3.7) must remain together (that is in the same room) and attentive throughout the process, so as to comply with the statutory requirement of 'presence';

(b)    the two witnesses both watch the testator date and sign the will;

(c)    each witness in turn then signs the will, watched by the testator and each other.

Following these steps complies with the statutory procedure and no further evidence should be needed beyond the will itself to show it has been validly executed. In fact, ensuring that the witnesses see each other sign, having already seen the testator sign, goes a little beyond the statutory requirements for the sake of further evidential proof should anyone decide to dispute what actually took place.

As will become apparent below, not all executions can follow these simple steps and there may be some additional requirements. Also, having regard to the provisions of section 9 of the WA 1837, particularly since it was amended by section 17 of the AJA 1982, an execution might still be valid despite the above sequence of events not being strictly followed, although such cases invariably require proof of certain facts by those seeking to establish the will's validity.

## 4.3  Formalities in section 9 of the Wills Act 1837

Section 9 of the WA 1837 (as amended by section 17 of the AJA 1982) provides as follows:

No will shall be valid unless—

(a)    it is in writing, and signed by the testator, or by some other person in his presence and by his direction; and

(b)    it appears that the testator intended by his signature to give effect to the will; and

(c)    the signature is made or acknowledged by the testator in the presence of two or more witnesses present at the same time; and

(d)    each witness either—

(i)    attests and signs the will; or

(ii)    acknowledges his signature in the presence of the testator (but not necessarily in the presence of any other witness),

but no form of attestation shall be necessary.

Particular elements of these requirements require further explanation since each has been the subject of much litigation in the past.

## 4.3.1    '… in writing'

There are no restrictions about the materials on which, or by which, a will may be written or as to the language used; nor is any particular form of words necessary. Schedule 1 to the Interpretation Act 1978 provides that, if any statute uses the word 'writing', that word is construed as including 'typing, printing, lithography, photography and other modes of representing or reproducing words in a visible form'. So, a will in shorthand or in Braille is acceptable, as is a will written in code as long as it is decipherable using extrinsic evidence.

The writing, even handwriting, need not be the testator's own and the writing need not be in the testator's native language. However, wills written in anything other than English (or Welsh, where appropriate) are best discouraged by the professional draftsman. Not only will a non-English will make the grant and administration process more difficult, but also there may be construction and interpretation issues because while English words and phrases may have accepted meanings when used in a will, the meaning of non-English words may be lost in translation, perhaps to the point where there is no exact equivalent in probate and succession law.

Some people today may be tempted to put their will into an electronic format, for example, storing on computer or even making a 'home movie' by sitting in front of a digital imaging device and reciting their testamentary wishes. This sort of refinement is perfectly in order as long as the 'will' is supported by a formal written will made in accordance with the usual statutory formalities. In other words, electronic formatting of a will is not by itself, at least not yet, acceptable as 'writing'.

Common sense dictates the use of paper but wills have been validly made on various substances, including a wall and even an eggshell. Similarly, the substance used to put words on the page has no limitation. If written partly in ink and partly in pencil, there is a presumption that the pencil writing was *deliberative only*; the words written in pencil will not be admitted to probate unless there is evidence proving that the testator intended them to be final. If the will is entirely written in pencil, or any other non-permanent substance such as chalk, then the will as a whole is valid, but obviously the use of such materials is never advisable and should not be used in practice unless no better writing materials are available.

Professionally made wills are now produced on a computer or similar device. Likewise, homemade wills may be made using the same technology but may otherwise be handwritten, or made using a commercial form containing standard printed clauses with blank sections which are either completed in manuscript or typed in.

The writing may extend to more than one page. There is no rule to say pages must be physically attached, although they must all be present together when the will is executed. However, unless the pages are physically joined, or it is obvious from the context that each page follows on from the previous one, the probate registry will call for further evidence to verify all pages are present and are to be read together.

### 4.3.2    '… signed by the testator'

Normally, the testator signs the will, preferably with his usual signature. The signature does not have to be the testator's full name and the use of initials alone has been accepted. Using a signature which is not the testator's real name is also valid if it can be verified the signature is in fact that of the testator by comparing it to his signature on other documents. Ideally, and to avoid any issues arising, the signature should be consistent with the way the testator is described in the will.

Various alternatives to a normal signature have been held as acceptable as a signature including:

(a)    the testator's mark, such as using a cross;

(b)    the testator's thumbprint;

(c)    the use of a rubber stamp;

(d)    the use of a word that can identify the testator, such as 'Mum'.

In other words, virtually anything written or impressed on the will and intended to be a signature can be effective. A good illustration of this point is *In the Goods of Chalcraft* [1948] 1 All ER 700 where the testatrix, who was dying, signed 'E Chal' but was so weak she could not complete her signature. It was held to be a sufficient signature on the basis that it was intended to be the best she could manage in the circumstances. In *In the Estate of Cook* [1960] 1 All ER 689, the will began with the name of the testatrix and ended with the words 'Your loving mother', which the court accepted was meant to be her signature.

In *Barrett v Bem* [2012] EWCA Civ 52, the Court of Appeal confirmed the trial judge's view that if a testator chooses to sign the will personally, as opposed to directing another person to sign on his behalf (see para 4.3.3), then he can be assisted by another person provided the testator makes some 'positive and discernible contribution to the signing process' as opposed to simply abstaining from preventing the signing. So, if the testator holds the pen but has to have his hand steadied while signing the will, then this appears to suffice as a signature. However, if the testator just holds the pen and his hand is guided across the page by a helper, this probably does not suffice because the signature is that of the helper rather than the testator. This would then raise the question of whether the testator had directed another to sign on his behalf (see para 4.3.3).

### 4.3.3    '... or [signed] by some other person in his presence and by his direction'

Section 9(a) of the WA 1837 permits a signature by another person. This is useful, and indeed necessary, if the testator is physically unable to sign or even make a mark on the will, although the facility is not limited to such cases. However, to be effective a third party's signature must be at the *direction* of the testator *and* made in the mental and physical 'presence' of the testator. In other words, both the testator and the person directed to sign must be together.

Anyone (including one of the attesting witnesses) may be directed to sign and can do so using his own or the testator's name.

Obviously, the fact a will appears to have been signed by someone other than the testator raises questions, not least with the probate registry when applying for the grant, as to whether the will truly represents the wishes of the testator. Consequently, the usual attestation clause (see para 4.3.9) in the will should always be amended to reflect that:

(a)    the will was first read to or by the testator or explained, and either way the testator appeared to understand it;

(b)    the will was signed by another on the testator's behalf in his presence, the testator having directed that the person signing should do so.

It is also helpful to explain in the attestation clause why the testator did not sign. This may not be necessary if the testator suffered from a permanent condition, such as blindness, because the impairment will be known to others as a matter of record. However, it is recommended if the testator's condition was of a temporary nature, such as a recent hand injury.

In *Barrett v Bem* [2012] EWCA Civ 52 (see para 4.3.2), the Court of Appeal considered whether a signature made by another was made at the *direction* of the testator. The testator had tried to sign himself but failed and had subsequently allowed his sister to do so. The court found that although the testator wanted to make a will and had tried, but failed, to sign it personally, this was not sufficient to amount to a 'direction' to his sister to sign the will on his behalf. The question was not whether the testator wanted to direct his sister to sign the will but whether, as a matter of fact, he actually did so. In the court's judgment, there had to be some positive communication for a valid 'direction' and the evidence fell short of establishing this was the case. Passive acquiescence was not enough.

As the will was signed by the testator's sister who was a beneficiary, those challenging the will also questioned whether her gift should fail if the will itself was valid. The trial judge ruled that section 15 of the WA 1837 (see paras 4.3.8 and 8.6) only makes a gift void if an attesting *witness* is the recipient; it has no application to someone signing at the direction of the testator. The Court of Appeal was not called upon to consider the question raised in the trial court but it echoed the view of the judge that it is undesirable for a beneficiary to execute a will in his own favour in any capacity. The fact a will is signed by a beneficiary, albeit on the testator's behalf in accordance with section 9, affects the issue of testamentary intention and so gives rise to 'suspicious circumstances' requiring the propounder of the will to prove knowledge and approval (see para 3.4.6).

### 4.3.4    '… testator intended by his signature to give effect to the will'

Prior to the AJA 1982, the testator had to sign at the foot or end of the will but this gave rise to problems where signatures appeared in margins and elsewhere on the page. The position now is that no location is specified in the amended section 9 of the WA 1837. The court just has to decide whether the testator intended the signature to give effect to the will.

In *Wood v Smith* [1992] 3 All ER 556, the testator, T, made a handwritten will which began 'My will by T of (address)'. T did not sign it at the end of the will, where the two witnesses signed. One of them pointed out to T that he had not signed. He replied 'Yes I have, I have signed it at the top. It can be signed anywhere'.

At first instance, the judge refused to accept this as a duly executed will, since the natural construction of the words in the WA 1837 'with intent to give effect to the will' was that T should sign *after* making the dispositive provisions and this had not happened here. The Court of Appeal rejected this argument, holding that as long as the writing of the will and the appending of the signature were all one operation, it did not matter where on the document or when, in the course of writing, the signature was appended.

This 'intention' of the testator may have to be established by evidence of due execution (e.g. from the attesting witness(es) or others present at the execution) if this cannot be deduced from the face of the will, as where the signature appears in an unusual position, or on an envelope containing the will.

If the will is written on more than one page (only the last being duly executed) and they are not securely fastened together, evidence of due execution will be needed. It will be sufficient to show that the pages were (at the time of execution) held together by the testator's finger and thumb, or pressed together on a table by the testator with his hand, or even that (though not touching) they were then in the same room under the testator's control.

Suffice to say, to avoid unnecessary complications later, the testator should be asked to sign at the end of the will, opposite the attestation clause, and also to sign at the bottom of each preceding page if there is more than one (although it is not necessary for the witnesses to sign previous pages).

Mention can be made here of *Marley v Rawlings* [2014] UKSC 2 where the court had to consider this aspect of section 9 of the WA 1837, as well as other issues (considered in Chapter 7). The deceased and his wife engaged a solicitor to make mirror wills but unfortunately each executed the will meant for the other by mistake. The mistake was not discovered when the wife died (presumably because everything passed by survivorship to her husband so the will was not required). On the husband's death, the mistake came to light. The Court of Appeal initially held the husband's will was invalid since he had not 'intended by his signature to give effect to the will he actually signed. What he had intended was to sign his own will and not that of his wife'. The Supreme Court disagreed, saying the husband had clearly signed the document in front of him and had done so with the intention of it being his will (even though it was not). In this way, the document the husband signed could be admitted to probate as his will and the court was then free to consider the problems raised by the document containing his wife's wishes rather than his own, which it did by rectifying the will under section 20 of the AJA 1982 (see para 3.4.5).

### 4.3.5     '… the [testator's] signature is made or acknowledged by the testator in the presence of two or more witnesses present at the same time'

There are several important points to consider here. First, the intended signature must be completed in the physical and mental 'presence' of at least two witnesses present at the same time. For physical presence, it is sufficient if the witnesses see the testator writing the signature, or at least could have seen the writing of the signature if they had looked. As regards mental presence, the witnesses do not need to know the testator is signing a will and certainly do not have to know the contents of the will. However, the witnesses must be aware (and so should be told, if necessary) what the testator is doing, i.e. the testator is signing *a* document and they as witnesses are to bear witness to the signing.

Alternatively, the testator's signature might already be on the will. This might be so if the testator has already written and signed the will before going to visit friends or neighbours to ask if they can witness what the testator has done. The testator does not need to sign the will again in the presence of the witnesses but, instead, can acknowledge the earlier signature in the joint presence of the witnesses, who must see, or have the opportunity of seeing, the signature. The signature must not, therefore, be covered (though the rest of the will can be). The acknowledgment by the testator may be by words or conduct but must be made to at least two witnesses simultaneously.

As to the necessary capacity of the witnesses, see para 4.3.7.

### 4.3.6    '… each witness either – (i) attests and signs the will; or (ii) acknowledges his signature in the presence of the testator (but not necessarily in the presence of any other witness)'

The witnesses should then be asked to sign the will. The exact position of a witness's signature is immaterial but it is usual for witnesses to sign beneath the testator's signature as evidence of intention to validate it.

In *Payne v Payne* [2018] EWCA Civ 985, the witnesses saw the testator add his signature and then filled in details of their name, address and occupation but had not signed the will form because it did not provide a place to write their signatures. The Court of Appeal compared the pre-1982 wording in section 9 of the WA 1837 with the substituted wording. The requirement that witnesses should 'subscribe' had been replaced with a need to 'sign'. The court's view was that the change in wording appeared to be designed to avoid archaic phraseology rather than introduce stricter formality requirements. Therefore, the word 'sign' should be interpreted as having the same meaning as 'subscribe'. As such, the provision merely required witnesses to write their name with the intention that writing it should operate as an attestation.

The testator must be physically and mentally present. Testators must either see the witnesses sign or be in such a position that they would have seen them if they had chosen to look (or could have seen if they had not been blind). If the testator loses consciousness before both witnesses have signed, the will is invalid because it must be signed in the mental, as well as the physical, presence of the testator.

Witnesses usually sign in the presence of each other, although this is not essential. In the event of a dispute, each witness can then provide evidence not only that he himself witnessed the testator's signature, but also that he was present when the other witness signed.

As with the testator's signature, section 9 of the WA 1837 allows a witness to acknowledge an earlier signature in the presence of the testator. This is not something to recommend at execution but is included in section 9 to save a will which might otherwise have been invalidly executed.

In *Couser v Couser* [1996] 3 All ER 256, the testator, T, completed and signed a printed will form. He took it to his friends, Mr and Mrs B, for witnessing. Mrs B signed the will, although her husband was not then present. Mr B later joined his wife and T. Mrs B objected that the will would not be valid if Mr B witnessed it now, but T persuaded Mr B to sign by showing him both his own and Mrs B's signatures. When Mr B signed, both T and Mrs B were present, although Mrs B continued to claim that the will was not valid.

It was held that, firstly, T had acknowledged his signature in the presence of two witnesses and, secondly, Mrs B's continued protests about the validity of the will were sufficient to show acknowledgement of her signature.

### 4.3.7    Capacity of the witnesses

Save for section 15 of the WA 1837 (see para 4.3.8), there are no particular rules as to who can, or cannot, be a witness, save that such a person must be able to satisfy the test for 'presence'.

In terms of physical 'presence', a blind person cannot be a witness (though a blind testator can still be in the 'presence' of a witness).

Someone who is intoxicated, asleep or unconscious and so unaware of what is going on is clearly lacking mental 'presence', and the same could well be argued of someone who was suffering from a mental illness. A young child, or anyone for that matter, who lacks awareness of what being a witness means, would also not be a valid witness.

There may be instances, such as a will being made in an emergency, where the choice of witnesses is limited but bearing in mind witnesses may be required to give evidence of due execution at a later date, they should ideally not be very old or very young. Similarly, they should not be too difficult to trace (and hence should be encouraged to write their address and any occupation under their signature). It may be better to avoid using someone who is merely a passing acquaintance or who might be about to move away from the area.

### 4.3.8    Witnesses and section 15 of the Wills Act 1837

An executor, beneficiary or the spouse or civil partner of a beneficiary is *prima facie* capable of being a competent witness and the validity of the will, in terms of its admissibility to probate, is not affected.

However, by virtue of section 15 of the WA 1837 (as amended), a beneficiary loses any beneficial interest given under the will if either the *beneficiary*, or that *beneficiary's spouse or civil partner*, has witnessed the will. If a witness later marries or enters into a civil partnership with the beneficiary, then the rule does not apply and so the beneficiary can still inherit. The aim of section 15 is to ensure an unbiased execution and that those who witness a will have no financial interest in the devolution of the estate. However, the section is often cited as outdated or at least in need of modification since it does not disqualify a cohabitee of a witness from inheriting under a will, no matter how lengthy the relationship with the witness.

If a will contains a charging clause allowing professional executors or trustees to charge for their services to the estate, this is no longer treated as a beneficial gift under the will. Instead, it is treated as an administrative provision. Hence, if a solicitor-executor with the benefit of such a clause is a witness, the solicitor or firm can still charge under the clause (section 28(2) of the Trustee Act 2000).

For more on section 15 of the WA 1837, including situations where it does not apply and its implications for those preparing wills, see, further, para 8.6.

### 4.3.9     Attestation clauses

An attestation clause is normally included at the end of the will where the testator and witnesses sign. It recites that the formalities required by section 9 of the WA 1837 have been complied with. A suitable form of wording is:

> Signed by the testator in our joint presence and then by us in [his][hers].

The lack of an attestation clause does not in any way invalidate a will because section 9 expressly says that 'no form of attestation shall be necessary'. Indeed, if it was a requirement, many homemade wills would fail as most lay will writers would be unaware of what such a clause was for.

However, if there is no attestation clause, the probate registry will require evidence of due execution from the witnesses or someone else present. This will contain their recollection of events and hopefully allow the registrar to find that the will was properly executed in accordance with section 9 of the WA 1837. If no evidence is obtainable, the court may admit a will to probate if it appears to have been duly signed and witnessed – but probably only after a hearing by a judge involving, inevitably, delay and extra expense.

Effectively, an attestation clause, like the one above, raises a *presumption* of due execution which avoids the need for further evidence and so should always be included in a will.

In *Sherrington v Sherrington* [2005] EWCA Civ 326, [2005] WTLR 587, the Court of Appeal held that the strongest evidence is necessary to rebut the presumption of due execution. The testator's will had been written out by his step-daughter and purportedly read out to him by telephone before he 'signed' it, in haste, on his way to an airport. The evidence of the witnesses, one of whom had scant English, suggested they had little knowledge of the requirements for wills and they did not know they were witnessing a will. Notwithstanding the unusual circumstances, the Court of Appeal upheld the validity of the will by saying that in the absence of the *strongest* evidence, the intention of the witness to attest is inferred from the presence of the testator's signature on the will, the attestation clause and the signature of the witness.

Although evidence to rebut the presumption of due execution must be strong, and so the burden of displacing it is great, such a claim did succeed in *Ahluwalia v Singh and others* [2011] EWHC 2901 (Ch). The will was held invalid after the claimant successfully alleged it was not signed by the testator in the presence of both witnesses when present at the same time, despite there being an attestation clause reciting this had been the case. Having heard evidence from the two witnesses, and finding one more credible than the other, the judge said the claimant had satisfied the burden of producing the strongest evidence. The evidential force of the presumption in favour of due execution did not outweigh the judge's finding that one witness had signed in the testator's presence when the other witness was not there.

The fact that a witness has no recollection of signing a will is not normally sufficient since memories are unreliable. What is needed is something more tangible such as proof that the witness was in a different place on the relevant date (see *Channon v Perkins* [2005] EWCA Civ 1808).

If the will is signed by someone other than the testator at his direction or, for example, if the testator is blind or illiterate, special forms of attestation clause should be used which additionally recite the fact the will, where necessary, was first read to the testator, etc (see, further, para 4.3.3).

## 4.3.10   Dating the will

A will does not have to be dated so far as section 9 of the WA 1837 is concerned. However, the lack of a date can cause difficulties in establishing that a particular will is, in fact, the last will of the testator and, therefore, the effective one in cases where there is more than one will in circulation. Problems can also arise with its construction, for example if the will refers to a gift of the car 'which I now own'. Such difficulties may be resolved by extrinsic evidence which pinpoints the date (see, also, para 12.3 as regards a problem in relation to the appointment of testamentary guardians).

The practice should be for the date to be inserted in the will just before the testator signs it. The date clause is traditionally either at the beginning of the will as part of the introduction, or at the end immediately before the attestation clause. Many practitioners prefer to put the date clause at the end because there is then less risk of its completion being overlooked as part of the execution process.

The case of *Corbett v Newey* [1996] 2 All ER 914 held that a will cannot be executed conditionally. In that case the testatrix executed her will and returned it to her solicitor saying it was not to be dated until she had made certain lifetime gifts. The will was later dated once the gifts had been completed but the Court of Appeal said the will was invalid because when she signed the will, she lacked the necessary testamentary intention (see Chapter 3). In other words, she did not intend by her signature to give effect to the will as required by section 9(b) of the WA 1837 (see para 4.3.4).

## 4.4    Practicalities of execution

There are two possible methods.

### 4.4.1    Supervised execution

The practitioner supervises the execution either at his office, or by attending at the place where the testator resides, either permanently or temporarily, such as a hospital.

This is the best method because the practitioner is in control of the execution and can see it is carried out correctly. The practitioner can also deal with any last minute issues that might arise, as well as being able to advise the testator on matters such as the safe keeping of the will and what to do if the testator wants to make changes.

### 4.4.2    Unsupervised execution

Alternatively, testators may want the will sent to them so they can deal with the execution of the will themselves. This may be requested in the belief it will save costs or simply because the testator finds it more convenient.

The problem here is that testators may never get round to executing their wills, or may do so but in a way that either makes the wills invalid or gives rise to a problem, such as where a beneficiary witnesses the will and loses his gift. Not only do such cases raise issues over the devolution of the testator's estate but there are likely to be claims from disappointed beneficiaries that the practitioner was in breach of duty in not ensuring that everything was done properly to make the will fully effective (see, e.g., *Esterhuizen v Allied Dunbar Assurance plc* [1998] 2 FLR 668, *Gray v Richard*

*Butler* [2000] WTLR 143 and *Humblestone v The Martin Tolhurst Partnership* [2004] EWHC 151 (Ch), [2004] WTLR 343 where the extent of a solicitor's duty to ensure valid execution is discussed).

Essentially, most, if not all, problems that can arise with an unsupervised execution can be largely eliminated by providing the testator with accurate and intelligible instructions to ensure everything is done as it should be. Many practitioners use a standard form for such instructions. This tends to reduce the risk of errors that might be introduced if writing a bespoke letter each time. Instructions to the testator should conclude with a request to return the dated and executed will to the solicitor so the execution can be checked to ensure, insofar as appears, that everything is in order.

## 4.5 Codicils

A codicil is a testamentary document which supplements the terms of an existing will by adding to it, amending it or revoking it, wholly or in part. In practice, only 'minor adjustments' should be made in this way. Major changes are best made by making a new will.

The requirements for execution of a valid codicil are the same as those discussed in this chapter for a will.

(See, further, para 6.3 as to the use and effect of a codicil.)

## 4.6 Wills made outside England and Wales and section 1 of the Wills Act 1963

If the testator's will fails to satisfy section 9 of the WA 1837 but was executed outside England and Wales, then it may be saved by coming within the terms of the Wills Act 1963.

Under section 1 of the Wills Act 1963, a will is generally valid if it accords with the internal law of the country in which it was executed, or in which the deceased was domiciled or habitually resident or of which he was a national, either at the time of its execution or his death (see, further, para 9.4).

## 4.7 Wills not subject to section 9 of the Wills Act 1837

### 4.7.1 Privileged wills

A wills practitioner is rarely, if ever, involved with the preparation and execution of a privileged will because by definition this type of will is usually made by someone at a time when that person is not able to seek professional assistance. However, a practitioner may encounter such a will after it has been made and may be required to advise on its effect.

Privileged wills can be made under section 11 of the WA 1837 by 'any soldier being in actual military service or any mariner or seaman being at sea'. The Wills (Soldiers and Sailors) Act 1918 extends the privilege so that, for example, 'soldier' includes members of the RAF.

The feature of a will made by anyone to whom the privilege applies is that all formal requirements of section 9 of the WA 1837 for the execution of a valid will are waived. Hence, the will can be made in any form and may even be an oral statement provided it shows an intention to dispose of property in the event of the testator's death. The testator need not know that he is making a will as such and the will is valid even if made by a minor. Since no attestation by witnesses is required, a gift to a witness in a privileged will is still effective and is not caught by section 15 of the WA 1837.

The privilege extends to soldiers in 'actual military service'. The meaning of this term includes activities closely connected with warfare, whether or not war has been declared and whether or not the testator has actually arrived at the scene of fighting. The fact there is no actual state of war or that the enemy is not a uniformed force engaged in regular warfare is irrelevant. Thus the privilege can attach to members of the armed forces engaged in active duty in 'trouble spots', even after hostilities might be regarded as having ceased so that the duties are akin to peace-keeping.

In applying the privilege to mariners or seamen 'at sea', this term is wider in its scope than 'actual military service' because the privilege applies to any seaman or mariner (whether or not in the armed forces) being at sea at all times and not only when warlike circumstances exist. The court has held that being 'at sea' includes the time preparing for and travelling to a port to take up a position on board a ship. However, the privilege does not apply to the will of a seaman made while on shore leave at a time when he or she is not a member of the crew of a particular ship and when he or she has not received orders to join a ship.

It is the circumstances in which the will is made that determine whether or not the testator is privileged. The circumstances at death are irrelevant. In *Re Servoz-Gavin* [2009] EWHC 3168 (Ch), the deceased was a radio officer in the Merchant Navy. In February 1990, he was about to leave for Bombay to join a ship registered in Panama and stayed with his cousin for 2 nights, while he was getting a visa. Before he left he said to her, 'If anything happens to me, if I snuff it, I want everything to go to Auntie Anne'. The deceased suffered a stroke in 1999 but survived until April

2005 when he died from a heart attack. His statement to his cousin was held to be a valid privileged will.

As to revocation of privileged wills, see para 5.8.

### 4.7.2 Statutory wills made by the court under the Mental Capacity Act 2005

Sections 16 and 18 of the MCA 2005, which came into force on 7 October 2007, provide for the Court of Protection to make an order for a will to be made on behalf of an adult who is incapable of making his own will. Such a will can deal with any of the patient's (P) property except foreign immovable property, which must be dealt with under the *lex situs* of the jurisdiction where it is located. Section 5 of the MCA 2005 provides that 'An act done, or decision made, under this Act for or on behalf of a person who lacks capacity must be done, or made, in his best interests'. There is an obvious difficulty in deciding what is in the best interests of a person in relation to what happens to his assets after his death. Section 4 of the MCA 2005 requires the court to take various factors into account including P's past and present wishes and feelings. In *Re Peter Jones* [2014] EWCOP 59, [2016] WTLR 661, the court held that this meant that where a person had a relatively recent will, the court could authorise a statutory will that makes good P's omissions but must not seek to correct his considered acts and decisions. In *NT v FS and others* [2013] EWHC 684 (COP), [2013] WTLR 867 the court made the point that the weight to be attached to different factors will inevitably differ depending on the individual circumstances of the particular case.

When applying for an order to execute a statutory will, any person who might be prejudiced by the new will, such as someone entitled under an existing will or on intestacy, must ordinarily be named as a respondent and in due course served with papers relating to the proceedings.

The will should be signed by the person authorised by the order, with the name of the testator or testatrix and with his or her own name, in the presence of two or more witnesses present at the same time, and these witnesses should attest and subscribe in the usual way (see Schedule 2 to the MCA 2005). The will is then authenticated with the official seal of the Court of Protection.

Where an order has been made for a will to be executed on behalf of a testator, the will is valid even though it is not sealed by the Court of Protection before the testator's death. The WA 1837 (apart from section 9) then applies to the will as though the will had been executed by the testator's own signature.

# 5 Revocation of Wills

## 5.1 Freedom to revoke wills

Testators are always free to revoke their will during their lifetime, provided they have the appropriate mental capacity. There are very few decided cases dealing with the mental capacity for revocation but according to *Re Sabatini* (1969) 114 SJ 35, a testator must have the same standard of mind and memory, and the same degree of understanding, when revoking a will, as when making it.

If a testator has entered into an agreement with another person to make a will in particular terms and not to revoke it unilaterally (a so-called mutual wills agreement), the testator is still free to revoke the will. However, the revocation will not necessarily achieve what the testator wants; if the other party to the agreement has died having carried out his part of the agreement, equity will impose a constructive trust over the part of the survivor's property that was subject to the agreement. The survivor may revoke the original will and make a different one but the new will cannot affect the destination of the property bound by the trust.

A similar principle applies if someone makes a new will and, by doing so, breaks a contract not to revoke an earlier one (see, further, paras 2.3 and 2.4).

## 5.2 Methods of revocation

There are three ways to revoke a will:

(a)   by later will or codicil;

(b)   by destruction;

(c)   by subsequent marriage or the formation of a civil partnership.

Subsequent divorce or dissolution of a civil partnership does not revoke an earlier will but does revoke a gift to the former spouse or civil partner and his or her appointment as executor (see para 5.6).

Other changes in circumstances, such as the birth of a child, separation, bankruptcy, etc have no effect whatsoever on an earlier will save for the implementation of any provisions in the will which might have been included in anticipation of such events ever occurring.

## 5.3    Revocation by a later will or codicil

Under section 20 of the WA 1837, a will can be revoked in whole or in part by a later will or codicil or by a written document executed in the same way as a will and declaring an intention to revoke the earlier will or codicil.

The clearest way in which a later will may revoke an earlier one is if it contains an express revocation clause. Such a clause should always be included in a will which deals with the whole of a testator's property.

A suitable form of wording is:

> I revoke all previous wills and codicils.

Even without an express revocation clause, a later will can revoke an earlier one by implication. However, the mere fact of making a later will does not automatically cause a *total* revocation of an earlier will, unless the two wills are incapable of standing together – in which case the later will alone prevails. In order to decide on the effect a later will has on earlier dispositions, a court has to exercise the functions of a court of construction (see, e.g. *Perdoni v Curati* [2011] EWHC 3442 (Ch)).

EXAMPLE

> Will 1 leaves, 'My Rolex watch to Fred, residue to Ray'.
>
> Will 2 made later leaves, 'My Rolex watch to John'. It does not contain a revocation clause or any provision dealing with residue.
>
> The gift in will 1 leaving residue to Ray continues to be valid and has to be carried into effect. Will 2 is silent as to what happens to residue, whereas will 1 made express provision for its disposal. In the circumstances, there is no inconsistency or incompatibility between the two wills, apart from the way the Rolex watch is dealt with. Hence, John takes the Rolex watch and Ray takes residue.
>
> If will 2 *had* contained an express revocation clause, John would have taken the Rolex watch but residue would have been undisposed of and so pass under the intestacy rules. If will 2 had no revocation clause but did contain an effective gift of residue, then will 1 would be revoked in its entirety by implication since all provisions dealing with the disposal of the whole estate are contained in will 2.

If the testator has already made a will which deals with property outside England and Wales, and now wants to make a new will dealing with property within England and Wales, the revocation clause needs careful thought. It should be worded so that it does not revoke the foreign will, for example:

> I revoke any previous wills and codicils to the extent that they dispose of my assets in England and Wales.

For issues in relation to foreign property generally, see Chapter 9.

Similarly, if the testator is making a codicil which is to revoke and replace part only of an earlier will, it is important to word the codicil appropriately. It is often more satisfactory to prepare a new will dealing with all of the assets (see para 6.3).

## 5.4 Revocation by destruction

A will can be revoked by 'burning, tearing or otherwise destroying the same by the testator or by some person in his presence and by his direction with the intention of revoking the same' (section 20 of the WA 1837).

Physical destruction without the intention to revoke is insufficient; a will destroyed accidentally or by mistake is not revoked. If its contents can be reconstructed (e.g. from a copy), an order may be obtained allowing the admission to probate of the reconstruction as a valid will.

Physical destruction is required: symbolic destruction (e.g. simply crossing out wording or writing 'revoked' across the will) is not sufficient. In *Cheese v Lovejoy* (1876–77) LR 2 PD 251 the testator wrote 'all these are cancelled' on the will and crossed out part of it. He then threw it away but a servant found and preserved it, producing it after the testator's death. The will was held to be valid. Although the testator had intended to revoke it, he had done nothing which could be regarded as 'burning, tearing, or otherwise destroying'.

Whether what has been done amounts to physical destruction is a question of degree. In *Re Adams* [1990] Ch 601, heavy scoring out with a ball point pen was held to amount to 'otherwise destroying'. The amount of interference with the will was far greater than mere crossing out.

If the testator destroys part of a will, this may amount to revocation of the whole will if the part destroyed is sufficiently substantial or important (e.g. the attestation clause). In *Hobbs v Knight* (1838) 1 Curt 768, where the testator cut off his signature, the whole will was held to be revoked. If the part destroyed is less substantial or important, then the partial destruction may revoke only that part which was actually destroyed. In *Re Everest* [1975] Fam 44, where the testator cut off the part of the will containing the residuary gift, the rest of the will was held to be unrevoked.

A testator who wishes to revoke by destruction should ensure that the will is completely destroyed. However, to prevent later uncertainty as to what happened to the will, it is preferable to revoke by an executed written document.

There is a presumption a will last known to be in the testator's possession but which cannot be found after death was destroyed by the testator with the intention of revoking it (see *Eckersley v Platt* (1865–69) LR 1 P & D 281). However, the strength of the presumption varies depending on circumstances. In *Rowe v Clarke* [2005] EWHC 3068 (Ch), the court held that 'the strength of the presumption in any given case depends on the character of the custody which the testator had over the will'. This testator had kept his papers in some disorder and had not attempted to keep the original will secure, so the presumption was very weak and was rebutted by the evidence. Importantly, the court also held the presumption can apply if there is no evidence the will was not in existence at the date of death. The person claiming revocation does not have to prove non-existence of the will.

If the destruction is carried out by anyone other than the testator, it must be done in the testator's presence and by the testator's direction. Otherwise, it is ineffective and cannot be ratified by the testator afterwards, although the testator could still effect a revocation by a duly executed written document.

## 5.5   Revocation by subsequent marriage or formation of a civil partnership

If the testator marries or forms a civil partnership after executing a will, the will is automatically revoked (section 18 of the WA 1837, as substituted by the AJA 1982).

At the time of writing, there is concern over 'predatory' marriages triggered by the sad story of Joan Blass who was married in secret to a much younger man when she was 90 and severely demented. Her family knew nothing of the marriage until after her death. The test of capacity to contract a valid marriage is relatively low so the new husband inherited her estate under the intestacy rules. In November 2018, a Marriage and Civil Partnership (Consent) Bill got its first reading but unfortunately it looks as if the Bill has been lost due to lack of parliamentary time – a Brexit casualty. The Bill would have changed the law so that entering into a new marriage or civil partnership would not automatically revoke a person's previous will.

The rule does not apply to a will made prior to a forthcoming marriage or civil partnership if it appears from the will that the testator was expecting to marry or form a civil partnership with a particular person and does not intend the will to be revoked (sections 18(3) and 18B(3) of the WA 1837).

The will must clearly recite: (a) an expectation of marrying or forming a civil partnership with a particular person; and (b) a wish that the will is not to be revoked.

In *Court and Others v Despallieres* [2009] EWHC 3340 (Ch), the will declared that it was not to be revoked by 'subsequent marriage, Civil Union Partnership nor adoption'. This did not satisfy the statutory requirements as there was no reference to an expected marriage or civil partnership with a particular person.

Unless the will states that it is conditional on the marriage or civil partnership taking place, it will take effect unless expressly revoked even if the expected marriage/civil partnership has not happened by the date of death.

EXAMPLE

> Fred and Frances are engaged. They make wills in expectation of marriage leaving everything to the other and then have a row and break off the engagement. Fred dies 10 years later without having changed his will. Frances will take his estate.
>
> A suitable form of wording for a will made in expectation of marriage is:
>
> > I am expecting to marry [NAME OF INTENDED SPOUSE]. My marriage to [her OR him] is not to revoke this will. This will is to take effect even if I die before marrying [NAME OF INTENDED SPOUSE].

Obviously, marriage or the formation of a civil partnership with anyone other than the person named in the will revokes the will.

Sections 18(4) and 18B(4)(6) of the WA 1837 allow dispositions in a will to survive marriage or the formation of a civil partnership provided it appears from the will that this was the testator's intention.

Sections 18(2) and 18B(2) of the WA 1837 provide that the exercise of a power of appointment by will remains effective notwithstanding a subsequent marriage or formation of a civil partnership. The appointment is saved irrespective of whether the will is expressed to be made in expectation of marriage or formation of a civil partnership. The exercise of the power of appointment is not saved from revocation where the property appointed would pass to the testator's PRs in default of appointment.

Note the effect of the Marriage (Same Sex Couples) Act 2013 which permitted the marriage of same sex couples as from 13 March 2014. From that date, all references to marriage, married couples, etc in existing legislation for England and Wales are amended to include marriage of same sex couples. References to such in wills, trusts and other private documents made after that date are similarly construed unless the context of the document provides otherwise. Section 9(1) allows existing civil partners to convert their civil partnership into a marriage, but an amendment made to section 18 of the WA 1837 provides that making such a change does *not* revoke an existing will or codicil.

Note also the Civil Partnerships, Marriages & Deaths (Registration Etc.) Act 2019 now makes civil partnerships available to mixed sex as well as same sex couples as from a date specified in regulations made by the Secretary of State (such date being no later than 31 December 2019). Section 2(5) of the Act provides that the Secretary of State may, by regulations, make provision for the conversion of marriages into civil partnerships.

## 5.6 Effect of divorce and dissolution

If the testator makes a will and is later divorced or if the civil partnership is dissolved (or the marriage or civil partnership is annulled or declared void) then, under section 18A of the WA 1837 (amended by the Law Reform (Succession) Act 1995 with effect from 1 January 1996) and section 18C the will remains valid but:

(a) provisions of the will appointing the former spouse or civil partner as executor or trustee take effect as if the former spouse or civil partner had died on the date on which the marriage or civil partnership is dissolved or annulled; and

(b) any property, or interest in property, which is devised or bequeathed to the former spouse or civil partner passes as if the former spouse or civil partner had died on that date.

This means that any substitutional provisions in the will which are expressed to take effect if the testator's spouse or civil partner predeceases will also take effect if the marriage or civil partnership is dissolved or annulled.

The provisions of sections 18A and 18C of the WA 1837 are subject to any contrary intention expressed in the will and the failure of gifts to the former spouse or civil partner is expressly stated to be without prejudice to any claim under the I(PFD)A 1975 (see para 2.2).

Sections 18A and 18C of the WA 1837 apply only to dissolutions or annulments decreed by a court and apply only at the decree absolute stage. A separation has no effect on a will. Anyone contemplating divorce or the dissolution of a civil partnership should always consider making a new will as quickly as possible.

## 5.7   Conditional revocation

Occasionally, a testator's intention to revoke his will may be conditional upon some future event (e.g. the testator destroys his will intending that it be revoked when he executes a new will). If that event does not in fact take place, the original will may be valid even though it has been destroyed. Extrinsic evidence is admissible to establish the testator's intention. The contents of the original will may be reconstructed from a copy or draft.

*In the Estate of Southerden* [1925] P 177 is a case where a husband had made a will in favour of his wife but believing that she would take his entire estate on intestacy he destroyed the will. Due to the size of his estate, she inherited only part of the estate on intestacy. The court held that the will remained valid as the husband's intention to revoke was conditional.

In *Re Jones* [1976] Ch 200, the intention to revoke was not conditional. The testatrix had made a will leaving a smallholding to certain beneficiaries. She told her bank manager that she was going to leave it elsewhere because of the beneficiaries' attitude to her and the fact that they had acquired their own property. She made an appointment to give instructions for a new will but died before attending. On her death, the will was found mutilated with the signature and the gift of the smallholding having been cut out. The will was held to be revoked since there was no evidence that what she had done was conditional on making a new will. By her mutilation of the will she intended to achieve its absolute revocation and such an inference was not necessarily inconsistent with her intention to make a new will at the earliest opportunity.

For a recent case where issues concerned with conditional revocation were considered, see *Blyth v Sykes* [2019] EWHC 54 (Ch).

## 5.8   Revocation and privileged wills

The requirements for making a privileged will are considered in para 4.7.1.

As regards revocation, as long as a testator still enjoys privileged status, he can revoke a will informally, regardless of whether or not the will was made informally.

Having been able to make a privileged will, the mere fact the testator subsequently loses privileged status does not of itself affect the validity of that will. However, having lost privileged status, then any revocation must generally be made in one of the formal ways described above.

There is an exception in section 3 of the Family Law Reform Act 1969 allowing minors who have made privileged wills to revoke them whilst still minors even though they no longer enjoy privileged status. However, it appears such revocation cannot be informal but must be by way of a formal attested document or by destruction if there was a written will capable of being destroyed.

# 6 Alteration to Wills and Use of Codicils

Section 21 of the WA 1837 provides that alterations made to a will after execution are invalid unless the alterations are executed like a will. The initials of the testator and witnesses in the margin beside the alteration are sufficient for this purpose.

## 6.1 Alterations made before execution

An alteration made before execution is valid but alterations are presumed to be made after execution. This means unless it can be proved that they were made before the will was executed, they will be ineffective. The safe course is, therefore, for the testator and witnesses to initial and date *all* alterations, whenever made.

## 6.2 Alterations made after execution

Unless executed like a will, the alteration is invalid and the original wording is admitted to probate so long as it is 'apparent'. Wording is regarded as apparent if it can be read by ordinary means, such as close inspection through a magnifying glass or holding the document up to the light.

What if the original wording is not apparent? If the original words have been obliterated in such a way they can no longer be read, those words have effectively been revoked by destruction. The rest of the will remains valid and takes effect with the omission of the obliterated words.

The court may decide that the testator's intention to revoke the obliterated words was conditional only. This inference is most likely where the testator attempted to replace the obliterated words with a substitution. The implied condition is that the testator intended to revoke the original words only if the substitution was effective. As it is not effective, the original words remain valid and, if they can be reconstructed (e.g. from a copy or draft), they will take effect.

EXAMPLES

In each of the following cases the original legacy was £1,000. The witnesses are dead and so there is no extrinsic evidence as to when the alterations were made:

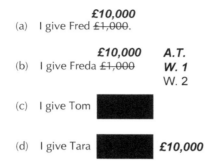

> **£10,000**
> (a)    I give Fred ~~£1,000~~.

> **£10,000**    **A.T.**
> (b)    I give Freda ~~£1,000~~    **W. 1**
>                                    W. 2

> (c)    I give Tom

> (d)    I give Tara                **£10,000**

In the absence of evidence of when the alterations were made, they are all treated as made after execution.

In clause (a), the alteration is unexecuted and is, therefore, inadmissible to probate. The original wording is apparent and so Fred takes the original amount of £1,000.

In clause (b), the alteration is initialled by the testator and witnesses and so 'executed like a will'. It is admissible to probate and Freda takes £10,000.

In clause (c), the obliteration is treated as revocation by destruction. Construing what is left of the clause, Tom takes nothing.

In clause (d), the obliteration is again treated as a revocation but with the intention of being conditional on the substituted amount being admitted to probate. As it cannot, the condition fails and so does the revocation. Provided the original wording can be established by any means, such as looking at a previous draft or using infra-red photography or other technology, Tara will take £1,000. If the original wording cannot be established, the will is admitted to probate with a blank space and, like Tom, Tara takes nothing.

## 6.3    Use of codicils

Another way of altering a will is to use a codicil. A codicil is a testamentary instrument which is executed in the same way as a will and which supplements the terms of an existing will either by adding to it, by amending it in part or by revoking it in part. Following death, both the will and codicil (of which there may be more than one) are admitted to probate.

A codicil normally 'republishes' a will so the original will is treated as if executed at the date of the codicil and incorporating the changes made by the codicil.

The effect of republication may be to alter the construction of the will, both as regards people and property.

EXAMPLES

(a)    Thomas makes a gift to 'my son's wife'. The wife at the date the will is made predeceases Thomas and so the gift lapses (i.e. fails). If the son remarries, the gift remains lapsed. However, if Thomas subsequently executes a codicil to the will, the will is republished and the gift in the will is construed as a gift to the son's wife at the date of the codicil (or, if the son has not remarried at the date of the codicil, the gift will be construed as made to the first person to fulfil that description) (see *Re Hardyman* [1925] Ch 287).

(b)    Therese makes a gift of 'my seaside cottage'. After the date of the will, she sells that particular cottage and buys another. The use of the word 'my' means the gift will be construed as a gift of the cottage she owned at the date the will was made and so the gift is adeemed (i.e. fails). (For ademption, see para 8.3.) However, if Therese subsequently executes a codicil, the will is republished and the gift will be construed as a gift of the cottage she owned at the date of the codicil (see *Re Reeves* [1928] Ch 351).

Great care is needed when drafting codicils to ensure the correct clauses in the will are being referred to, revoked, etc and that the new clauses 'work' when read in conjunction with the original clauses. For a typical illustration of the problems that can arise, see *Re Morris* [1971] P 62, where a solicitor prepared a codicil which was intended to revoke clause 7 (iv) of the will but in error the codicil revoked the whole of clause 7.

The widespread use of technology in producing wills means it will normally be simpler and more satisfactory to generate a new will incorporating desired changes, particularly if the practitioner who made the original will is instructed to make the changes and still has the will 'on file'.

# 7 Construction and Interpretation of Wills

## 7.1 Introduction

A will should mean what the testator intends it to mean.

However, if the testator's intention is not clear, then it ultimately falls to the court to determine what the testator intended. The court applies certain established principles of construction to the meaning of particular words and phrases and is assisted by a number of statutory provisions to determine the will's meaning.

This chapter considers common rules of construction as applied to a will. The issues covered here are important:

(a) Firstly, to the practitioner who is engaged in advising a testator on the terms of a new will and who is then faced with the task of drafting it. An awareness of the rules of construction is essential, not least because the practitioner needs to know when it may be necessary to vary the meaning that might otherwise be implied by the court or statute. In most cases, statutory rules of construction are subject to a contrary intention expressed in the will.

(b) Secondly, to the practitioner advising PRs and beneficiaries who need to know how a will should be interpreted following the death. PRs must carry out the terms of a will exactly as the testator intended to the extent the law allows. Failure to do so makes them liable to those who should have been the recipients of the testator's property.

A will which is professionally drawn ought to be clear and readily understood, at least by lawyers and other professionals. However, even professionally drawn wills can contain mistakes and ambiguities making it impossible to say, with confidence, what the will actually means. Such problems are likely to be more common with homemade wills. If difficulties arise, the PRs cannot prudently administer or distribute the estate until they are adequately protected against any comeback from parties who may have a different view on the will's meaning.

PRs can seek such protection in various ways, including the obtaining of insurance or getting all beneficiaries who are affected by the ambiguity, etc to come to an agreement as to how the will is to be construed (if this is possible). Otherwise, the PRs must obtain a determination from the court to say what the will means and how they should give effect to its terms. Obviously, this imposes an additional costs burden on the estate, notwithstanding the possibility of recovery via a negligence claim against the will maker.

## 7.2   General principles of construction

### 7.2.1   Jurisdiction

Any questions of construction which arise are normally dealt with by the Chancery Division by means of an application under CPR, rule 64.2 using the non-contentious procedure under CPR, Part 8. The claim will usually ask for a determination on a particular question, such as who is entitled under a particular provision. CPR, PD 64 gives examples of the sort of claims which may be made.

The Family Division's jurisdiction on construction or interpretation of a will, as applied by the probate registry, is limited to determining title to the grant of representation. If this involves the construction of a clause or phrase, or even the will as a whole, to determine a potential grantee's right to benefit (and hence to apply for a grant), an application must be made to the Chancery Division.

### 7.2.2   Court's function in construing a will

The role of the court is to ascertain the intention of the testator as expressed in the will when read as a whole. It is not the court's function to re-write the will, nor guess at what the testator might have intended.

In *Royal Society for the Prevention of Cruelty to Animals v Sharp and others* [2010] EWCA Civ 147, [2011] STC 553, Patten LJ in the Court of Appeal said it is dangerous to approach the assessment of the testator's intentions other than through the language of his will. This case concerned the burden of inheritance tax, the outcome of which fell to be decided on what was intended in a professionally drawn will, and he was critical of the judge at first instance who sought to find a different interpretation from that which appeared on the face of the will. He said:

> Although solicitors do make mistakes, there needs to be something in the language of the document or its admissible background to justify that inference. More importantly, those factors must be such as to permit the Court to give the words actually used a meaning which is not strictly in accordance with the usual rules of grammar or vocabulary.

He went on to say that this is in accordance with the approach to the construction of contracts taken by the House of Lords (as it then was) in *Investors Compensation Scheme Ltd v West Bromwich Building Society* [1998] 1 All ER 98.

This view was subsequently taken up by the Supreme Court in *Marley v Rawlings* [2014] UKSC 2, where Lord Neuberger said interpreting a will is essentially the same exercise as interpreting commercial documents such as contracts, notices and patents:

> When interpreting a contract, the court is concerned to find the intention of the party or parties, and it does this by identifying the meaning of the relevant words, (a) in the light of (i) the natural and ordinary meaning of those words, (ii) the overall purpose of the document, (iii) any other provisions of the document, (iv) the facts known or assumed by the parties at the time that the document was executed, and (v) common sense, but (b) ignoring subjective evidence of any party's intentions. ... When it comes to interpreting wills, it seems to me that the approach should be the same. Whether the document in question is a commercial contract or a will, the aim is to identify the intention of the party or parties to the document by interpreting the words used in their documentary, factual and commercial context.

His Lordship's conclusion, as he acknowledged, was not revolutionary. Over a century ago in *Boyes v Cook* [1880] LR 14 Ch D 53, CA, the court said when interpreting a will, it should 'place [itself] in the [testator's] arm chair'. The old so-called 'armchair rule' was consistent with the modern approach to interpretation by reference to the factual context in which the will was made. Nonetheless, courts now place reliance on Lord Neuberger's approach, both as an objective in determining construction issues and as justification for interpreting a will in a way that may not be entirely obvious.

For example, in *Reading v Reading* [2015] EWHC 946 (Ch), the judge construed 'issue' as including step-children, contrary to its usual meaning, since there were indications, both in the will as a whole and in the factual background, that this was the testator's intention.

Again, in *The Royal Society v Robinson* [2015] EWHC 3442 (Ch), the will was expressed to apply only to the testator's property 'in the United Kingdom'. Both at the time of the will and at his death, the testator's major assets were bank accounts in Jersey and the Isle of Man. The normal meaning of 'United Kingdom' is limited to England and Wales, Scotland and Northern Ireland, where the testator had virtually no assets at all, and does not extend to the Channel Islands or Isle of Man. However, given the factual background the judge felt able to give 'United Kingdom' an extended meaning.

## 7.3   Applying basic rules of construction

In determining the testator's intention through the language of the will, the courts apply various rules of construction. Unfortunately, there is no pre-determined checklist of steps that need to be taken, not least because every case is different. However, as a starting point, the court applies two basic presumptions:

(a)   Non-technical words are given their ordinary meaning, or that intended by the testator when there are several ordinary meanings. In *Perrin v Morgan* [1943] AC 399, the House of Lords had to consider the use of the word 'money', a word that can have several ordinary meanings, ranging from 'cash' to the whole of a person's property (as in 'it's his money she's after'). In such a case, the court construes the word in the context of the will (with the aid of any admissible extrinsic evidence, see para 7.4). The testator in *Perrin v Morgan* had made a gift of his 'money' and also provided for a gift of residue. It was decided that the word 'money' referred to all his personal property.

(b)   Technical words are given their technical meaning. So, in *Re Cook* [1948] 1 All ER 231, ChD, a testatrix gave 'all my personal estate whatsoever' to her nephews and nieces. It was held that her realty (which comprised the bulk of her estate) did not pass under her will but under the intestacy rules.

However, these presumptions may be rebutted under the so-called 'dictionary principle' if from the will (and any admissible extrinsic evidence, see para 7.4) it is clear that the testator has used the word(s) in a different sense from their ordinary or technical meaning. So, the testator can, in effect, make 'big' mean 'small' or the term 'personalty' include 'realty' if he makes the sense in which he is using the words clear in his will, for example by including a definition clause.

However, the courts cannot invent meanings. In *Anthony v Donges* [1998] 2 FLR 775 , T's will gave his widow 'such minimal part of my estate ... as she may be entitled to under English law for maintenance purposes'. The widow contended this meant she should receive the same value property as she would have been entitled to in a claim for *reasonable financial provision* under the I(PFD)A 1975. The court held it could not speculate as to what the testator might have intended and since the words had no determinable meaning, the clause was void for uncertainty.

## 7.4   Using extrinsic evidence as an aid to construction

Generally, the court must construe only the words written in the will itself and so cannot admit extrinsic evidence of the testator's intention. If it could freely take evidence from outside the will (e.g. letters to and from relatives, things said, or alleged to have been said, by the testator), it would make section 9 of the WA 1837 redundant. As seen in para 4.3, section 9 lays down strict formalities for the way in which testamentary wishes must be executed in a written will.

However, the courts have established circumstances where extrinsic evidence has been admissible, notably:

(a)   *If the words used are not apt to fit the surrounding circumstances* (sometimes referred to as 'the armchair rule', *Boyes v Cook* (1880) LR 14 Ch D 53 CA – see para 7.2.2): so, in *Thorn v Dickens* [1906] WN 54, the will left 'all to mother'. This seemed clear enough but when the will was made, the testator had no mother living. Extrinsic evidence of the testator's circumstances showed he was in the habit of calling his wife 'mother' and she was able to take. If his actual mother had been alive, then she would have been the beneficiary and no extrinsic evidence would have been admissible to establish he intended his wife to benefit.

(b)   *If there is a latent ambiguity*: this occurs if the words on the face of the will seem clear but, when effect is given to them, it is found the words can apply to two or more people or items of property. In *Re Jackson* [1933] Ch 237, ChD, a legacy to 'my nephew Arthur Murphy' produced three people who could each claim they answered the description. Extrinsic evidence, including statements made by the testator, was held admissible to establish which one was intended as the legatee. Had such evidence not given the answer, the gift would have failed for uncertainty.

For deaths after 31 December 1982, section 21 of the AJA 1982 specifically allows extrinsic evidence, including evidence of declarations as to the testator's intention, to be admitted to assist in the interpretation of a will if:

(a)   *any part of it is meaningless*: so, if the testator uses words or symbols which have no meaning to anyone else, extrinsic evidence will be admissible to assist interpretation of the will;

(b)   *the language used in any part is ambiguous on the face of the will*: this would be a patent ambiguity, i.e. one which is immediately obvious. Extrinsic evidence would be admissible to aid interpretation of such phrases as 'my money' or 'my possessions' if not clear;

(c)   *evidence, other than evidence of the testator's intention, shows that the language used in any part of the will is ambiguous in the light of surrounding circumstances*: this is, in effect, the old rule on latent ambiguity but it goes further, by providing that extrinsic evidence (apart from evidence of the testator's intention) can now be admitted to raise the possibility that such an ambiguity exists. So, if there is a gift to 'my cousin Jane Smith' and extrinsic evidence of the surrounding circumstances shows that not only did the deceased have a cousin of that name but so did his wife, then evidence will be admissible to determine who is entitled. Evidence of the deceased's intention cannot be introduced to raise the ambiguity in the first place because only evidence of the circumstances is admissible at this stage. However, once the ambiguity has been 'identified', extrinsic evidence of the testator's intention is admissible to attempt to resolve it.

On the question of admissibility of extrinsic evidence, in *Re Williams (Deceased)* [1985] 1 WLR 905, the judge emphasised that extrinsic evidence, in this case a letter written by the testator to her solicitor containing instructions, is only admissible as an *aid* to construction. It is not admissible to vary or contradict what is otherwise clear language in the will. So, the court will not allow its introduction as a means of enabling it to rewrite the will just because it feels the outcome is a meaning the testator probably did not want. If the court wishes to rewrite a will, it can only do so, if at all, under the rectification provisions (see para 7.6).

## 7.5   From which date does a will speak?

### 7.5.1   Section 24 of the Wills Act 1837 – a will speaks from death as regards property

Suppose Freda's will states 'I give my brother all my legal text books'. When Freda made the will she had ten books but when she died she had 20. Does the brother inherit only the ten books owned when the will was made or can he claim all 20 books at the date of death? Does it matter if the 20 books at death are all new editions, ten of which have replaced old editions owned when the will was made, and which no longer have a place in Freda's library when she dies?

By section 24 of the WA 1837, unless a contrary intention appears from the will, it speaks and takes effect as regards *property* as if it had been executed immediately before the death of the testator. So, if the subject-matter of the gift is generic and described in such a way as to be capable of increase or decrease between the date of the will and the date of death, then the will is said 'to speak from death'. In the above example, the brother is entitled to all 20 books that satisfy the description when Freda dies. The same principle would apply to a gift of 'all my shares in ABC plc'.

However, the rule gives way to a contrary intention in the will. Consider a gift of 'my 2,000 shares in ABC plc'. In this case, the testator has clearly identified the 2,000 shares owned at the date of the will and if those shares are sold the gift fails even if the testator subsequently acquires others.

A contrary intention may be expressed in other ways. For example, 'I give my house to …'. In this case, due to the use of the word 'my', the court is likely to infer the gift is intended to pass the item owned by the testator at the date the will is made. Unlike the gift of 'all my legal text books', this is not a gift by generic description capable of increase or decrease but rather a gift of a particular asset. So the court is likely to say it means the house owned when the will was made, rather than a different one owned at the date of death. The importance of this construction is that if the original house no longer exists at the date of death, the gift fails because of ademption (see para 8.3).

Other words and phrases attached to a gift may also show a contrary intention to exclude section 24 of the WA 1837, as in 'the house where I now live' or 'the car which I currently own'.

If the testator intends to pass a specific asset which is likely to be replaced after the date of the will, a house or car being obvious examples, and the testator wants the beneficiary to take whatever happens to be owned at death, then clear words must be used to prevent ademption. A gift of 'the house which I own at the date of my death' or ' any motor car I own when I die' will pass whatever property is owned at death and regardless of whether it was the same item at the time the will was made. Only if the testator dies owning no item matching the description does the gift fail.

## 7.5.2    Section 24 of the Wills Act 1837 does not apply to people

The rule of construction in section 24 of the WA 1837 applies only to property and not to people. As to the beneficiaries (or objects) of the gift, in the absence of any contrary intention, the will speaks from the date of execution.

A gift to 'John's eldest child' will be construed as a gift to the person fulfilling that description *at the date of the will*. If that person predeceases the testator, the gift fails. It does not benefit the person who happens to be John's eldest child living when the testator dies. Of course, if the gift had continued by saying 'as is living at my death', then the intention is clear and allows the 'new' eldest child to take.

If there is a gift to a beneficiary by description, such as 'to the wife of Charles' and no one fulfils that description at the date of the will, the gift is construed as one to the first person to fulfil the description – i.e. to the first person Charles marries after the date of the will. Once someone has fulfilled the description (whether at the time the will was made or later), the gift is construed as being to that person even if they no longer fulfil the description, as where Charles obtains a divorce and remarries someone else before the testator's death.

This rule regarding objects does not apply to class gifts, including those where there is an 'individual gift' to each member of the class (see para 7.7).

### 7.5.3 Codicils and republication consequences

If a testator later makes a codicil to his will, the effect is usually to republish the will so that for relevant purposes, it is now said to speak from the date of execution of the codicil rather than from the date of the will's original execution.

This can be important when applying the above rules, particularly to a case where section 24 of the WA 1837 is excluded by contrary intention and a specific asset is replaced between the date of the will and the date of the codicil. Since the effect of republication is to update the will to the date of the codicil, it prevents the failure of a gift which would otherwise have been adeemed (see, also, para 6.3).

## 7.6 Omitting, changing and supplying words

Section 20 of the AJA 1982 allows the court in *limited circumstances* to rectify the will to carry out the testator's intentions.

The court may exercise this power only if satisfied the will as drawn fails to carry out the testator's intention as a result of:

(a) a clerical error; or

(b) a failure to understand the testator's instructions.

In *Bush v Jouliac* [2006] EWHC 363 (Ch), a solicitor drafted a will and omitted to include a clause to exclude the effect of section 33 of the WA 1837 (see para 8.4.3). As a result, the property passed under section 33 to the issue of the deceased's son who had predeceased, this being contrary to what the deceased had clearly intended. If the solicitor had omitted the exclusion clause because he was ignorant of the legal effect of section 33, then the court had no power to rectify just because the draftsman was mistaken as to the legal consequences of the words used. However, if the omission was the result of a clerical error in failing to include the necessary exclusion clause, then rectification was possible. Evidence of a clerical error was accepted and rectification of the will was allowed.

A similar result was achieved in *Brown and Another v Bimson and others* [2010] EWHC 3679 (Ch), where the draftsman of a will was held to have made a clear clerical error in omitting a power to advance capital, despite having advised the testator in a letter of advice preceding execution of the will that such a power would be available. Had the clerical error not been rectified, it would not have been possible to make capital payments to the deceased's husband who was the life tenant. In common with many rectification applications, this case was unopposed and the solicitors who erroneously drafted the will agreed to bear the costs.

In *Marley v Rawlings* [2014] UKSC 2, the Supreme Court considered whether Mr Rawlings' mistake in signing his wife's will instead of his own could be classified as a 'clerical error' for the purpose of a rectification claim. Lord Neuberger initially quoted from *Bell v Georgiou* [2002] EWHC 1080 (Ch), where it was said a 'clerical error' occurs when someone, who may be the testator himself, or his solicitor, or a clerk or a typist, writes something which he did not intend to insert, or omits something which he intended to insert. Whilst accepting 'clerical error' could have a narrow meaning, he then said:

> ... 'clerical error' is an expression which has to be interpreted in its context ... it seems to me that the expression 'clerical error' in section 20(1)(a) should be given a wide, rather than a narrow, meaning.

He went on to say that if necessary the whole will could be rectified to give effect to what was the clear intention of the testator. In this case, the lawyer supervising the execution of the wills had, by his own admission, made a mistake when he gave Mr Rawlings the wrong will to sign. Lord Neuberger said:

> There was an error, and it can be fairly characterised as 'clerical', because it arose in connection with office work of a routine nature. Accordingly, given that the present type of case can, as a matter of ordinary language, be said to involve a clerical error, it seems to me to follow that it is susceptible to rectification.

The Supreme Court allowed rectification of the will Mr Rawlings had signed by replacing the typed words within it (the words representing his wife's wishes), with those contained in the document signed by his wife (and which he thought were in the will he signed). In this way, the will signed by Mr Rawlings would end up containing the words he assumed were there to carry out his wishes.

Very few rectification claims are likely to be based on the will drafter's failure to understand the testator's instructions. An example would be the drafter failing to appreciate the testator had assets outside the United Kingdom and including a provision limiting the will to UK assets only.

The time limit for an application under the section is 6 months from the date of the grant, although a later application is possible with leave of the court. PRs who distribute the estate after 6 months from the date of grant but before an application for rectification are protected.

If all relevant beneficiaries agree to rectify, the matter can be dealt with as a post-death variation to the terms of the will (see para 8.2.1).

## 7.7    Class gifts and the class closing rules

A class gift is a gift of property to be divided amongst persons who fulfil a general description, for example, 'the children of X' or 'the children of X who attain the age of 21'. The size of each beneficiary's share will depend on the number of beneficiaries who fit the description. In the above examples, this cannot be known until, at the earliest, it is certain X can have no more children. However, the second example raises the possibility that it could be later due to the added age contingency having to be satisfied. Until the total number of class members is known, the PRs cannot be certain of the size of each person's share. They therefore face the risk of a new class member appearing at a time when they might have distributed all the property. Consequently, they may be reluctant to make any distribution, even to those who are entitled, until all potential members of the class are known.

The courts have devised *class closing rules* to overcome the problem of delay by providing a 'close-by' date, after which no further members of the class may join. Potential beneficiaries born after the class has closed and who were not *en ventre sa mère* at that time, are not entitled. The rules vary in detail according to the type of gift but, broadly, the class closes as soon as there is one beneficiary who attains a vested entitlement and is thus able to call for an immediate distribution of his share.

As rules of construction, the class closing rules are not applied if the testator has shown a clear contrary intention in his will. An emphatic phrase such as 'whenever born' or 'at whatever time they are born' is needed to exclude the operation of the rules.

The class closing rules differ according to the type of gift involved but offer only a partial solution. There may still be instances where the class has the potential for remaining open longer than is administratively convenient. In those cases, the will drafter should consider an express provision to close the class.

(See, also, para 7.8 as to defining membership of the class and para 22.3.3 as regards drafting considerations to vary the class closing rules.)

References in the following rules to persons 'living' or 'in existence' include persons *en ventre sa mère* at the time and subsequently born alive.

### 7.7.1    Immediate vested gift

An example is a gift 'to the children of X'. The class will close at the date of the testator's death if there is any child of X then living. No child (except one *en ventre sa mère* at that date) born thereafter can be included in the class. If there are no children of X then living, the class remains open until X dies.

### 7.7.2    Deferred vested gift

An example is 'to A for life remainder to the children of X'. Here, the class will close when the 'postponement' ends (i.e. on the death of A), provided a member of the class has by then attained a vested interest. So, any children of X born before A's death qualify (whether born before or after the testator's death). If a child who has attained a vested interest predeceases the life tenant, the child's estate benefits. (This will not be the case if there is a contrary intention in the will making it clear the child must be living at A's death to be included.) If, on the death of A, no one has attained a vested interest, the class remains open until X dies.

### 7.7.3    Immediate contingent class gift

An example is 'to the children of X who attain the age of 18'. The class closes at the date of the testator's death if any member of the class then living has already fulfilled the contingency. The class will therefore comprise any such child who has already attained the age of 18 plus any others then living who subsequently attain the age of 18. The share of any child who dies without fulfilling the contingency accrues to those members of the class who do; if a child dies having fulfilled the contingency but before distribution, the child's estate inherits.

If, at the date of the testator's death, no member of the class has fulfilled the contingency, it remains open until such time as the first member does so.

### 7.7.4    Deferred contingent class gift

An example is 'to A for life remainder to the children of X who attain the age of 18'. Here, the class will close on the death of A if, by that time, any child of X has fulfilled the contingency. Any others then living, who subsequently fulfil the contingency, are also entitled. Again, the potential shares of any who die without fulfilling the contingency accrue to those who do; if a vested interest has been obtained but the beneficiary dies before distribution, the estate of the deceased class member inherits.

If no class member has attained a vested interest on the death of A, the class remains open until such time as the first child of X fulfils the contingency.

### 7.7.5    Early closing of a deferred class gift

The courts have also provided for 'early closing', where there is a deferred class gift and the prior interest fails because the intended life tenant predeceases the testator. The gift to the class is accelerated so as to become an immediate class gift. The class closing will be determined by the rules appropriate to *immediate* vested or contingent class gifts as the case may be.

If the life interest terminates because the life tenant disclaims or surrenders his interest, it seems probable there will be no acceleration of the closing of the class (see *Re Harker's Will Trusts* [1969] 1 WLR 1124, where the court refused to follow a contrary view taken in *Re Davies* [1957] 1 WLR 922).

### 7.7.6    Class gifts, substitution and section 33 of the Wills Act 1837

Section 33 of the WA 1837 (as substituted by section 19 of the AJA 1982) provides that, in the absence of a contrary intention, if the class gift is to the *children or remoter issue of the testator* and a member of the class predeceases the testator leaving issue who survive the testator, such issue take *per stirpes* the share which their parent would have taken (see, further, para 8.4.3).

Whilst this statutory substitution is an important provision, it has limitations because it *applies only to gifts in favour of the testator's own children or remoter issue*. It does not apply to other class gifts, for example, 'to my brother's children' where a member of the class who predeceases the testator simply drops out of the class irrespective of whether they leave surviving issue or not.

Of course, it is always open to the will maker to provide expressly for the substitution of a predeceased member's issue and this possibility should be considered with the testator. In cases where section 33 of the WA 1837 would apply, the discussion should clarify whether or not the testator actually wants issue to benefit by substitution. If not, section 33 must be excluded; even if the testator does want issue to be substituted, it is preferable to include an express substitution provision so that those reading the will after the testator's death are in no doubt as to the testator's wishes.

### 7.7.7    Individual gifts to members of a class

A gift of an individual amount to each member of a class, for example '£500 to each of the children of X' is not strictly a class gift because the amount taken by each beneficiary is fixed; all that may be uncertain is how many beneficiaries are so entitled and hence how much property is required to fund the legacy. However, the problems here are not dissimilar to those arising in relation to a true class gift because, until the death of X, the PRs will not know how much property to set aside.

The rule here is that all persons answering the description at the date of the testator's death are eligible to participate but if there are none alive at that time, the gift fails completely. Either way, any beneficiary born after the testator's death, unless *en ventre sa mère*, will not benefit. (If the gift in the example had followed a life interest, the rule would be applied as at the date of death of the life tenant.)

Again, testators are free to impose their own rules if they wish. So a provision of '£500 to each of X's children whether born before or after my death' is permissible, although administratively inconvenient.

## 7.8   Defining children and other relatives

The following rules apply generally to gifts to 'children' whether vested or contingent. They apply also to a class gift to any other relatives by description whether or not they are relatives of the testator, for example, 'my brothers', 'my sister's children', 'my nephews', etc. If the effect of these rules is not in keeping with what the testator wants, then the draftsman must include words which clearly show a contrary intention.

## 7.8.1   Relationships generally

Problems are unlikely to arise if the testator refers to intended beneficiaries by name but often the intention is to create a class gift (see para 7.7) so that beneficiaries born after the date of execution of the will can be included. Care must be taken to avoid any misunderstanding when describing the potential members of the class. Without more, a gift in favour of 'my nephews' is construed as including only the *testator's* nephews (having regard to the rules discussed below) and not those on his spouse's, civil partner's, or partner's side of the family, notwithstanding having been treated as his own. In particular, a reference to 'my children' would not, in the absence of adoption (see para 7.8.5), include step-children. It follows that a testator wishing to benefit relatives who are not otherwise within the terms of a gift must include express words in the will to show a contrary intention that excludes the usual rules.

## 7.8.2   Children, etc

*Prima facie*, a gift to 'children' is construed as including all children of the testator but not grandchildren or great grandchildren (although if a gift is to the testator's own children, section 33 of the WA 1837 will create a statutory substitution unless excluded).

A gift to 'issue' means direct descendants in every degree and so extends beyond 'children' to 'grandchildren', 'great grandchildren', and so on.

## 7.8.3   Legitimated children, etc

By virtue of the Legitimacy Act 1976, a legitimated child (i.e. one born outside marriage whose parents subsequently marry) is entitled in the same way as if born legitimate, subject to a contrary indication in the will. This is so whether the legitimation occurred before or after the testator's death. If the disposition under a will depends upon the date of birth, the rules of construction are similar to those discussed at para 7.8.5 in respect of adopted children.

## 7.8.4   Children, etc whose parents were not married

As regards a will or codicil executed before 1970, the common law rule was that a gift to 'children' (or other relatives) is construed *prima facie* as embracing only legitimate children. As regards wills made after 31 December 1969, the position is now determined by statute.

Section 1(1) of the Family Law Reform Act 1987 (FLRA 1987) applies to any will or codicil made on or after 4 April 1988 so that references therein are construed without regard to 'whether or not the father and mother of either [person] or the father and mother of any person through whom the relationship is deduced have or had been married to each other at any time'. In other words, a reference to 'my children', 'X's children', etc includes both legitimate and illegitimate persons within the description. A gift 'to my grandchildren' includes all the testator's grandchildren, even the illegitimate child of an illegitimate child.

This rule is applied subject to any contrary intention shown in the will.

Section 15 of the Family Law Reform Act 1969 applies to wills or codicils made after 1969 but before 4 April 1988. It contains provisions broadly the same as those in the FLRA 1987 and is again subject to a contrary intention shown by the testator.

## 7.8.5     Adopted children, etc

The position of adopted children is (in construing the will of a testator dying after 1975) governed by the Adoption Act 1976 and the Adoption and Children Act 2002, which apply to adoption orders (whether made before or after the testator's death) made by a court in the United Kingdom, the Isle of Man or the Channel Islands, and to certain foreign adoptions.

An adopted child is to be treated as the legitimate child of the person or persons who adopt(s) the child and is not to be treated as being the child of anyone else. In other words, the adopted child is no longer regarded as the child of the natural parents for the purposes of interpreting the natural parents' wills, or the distribution of their estates on intestacy.

If the disposition in a will depends on a date of birth, then, subject to any contrary intention being shown, the disposition is construed as if:

(a)     the adopted child had been born at the date of adoption;

(b)     two or more children adopted on the same date had been born on that date in the order of their actual births.

So, if there is a gift to 'such of X's children living at my death' and X adopts a 3-year-old child one year after the testator's death, that child is not included in the gift because the child was not X's child at the time of the testator's death. The child is excluded in the same way as any natural child.

However, these rules do not affect any reference in the gift to the age of a child. So, for example, if a gift is contingent on attaining the age of 18, an adopted child achieves a vested interest when actually reaching aged 18 and not 18 years after the adoption.

## 7.8.6    Gender recognition

The Gender Recognition Act 2004 provides that 'where a full gender recognition certificate is issued to a person, the person's gender becomes for all purposes the acquired gender'.

The Act applies only to a will made after the Gender Recognition Act 2004 came into force on 4 April 2005 (section 15). So, if a will, made after this date, makes provision for 'my nieces', then someone born a nephew will be eligible to benefit after acquiring full female gender recognition under the Act.

Section 17 of the Gender Recognition Act 2004 relieves trustees and PRs from any duty to enquire whether a gender recognition certificate has been issued to a person or revoked, even if that fact could affect entitlement to the estate they are distributing. However, the beneficiary may still enforce a claim by following property into the hands of anyone who has received it instead.

Section 18 of the Gender Recognition Act 2004 gives a power to the court where the devolution under the will is different to what it would have been but for the acquisition of a full gender recognition certificate, thus defeating someone's expectations. The court may, if satisfied it is just to do so, make such an order as it considers appropriate in relation to the person benefitting from the different disposition of the property. So, if the will gives property to 'my eldest daughter at the date of my death' and the testator has an older son who acquires a female gender under the Act, thus displacing the daughter who would otherwise have taken, the latter can apply to the court for an order in her favour.

## 7.8.7    Children born following fertilisation techniques or surrogacy arrangements

At common law, a child's legal parents are the child's genetic parents. However, the Human Fertilisation and Embryology Acts of 1990 and 2008 contain provisions to determine parentage in cases of assisted reproduction and the making of parental orders if a child is born into a surrogacy arrangement (see, also, para 22.3.3, Meaning of 'child'). The result is that, provided the requirements of the Act are complied with, a child conceived with donor sperm and eggs can be treated as the child of two individuals with whom there is no genetic link.

Although a testator is free to exclude these provisions in a will, the best advice is probably not to do so. For example, if a testator made a gift 'to all my nephews' and said that any nephew born as a result of assisted reproduction or surrogacy who was not genetically related to the testator was excluded from the class, it causes serious problems for the PRs. Before distribution they would have to ascertain from the parents of each nephew whether any assisted reproduction had taken place because failure to do so might result in a benefit being paid to someone the testator had expressly excluded.

## 7.8.8 Spouses and civil partners

The Civil Partnership Act 2004 amended many statutes so that the status of a registered civil partner is the same in most respects as that of a spouse. However, there is nothing in the Act to say that references in a will or other document to terms such as 'spouse', 'husband', 'wife', or 'marriage' must now be construed as including 'civil partner' or 'civil partnership'.

So, if a will contains a discretionary trust for, say, children, and the testator wants the class of beneficiaries to include not just husbands and wives of children but also their civil partners, then express words must make this clear. The position is not the same for same sex spouses: references to spouses in wills, trusts and other private documents made on or after 13 March 2014 will include same sex spouses unless the context of the document provides otherwise (see, further, para 22.3.3 and para 5.5 as regards same sex marriages).

# 8 Why Gifts in Wills Might Fail

## 8.1 Reasons for failure

There are many reasons why gifts in a will can fail:

(a)  disclaimer;

(b)  ademption (property matching description not owned at death);

(c)  lapse (beneficiary predeceases testator);

(d)  forfeiture (beneficiary convicted of killing the testator);

(e)  section 15 of the WA 1837 (beneficiary or spouse/civil partner of beneficiary witnesses will);

(f)  uncertainty;

(g)  gift contrary to public policy;

(h)  gift induced by force, fear or undue influence;

(i)  doctrine of satisfaction (lifetime gift satisfying gift in the will).

If the gift cannot take effect, its subject matter will pass with the residue of the estate. If the residuary gift fails, the property is undisposed of and passes under the intestacy rules to the deceased's next of kin.

A gift can also fail, in whole or in part, due to abatement if there are insufficient assets left to fund the gift once the debts of the estate have been paid.

## 8.2 Disclaimer

### 8.2.1 Refusal to accept property

Those making wills need to know their wishes may not take effect.

No one can force another to accept an inheritance. Beneficiaries are free to disclaim (that is, refuse to accept) property given to them. However, it is not usually possible to pick and choose; unless the will provides to the contrary, the whole of a gift must be disclaimed or accepted. If, however, a will gives one person two separate gifts, one may be accepted and the other disclaimed. Once a person has accepted any benefit from property (e.g. income from, or interest earned, by it), it is too late to disclaim.

Subject to the above, there is nothing to stop a beneficiary disclaiming, nor (for reasons given below) accepting the property and then giving it away by re-directing to someone else, called a 'post-death variation', but there are potential tax consequences unless statutory requirements are satisfied (see para 8.2.2).

A voluntary disclaimer made during the testator's lifetime is ineffective (see *Smith v Smith* [2001] 1 WLR 1937) because, until death, a will has no effect. The beneficiary has nothing to accept or disclaim.

A disclaimer does not need to be in any particular form. According to *Re Cook* [2002] STC (SCD) 318, it can be by conduct. However, it is preferable for the disclaiming beneficiary to write a short statement to the deceased's PRs who should insist on having something on the file before distributing the property in reliance on the disclaimer.

A person disclaiming has no control over the destination of the disclaimed property. It passes to whoever is next entitled by application of normal succession rules; a disclaimed non-residuary gift falls into residue and if residue is disclaimed, it passes on partial intestacy.

However, there is potential for uncertainty. For example, a substitutional gift expressed to apply if the principal beneficiary 'predeceases or fails to survive me by 28 days' does not on the face of it take effect if that beneficiary disclaims as they have neither predeceased nor failed to survive. Section 2 of the Estates of Deceased Persons (Forfeiture Rule and Law of Succession) Act 2011 now says a person disclaiming is *deemed* to have died immediately before the testator, suggesting the disclaimed property should now pass to the substitute beneficiary. However, the wording of section 2 is not clear and the fictional pre-deceasing may apply only if the disclaiming beneficiary is a child or remoter issue of the testator. Given the potential uncertainty as to how disclaimed property should be dealt with in some cases, coupled with the fact the disclaiming beneficiary has no say in where the property goes, a beneficiary wanting to give up a benefit will normally prefer to enter into a post-death variation (see para 8.2.2). This allows the beneficiary to determine not only who gets the disclaimed property, but also the terms on which it is taken.

## 8.2.2    Tax implications of disclaimers and post-death variations

Although this chapter is primarily concerned with failure of gifts, it would be wrong not to mention the tax implications of disclaimers and post-death variations as they are very important to beneficiaries.

Normally when someone makes a lifetime gift of property (which includes refusing to take property or redirecting it), they are treated as:

(a)    making a potentially exempt transfer for inheritance tax purposes which becomes fully chargeable to tax if they die within 7 years of the transfer; and

(b)    making a disposal which could give rise to a charge to capital gains tax if it is of an asset which has increased in value between acquisition and disposal.

EXAMPLE

> Ben is left a seaside cottage by his aunt; she leaves the rest of her estate to charity. The cottage was valued at £400,000 when she died. Ben does not want the trouble of maintaining a second home but knows his son, Sam, would like the property. One year after the death, Ben transfers the cottage to Sam when it is worth £420,000.

> Ben makes a potentially exempt transfer for inheritance tax of £420,000 and a disposal for capital gains tax purposes, realising a chargeable gain of £20,000.

However, there are two statutory provisions which allow Ben to have the gift read back into his aunt's will for inheritance tax and/or capital gains tax. For the purpose of these two taxes, the aunt is then treated as having left the property directly to Sam.

The provisions are section 142 of the Inheritance Tax Act 1984 (IHTA 1984) and section 62(6) of the Taxation of Chargeable Gains Act 1992. Both provisions apply if property is disclaimed or the destination is varied in writing within 2 years of death.

In the case of a disclaimer, there are no other requirements. In the case of a variation, it must include a statement that the gift is to be treated as the deceased's for the purposes of one or both of the two statutory provisions. If a variation favours a charity, evidence must be obtained to show the charity has been informed, for example, its written acknowledgement, before it is effective for inheritance tax purposes – such a variation allows a claim for the charity exemption and a refund of inheritance tax in appropriate circumstances.

In the above example, a disclaimer will not achieve Ben's purpose as the cottage would pass as part of the residue to charity. A variation allows Ben to ensure the cottage goes to Sam.

Ben will certainly want the gift treated as his aunt's rather than his for inheritance tax purposes as he will not want to risk a liability to tax should he die within 7 years.

On these figures he will also want the gift treated as his aunt's for capital gains tax purposes as the £20,000 gain exceeds his annual exemption. However, if the cottage had decreased in value by £20,000, he might prefer to treat the gift as his for capital gains tax to give him a £20,000 loss which he can set against any gains he makes in the current tax year or may make in future tax years. If that is what he wants, his variation should omit the statement under the Taxation of Chargeable Gains Act 1992.

## **8.3**　Ademption

Section 24 of the WA 1837 provides that:

> … every will shall be construed, with reference to the real estate and personal estate comprised in it, to speak and take effect as if it had been executed immediately before the death of the testator, unless a contrary intention shall appear by the will.

This means that a gift of 'all my shares' or 'all my jewellery' takes effect to dispose of all the property meeting that description owned by the testator when he died, whether or not the testator owned it at the time the will was made. Only if the deceased owns no such items at the date of death will the gift fail.

However, testators often want to make a gift of a particular item or group of items of property owned at the date they make the will. The description of the property will indicate that it is a particular item and if the testator no longer owns that property at death, the gift is said to be 'adeemed' (i.e. it fails).

Ademption usually occurs because the property has been sold, given away or destroyed during the testator's lifetime. The disappointed beneficiary receives nothing by way of compensation unless the will made express provision, for example 'I give my house "The Willows" or any house I may own at the date of my death to [X]'. Even here, the gift will fail if the deceased owns no house at that date, perhaps because the deceased has sold and moved into residential care.

Problems may arise if the asset has been retained but has changed its nature since the will was made. For example, the will may make a specific gift of company shares, but by the date of death the company has been taken over so the testator's shareholding has been changed into a holding in the new company. In such a case, the question is whether the asset is substantially the same, having changed merely in name or form, or whether it has changed in substance. Only if there has been a change in substance is the gift adeemed.

In *Re Dorman* [1994] 1 WLR 282, the deceased left the money in a named deposit account to a beneficiary but by the date of her death the money had been moved to an account earning a higher rate of interest. The court held that the accounts were similar and had been funded in the same way so that there was no change of substance and the gift could take effect as a gift of the money in the new account. In *Re Slater* [1902] 1 Ch 665, a testator made a gift of shares in Lambeth Waterworks Company. By the date of death, the company had been taken over and amalgamated with other companies to form the Metropolitan Water Board, which issued its own stock to replace shares held in the old companies. The Court of Appeal held that the legacy was adeemed as the stock was held in an entirely different organisation.

Another area of potential difficulty occurs where the testator disposes of the property described in a specific gift but before his death acquires a different item of property which answers the same description; for example a gift of 'my car' or 'my piano' where the original car or piano has been replaced since the will was made. It has been held that the presumption in such a case is that the testator meant only to dispose of the particular asset he owned at the date of the will and so the gift is adeemed. By referring to 'my' car or piano, the testator is taken to have shown a contrary intention to section 24 of the WA 1837. However, this presumption is not particularly strong and the construction may vary according to the circumstances, for example the respective values of the original and substituted assets may be taken into account.

A testator may wish to add to or change a will in a minor way and so may execute a supplementary codicil. A codicil is a supplement to a will which, to be valid, must be executed in the same way as a will (see para 6.3). The significance of a codicil in the context of a gift of property is that it republishes the will as at the date of the codicil. Thus, if the testator makes a will in 1990 leaving 'my gold watch' to a legatee, loses the watch in 2001 and replaces it shortly afterwards, the gift of the watch in the will is probably adeemed. If, however, the testator executes a codicil to the will in 2003, the will is read as if it had been executed in 2003 and so the legatee will take the replacement watch (see, also, paras 7.5 and 21.2.4).

## 8.4 Lapse

### 8.4.1 Basic rule

A gift in a will fails or 'lapses' if the beneficiary dies before the testator. If a gift of a particular item or a gift of cash lapses, the property falls into residue. If a gift of residue lapses, the property passes under the intestacy rules, unless the testator has provided for the possibility of lapse by including a substitutional gift in the will.

Where a gift is to individuals 'jointly' or is a gift to members of a class, it will not lapse unless all the beneficiaries predecease the testator. If just one person survives, that person takes the whole gift. If the gift is to a number of people 'equally' or 'in equal shares', the share of any beneficiary who predeceases will lapse unless the will provides that it is to be added to the shares of the surviving beneficiaries or is to pass to a substitute beneficiary.

Where no conditions to the contrary are imposed in the will, a gift vests on the testator's death. This means that provided the beneficiary survives the testator, for however short a time, the gift takes effect. If the beneficiary dies soon after the testator, the property passes into the beneficiary's estate.

However, if a gift is made conditional or contingent on a future event, typically attaining a stated age, then the gifted property does not vest until the condition or contingency is satisfied. If the beneficiary dies in the meantime, the gift fails, i.e. 'lapses'. Nothing passes to the beneficiary's estate and the property devolves as with any lapsed gift unless the testator has contemplated the failure by including a substitutional gift in the will.

It is common to provide in a will for a survivorship clause that beneficiaries take only if they survive a stated period, often 28 days. This allows the testator to make express provision for what is to happen if the beneficiary survives only for a short period (see, also, para 8.4.2).

### 8.4.2    If the order of deaths is uncertain

The principle outlined above means that if the deaths of the testator and beneficiary occur very close together and there is no survivorship clause, it is vital to establish who died first.

The law of succession does not accept the possibility that two people might die at the same instant. If the order of deaths cannot be proved, section 184 of the LPA 1925 provides the deaths are deemed to occur in order of seniority so the elder is deemed to have died first. If the testator was older than the beneficiary, the gift takes effect and the property passes as part of the beneficiary's estate.

EXAMPLE

> Hari and Wilma are married and are killed in a car accident. The order of their deaths is uncertain. Hari is 30 and Wilma is 29. They have no children but each has a surviving mother. Their wills leave everything to the other with no survivorship clause or substitutional gifts.

Hari is deemed to die first and his estate goes to Wilma. The gift to Hari in Wilma's will lapses. Her estate (which now includes Hari's) passes to Wilma's mother on application of the intestacy rules.

This is unlikely to be what Hari would have wanted. Had his will included a survivorship clause, he could have left his estate to his own chosen beneficiary, perhaps his mother, if Wilma failed to survive him by, say, 28 days.

If Wilma's mother is generous, she could vary the destination of part of Wilma's estate to leave property to Hari's mother (see para 8.2.2).

### 8.4.3    If children or remoter issue of the testator predecease

'Issue' are straight line descendants of a person, namely children, grandchildren, great grandchildren, and so on. The term does not include collateral relatives, such as siblings, nephews and nieces.

Section 33 of the WA 1837 applies to all gifts by will to the testator's children or remoter issue unless a contrary intention is shown in the will. Its effect is to incorporate an implied substitutional provision into such gifts so if a will contains a gift to the testator's child or remoter issue and that beneficiary dies *before* the testator, leaving issue of his own who survive the testator, the gift does not lapse. Instead, it passes to the beneficiary's issue. The issue of a deceased beneficiary take the gift their parent would have taken in equal shares. No one can take under the section if his parent is living.

EXAMPLE

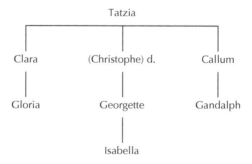

Tatzia leaves her estate to her three children, Clara, Christophe and Callum. Christophe predeceases her. His daughter, Georgette, takes the one-third share he would have taken, had he survived Tatzia. If Georgette had siblings, she and the siblings would have divided Christophe's share equally.

Isabella takes nothing because her mother, Georgette, is alive. Had Georgette also predeceased Tatzia, Isabella would have taken Christophe's share.

Section 33 does not apply if the will shows a contrary intention, usually shown by including an express substitution clause.

EXAMPLE

If any child predeceases me, the share which that child would have taken is to go to [      ].

Including an express substitutional gift rather than relying on the implied one under section 33 is always to be preferred even if the intended outcome is to benefit the child's issue anyway. The main reason is to express on the face of the will for the benefit of the testator what is to happen to the child's share so that if the testator wishes, they can consider an alternative. Furthermore, it allows provision for substitution in a case where the child survives the testator but then dies before satisfying any expressed contingency – this being a situation where section 33 would not apply. Also, apart from avoiding the uncertainty discussed below, the testator can impose a different contingency on the issue taking by substitution.

In *Ling v Ling* [2002] WTLR 553, the gift was to those of my children 'living at my death'. The court held this was not a contrary intention. The words 'living at my death' simply stated explicitly what would otherwise be implicit – that a class is composed of those members living at the testator's death. To exclude section 33, it would have been necessary to state issue were not to be substituted for a deceased child.

In *Ling v Ling*, the gift to the children was contingent on them attaining 21 and the judge expressed the view that if a child predeceases, any issue taking under section 33 must satisfy the same contingency.

Since *Ling v Ling*, two cases, *Rainbird v Smith* [2012] EWHC 4276 (Ch) and *Hives v Machin* [2017] EWHC 1414 (Ch) have each considered section 33 in the context of a similarly worded class gift leaving property to the testator's surviving children with the proviso 'and if more than one in equal shares'. In determining if these words excluded section 33, so preventing the issue of a predeceased child from taking, in *Rainbird v Smith* the judge held they did, while the judge in *Hives v Machin* took the opposite view. In both cases, the will drafters had assumed the words used were sufficient to exclude section 33 so the share of a predeceased child accrued to the survivors rather than passing down to the dead child's issue.

These cases are a warning to will drafters that the only way to be certain the statutory substitution for issue under section 33 is excluded (assuming this is what the testator wants) is to include express words saying so.

EXAMPLES

> I DECLARE the provisions of section 33 Wills Act 1837 (as amended) shall not apply to [this gift] [this my will].

> I DECLARE that the share of a child who predeceases me shall be divided between such of my other children as survive me, equally if more than one, and shall not pass to the children of the predeceased child.

The Estates of Deceased Persons (Forfeiture Rule and Law of Succession) Act 2011 provides a person disclaiming (see para 8.2) or whose interest fails through application of the forfeiture rule (see para 8.5) is deemed to have died immediately *before* the testator and the estate is distributed accordingly. If the person in question is a child (or remoter issue) of the testator, the property automatically passes to that person's living issue as provided for by section 33, subject to any contrary intention shown by the will.

# 8.5   Forfeiture

The forfeiture rule provides, as a matter of public policy, a person should not be able to inherit from a person he has been convicted of unlawfully killing.

The rule applies to both murder and manslaughter but not in cases where the killer was found not guilty by virtue of insanity. 'Unlawful killing' includes aiding, abetting, counselling or procuring the death of another person, for instance by assisting with his suicide, a crime under section 2 of the Suicide Act 1961. See *Dunbar v Plant* [1998] Ch 412 and, more recently, *Ninian v Findlay* [2019] EWHC 297 (Ch).

In cases of manslaughter (but not murder), the killer can apply within 3 months of conviction for relief from forfeiture under the Forfeiture Act 1982. The time limit is strict and the court has no discretion to extend the period (see *Land v Land* [2006] EWHC 2069 (Ch), [2007] 1 All ER 324).

At one time, the forfeiture rule could produce unfair results.

EXAMPLE

> Kevin murdered his parents. Their wills leave everything to him and his sister in equal shares, and if either predeceases leaving children, the share of the predeceased child is to go to their children. Kevin has two children.

> Kevin's interest is forfeited. The substitutional gift cannot take effect because Kevin has not predeceased and neither, for the same reason,

can section 33 of the WA 1837 apply. His share, therefore, is undisposed of property and will pass on partial intestacy.

The forfeiture rule applies in the same way on intestacy and so Kevin forfeits his entitlement *to one half of the undisposed of property*. His children cannot replace him because he has not predeceased his parents. His share, therefore, passes to his sister and not to his children.

However, the Estates of Deceased Persons (Forfeiture Rule and Law of Succession) Act 2011 now provides, for deaths on or after 1 February 2011, that a person who forfeits an entitlement is treated as having predeceased the person killed. Whilst the effect of this provision is not entirely certain insofar as it relates to an interest forfeited in a will, it is clear it does apply if the convicted person is the testator's child or remoter issue. Hence, in the above example, the substitutional gift to Kevin's children will now take effect.

# 8.6   Beneficiary witnesses will

## 8.6.1    Effect of section 15 of the Wills Act 1837

Under section 15 of the WA 1837, a gift by will fails if the beneficiary, his spouse or civil partner witnesses the will. The will itself remains valid. The rule exists to ensure wills are reliably witnessed by independent persons.

EXAMPLE

Ted's will leaves £100,000 to his godson, Gregor, residue to Oxfam.

Ted's will is witnessed by Gregor's civil partner, Pete.

The legacy to Gregor fails but the will is valid and everything passes to Oxfam.

## 8.6.2    Situations where section 15 of the Wills Act 1837 does not apply

### (a) Legatee takes on trust for someone else

The section does not apply if the gift is to a person as a trustee. So, if in the above example the £100,000 had been given to Gregor on trust for his children, the gift would have taken effect even though Gregor's civil partner had witnessed the will.

## (b) Will witnessed by two other witnesses

In the case of a testator dying on or after 29 May 1968, the Wills Act 1968 provides that a witness who is a beneficiary, or is the spouse or civil partner of a beneficiary, can be disregarded if the will is duly executed without that particular witness.

EXAMPLE

> Ted's will (which leaves £100,000 to Gregor, residue to Oxfam), is witnessed by Gregor's civil partner, Pete, and two independent witnesses.
>
> The gift to Gregor can take effect.

## (c) Gift made or confirmed by independently witnessed codicil

If there are later confirmatory codicils which are not witnessed by the beneficiary, or the beneficiary's spouse or civil partner, the gift can take effect.

In *Re Trotter* [1899] 1 Ch 764, T made a gift by will to B who also witnessed the will. There were two later codicils to the will. B did not witness the first but witnessed the second. The court held that as there was one independently witnessed codicil, the gift could take effect.

## (d) Subsequent events irrelevant

It is the position at the date of execution which is relevant. Subsequent events are ignored. Thus, if a witness marries or forms a civil partnership with a beneficiary after witnessing the will, the gift remains valid (see *Thorpe v Bestwick* (1880–81) LR 6 QBD 311).

## 8.6.3    Implications for those preparing wills

If a will is sent to a client for execution, there must be a clear explanation of who can and cannot be a witness.

In *Ross v Caunters* [1980] Ch 297, a will was returned after execution to the solicitor who had prepared it. The solicitor had not warned the client a spouse of a beneficiary should not be a witness and did not question the fact the witness had the same surname as a beneficiary. When it turned out after the testator's death the witness was married to the beneficiary, the solicitor was found to be negligent and liable to the disappointed beneficiary.

(See, also, *Humblestone v Martin Tolhurst Partnership* [2004] EWHC 151 (Ch), where the court held the normal retainer for a solicitor where a will is prepared by a firm and returned to it for safe keeping after execution, requires the firm to check that, on its face, and on the facts then known to it, the execution of the will is ostensibly valid.)

## 8.7   Uncertainty

A gift in a will fails if it is impossible to identify either the subject matter or the intended beneficiary.

### 8.7.1   Uncertainty of subject matter

Gifts of 'some of my best table linen' (see *Peck v Halsey* (1726) 2 P Wms 387) and 'of a handsome gratuity' (see *Jubber v Jubber* (1839) 9 Sim 503) have been held void for uncertainty. However, now it is possible to admit extrinsic evidence of a testator's intention under section 21 of the AJA 1982 (see para 7.4), it may be possible to establish what the testator intended.

A gift which allows a beneficiary to select such items as the beneficiary wishes is not void for uncertainty as long as the range of items from which the selection is made is certain. It is sensible if giving such a power to provide that in the event of any dispute, the decision of the PRs is final.

### 8.7.2   Uncertainty as to beneficiaries

A gift to 'the son of A' failed where A had several sons (see *Dowset v Sweet* (1753) 27 ER 117). It is, therefore, important to check carefully names of individuals and institutions intended to benefit. Again, it may now be possible to ascertain the testator's intention by admitting evidence under section 21 of the AJA 1982.

See, for example, *Harris v Beneficiaries of the Estate of Margaret Alice Cooper (Deceased)* [2010] EWHC 2620 (Ch), where extrinsic evidence was admitted to establish who the testatrix had meant by 'my surviving relatives'. See, also, *Pinnel v Anison* [2005] EWHC 1421 (Ch), where the court said it would be slow to find a gift void for uncertainty.

In the case of charities, there is an exception to the rule a gift fails if the beneficiary is not sufficiently identified. Provided it is clear from the will the gift was intended to be used for exclusively charitable purposes, the court will direct a scheme to give effect to the testator's wishes. If a gift is to a named institution but the name is incorrect, for example 'to Cancer Research', it is possible to apply to the Attorney General who has power under the Royal Sign Manual to direct which charity should take.

## 8.8   Contrary to public policy

A gift which is for an illegal or immoral purpose or which is contrary to public policy cannot take effect. The forfeiture rule considered at para 8.5 is one example of a gift contrary to public policy.

## 8.9   Gift induced by force, fear or undue influence

If a will is made as a result of force, fear, fraud or undue influence, it is not regarded as the act of the testator and will be refused probate. The person alleging the force, fear, fraud or undue influence must establish it since there are no presumptions.

See further para 3.4.

## 8.10   Doctrine of satisfaction

There is an equitable presumption (called the presumption of satisfaction) that parents intend to treat their children equally and would not wish to benefit one child twice over at the expense of the others.

Therefore, if a parent makes a will leaving property to children and subsequently makes a substantial lifetime gift to one of the children, the presumption is the lifetime gift 'satisfies', in whole or in part, the legacy which is thereby extinguished or reduced.

EXAMPLE

> Dad's will leaves each of his three children £100,000. His youngest son then wants to buy a house and Dad gives him £60,000 as a deposit.
>
> Following Dad's death, his youngest son will be treated as having received part of his legacy already. If Dad had given him £200,000, his legacy would be reduced to nothing.

The presumption applies equally to mothers and fathers (see *Cameron v Cameron* [1999] Ch 386) and to gifts of land as well as gifts of personalty (see *Race v Race* [2002] EWHC 1868 (Ch)).

Since it is only a presumption, it can be rebutted if, for example, it is clear the parent wanted to prefer one child over the others. In *Casimir v Alexander* [2001] WTLR 939, ChD, a father gave one daughter a house. The daughter had cared for the parents for many years and the father regarded her as having 'earned' the gift.

The presumption does not apply if the lifetime gift precedes the making of the will. Similarly, it does not apply if, in the example above, Dad has executed a codicil confirming each of the £100,000 legacies after giving the deposit to his youngest son.

## 8.11    Abatement

A gift may abate, that is fail, wholly or in part, if there are insufficient assets in the estate to satisfy it. The basic rule is that rights of creditors take preference over those of beneficiaries and so the former must be paid first out of available assets. Only when debts and funeral and testamentary expenses have been satisfied can effect be given to the beneficial interests in the will.

Subject to any specific instructions given by the testator, creditors will be paid first from available residue, then from the funds necessary to pay general legacies and, finally, assets which are the subject of specific legacies will be used. As to the meaning of general and specific legacies, see para 13.2 and see, also, Appendix 1.

EXAMPLE

> Trevor dies leaving an estate worth £100,000. He also has debts (including funeral and testamentary expenses) of £82,000. His will provides for:
>
> (a)    his gold watch (worth £8,000) to Alex (a specific legacy);
>
> (b)    his Aviva plc shares (worth £16,000) to Barry (a specific legacy);
>
> (c)    a pecuniary legacy of £10,000 to Carol (a general legacy);
>
> (d)    residue to Richard.
>
> The total value of the legacies in (a), (b) and (c) is £34,000 and so (ignoring debts) residue is worth £66,000. However, the debts of £82,000 must be paid before any gifts can take effect.
>
> The £66,000 potentially available as residue will be used first. In terms of Richard's anticipated inheritance, he takes nothing because the residue has abated to nothing.
>
> To satisfy the outstanding £16,000 of debts, the £10,000 set aside for Carol's pecuniary legacy will be taken next because this is a general legacy. Therefore, she too receives nothing because her legacy has also abated to nothing.

That leaves £6,000 of debts remaining and at this stage resort is made to the property which is the subject of the two specific gifts in (a) and (b). The position here is that the two gifts being in the same category will abate rateably according to value which in this case is 1:2. Therefore, the gold watch will effectively bear £2,000 and the Aviva shares £4,000. Each beneficiary has the choice of either paying the requisite amount to the executors from their own resources or the asset (or such part of it in the case of the Aviva shares) would have to be sold to raise the funds.

It is possible for the testator to vary the usual rules on abatement by providing that some legacies are to be paid in priority to others (see para 13.6.4).

Of course, it is possible for a testator to leave more debts than the total value of his estate, in which case none of the gifts in the will can take effect at all. Such an estate is said to be insolvent and the available assets must be applied towards the payment of debts following the order prescribed by the Administration of Insolvent Estates of Deceased Persons Order 1986 (SI 1986/1999). Nothing said by the testator in the will as to the variation of this order is of any effect.

# 9 Wills Dealing with Property Abroad

It is becoming much more common for individuals to own foreign property. The property may be investments or land and is typically a holiday home. The problem is knowing whether a will executed here under the law of England and Wales is going to be effective to deal with assets located outside the jurisdiction; similarly, whether a will executed abroad is capable of dealing with assets here. Whether or not the will is effective may depend on a number of factors, not least:

(a) the location and status of the testator, in the sense of domicile, nationality or degree of residence, at the date of either the will, or death or both;

(b) the nature of the property as to whether it is classified as 'movable' – broadly equivalent to 'personalty', or 'immovable' – broadly meaning an interests in freehold or leasehold land;

(c) the domestic law and the private international law of the country or state seeking jurisdiction and its interaction with the law of any other country or state, such as that where the will was made, where the property is located or with which the testator had a connection as in (a) above.

(d) the extent, if at all, to which the EU Succession Regulation (EU/650/2012) (also known as Brussels IV) applies (see para 9.4).

Dealing with such issues is far beyond the scope of this book and the reader must refer to a specialist work. However, this chapter can offer some guidance as to the issues that can be encountered.

## 9.1 Problems caused by owning foreign property

Subject to the EU Succession Regulation (see para 9.4) and limited areas covered by international treaties, there is no internationally agreed form of private international law. In addition to its own domestic legal system, each country also has its own system of private international law. Different countries have different ways of connecting the individual to the legal system.

For example:

(a)    domicile (the country or state in which the individual regards himself as permanently based and having his 'centre of operations');

(b)    nationality;

(c)    location of assets;

(d)    habitual residence.

The result is there may be more than one country claiming jurisdiction over an estate because one country uses domicile, another nationality and another location of assets, and this will inevitably cause difficulties.

Problems also arise because some jurisdictions, like England and Wales, use a common law system normally starting from the premise that testators should be free to dispose of their assets as they wish. Other jurisdictions including many in continental Europe and South America use a civil law system or civil code conferring fixed inheritance rights on certain family members – usually spouses and children. This is referred to as 'forced heirship' (see para 9.2).

Furthermore, civil law systems often have a matrimonial property regime so each spouse is treated as owning 50% of all assets acquired after marriage. Therefore, each spouse is able to deal with only his or her interest in the matrimonial assets, irrespective of who provided the funds. This is referred to as 'community of property' (see para 9.3).

Inevitably, therefore, there are conflicts when trying to decide what is to happen to assets in cross-border estates.

## 9.2   Forced heirship

The principle that certain relatives must receive a fixed proportion of the assets can extend even to lifetime gifts. For example, a child may be able to recover assets given away by the deceased before death.

Some countries, for example Italy (before it accepted the EU Succession Regulation), refer back to the country of nationality for the law relating to succession for all types of property. Thus, Italian forced heirship rules would not apply to any assets left by UK citizens, no matter where they were domiciled. However, other countries do not refer back to nationality and so forced heirship rules may apply to non-nationals.

While many cases that would have been subject to forced heirship may now escape due to the effect of the EU Succession Regulation (see para 9.4), in most countries, these forced inheritance rules do extend to non-nationals. Commonly, the domestic law is applied to land, while the law of the country of domicile (or habitual residence) is applied to movable property.

For example, if an English person dies owning land in Brazil, under the Brazil Civil Code, effect can be given to an English will unless application of Brazilian law is more favourable to any spouse or children of the deceased. Brazilian law requires a reserved portion equal to 50% of the estate to be distributed to so-called necessary heirs, namely existing descendants, ascendants and surviving spouse. However, Brazil refers back to English (private international not domestic) law for the movables. England would then, in the case of a deceased person with English domicile, apply its own domestic law to the movable property, either under the deceased's will, or intestacy if otherwise undisposed of.

An English court will only apply forced heirship restrictions to the disposition by will of movables if the testator dies domiciled in a country, the law of which imposes them (see *In re Angus' Will Trusts* [1960] 1 WLR 1296).

It is often possible to change the nature of an asset relatively easily. For example, if land is held through shares in a company, the asset owned is shares not land and will escape the forced heirship rules applicable to land. Owning land through a company may, however, have adverse capital gains tax consequences and so it is important to take local legal advice on the nature of forced heirship rights and the best form of ownership vehicle.

It will often be worthwhile appointing both a UK and a foreign adviser. The foreign lawyer should be suitably placed to advise on local succession and tax issues; however, he is unlikely to appreciate the UK tax and succession issues. In this regard, there is an advantage to instructing a UK-based (international) estate planning and tax specialist; they can advise on the UK issues and co-ordinate with the foreign lawyer to make sure the solution fits both the UK and foreign angles.

## 9.3  Community of property

Community of property between husband and wife gives each of them rights in each other's property throughout marriage, with such rights continuing after the death of one of them. Most civil law jurisdictions have a default regime that will apply subject to contrary agreement or election. In France, for instance, the default regime is that of community of marital gains so that 50% of assets acquired during the marriage will be treated as being owned by each of the spouses and only the deceased's 50% will pass with the rest of the estate on death.

Where community of property applies, the husband and wife may be precluded from giving it away, or giving away more than their respective share.

The community rights which arise under a foreign law on marriage will not be lost by a subsequent change of domicile to a jurisdiction (such as England) which has no such rights. An attempt by will to dispose of more than the freely alienable share in the community property will fail, even if the person concerned died domiciled in England (see, e.g., *Celestine De Nicols v Curlier and others* [1900] AC 21).

In some jurisdictions, couples can elect at the date of the marriage whether or not they want community of property to apply.

Under the French rules, for instance, the parties may elect for there to be an accruer clause in the contract so that on the death of one spouse the communal property passes outright to the surviving spouse by survivorship. Any such adjustments to the default regime would have to have been evidenced by a notarial act. This may be a simple way to achieve an equivalent structure to joint ownership, though it will not usually be allowed where there are children of a previous marriage who have forced heirship rights, as otherwise it would be an easy means to circumvent these.

Therefore, in the case of clients with holiday homes, it may be that the property will pass outside any will and not be subject to forced heirship.

## 9.4   The EU Succession Regulation

The EU Succession Regulation (EU/650/2012 (also known as Brussels IV) was formally adopted by the European Parliament and Council on 4 July 2012. It is binding in all EU member states (except the United Kingdom, Ireland and Denmark, which exercised their right to opt out). With effect from 17 August 2015 it determines private international law for those member states bound by it.

Brussels IV aims to reduce previous difficulties and uncertainty by introducing common rules dealing with conflict of laws for those EU member states to which it applies if somebody dies on or after 17 August 2015. It may also change the effect of wills made before that date. Although Brussels IV does not apply in the United Kingdom, it still affects the way private international law of England and Wales (as well as that of Scotland and Northern Ireland) interacts with the laws of the EU member states which are bound by it.

Since the United Kingdom is not bound by Brussels IV, there will be no change in the way it affects the United Kingdom after it leaves the European Union. The United Kingdom is already a 'third state' along with Ireland and Denmark as a result of opting out of Brussels IV. As a non-EU country the United Kingdom will continue to be a 'third state'.

For deaths after 17 August 2015, unless otherwise provided for in Brussels IV, the law that applies to succession matters, for both immovable and movable property, is the law of the state in which the deceased was habitually resident at death (Article 21(1)), unless it is clear from all the circumstances the deceased was manifestly more closely connected at death with another state – in which case the law of that state applies by default instead (Article 21(2)).

However, this general rule is overridden if the deceased has chosen the law of any nationality he has when making the choice, or at the time of death, to govern succession to his estate as a whole (Article 22(1)). Such choice can be made in a will or codicil. (If a testator makes a will in accordance with the law of his nationality, the testator may be treated as having chosen to apply that law even if the will does not expressly say as much.)

A choice made by a national of any state will be respected in the EU states which adopted Brussels IV.

For most people, choosing to apply the law of their nationality by express provision will ensure their estate is governed by the law with which they are most familiar.

The United Kingdom does not have one law of succession; there are different succession laws applying to England and Wales, Scotland and Northern Ireland. Hence a person domiciled in any part of the United Kingdom who wants to choose the law of his nationality must choose the law of the part of the jurisdiction with which he is most closely connected.

Consider the example of Paul who is a British citizen domiciled in England and Wales. He was born in Wales and since then lived most of his life in England but has owned a second home in France for many years where 'off and on' he has spent time. He has a wife and two children. He is estranged from his family and has been spending most of his time in recent years with his close friend at the French house, which is where Paul died. His will made in England leaves the French house to his close friend.

On Paul's death, France will apply Brussels IV. If Paul made no express provision in his will, the interaction between Brussels IV and English private international law *could* result in the French house devolving according to French law as immovable property located in France on the basis Article 21(1) applies. If so, French forced heirship rules apply (as they would have done before Brussels IV came into force), with the result Paul's family may be able to take the French house in priority to the close friend.

However, if Paul included a choice of English law in his will, France has to apply English law to the property under Article 22(1) allowing the close friend to inherit it. (Although English law says the French house is subject to French law, in these circumstances Brussels IV prevents France from accepting any attempt by the English court to have French law applied.) English law will apply to Paul's other assets (including the contents of the French house since these are movables) regardless of any choice of law.

## 9.5  How many wills?

Ideally, a testator will use different wills to deal with assets in different countries.

There are a number of reasons for this:

(a)    A local lawyer will be able to advise on any problems of inheritance in that jurisdiction arising from fixed inheritance laws (although, ideally, these should have been investigated at the date the property was acquired).

(b)    A local lawyer will be able to advise on the tax payable as a result of leaving property in the way proposed. Many jurisdictions charge tax at different rates depending on how close the relationship is between the deceased and those inheriting.

(c)    A will made in the language and form of the local jurisdiction will be familiar to local institutions and will, therefore, make it easier to deal with those assets.

(d)    Civil law and Islamic jurisdictions do not recognise the concept of executorship in its English sense and assets usually vest in the heir direct. Executors appointed under an English will are, therefore, unlikely to be able to take any effective steps to acquire title to the foreign assets.

(e)    Similarly, many jurisdictions do not recognise trusts so a will leaving property to a spouse for life or on discretionary trusts may cause problems.

If making more than one will, it is important to ensure that each will deals only with assets situated in the particular jurisdiction and does not contain a revocation clause which revokes 'all other wills'.

What happens if there is a mistake and the later will revokes all wills or purports to deal with all property? Normally, the latest will prevails. However, it may be possible to construe a revocation clause as intended to apply only to other wills in that jurisdiction.

This was done in *Re Wayland's Estate* [1951] 2 All ER 1041, where a British subject domiciled in England made a will in Brussels expressed to deal only with his Belgian property. A few months later he made a will in England which contained a general revocation clause but which also included a declaration, '… this will is intended to deal only with my estate in England'. When giving instructions for his English will, he informed the solicitor that he had made a Belgian will in respect of his Belgian estate, and, before and after making his English will, he wrote to his Belgian solicitor in regard to the custody of his Belgian will.

The court held that the revocation clause in the English will was intended to revoke all former wills dealing with English property, and was not intended to, and did not, revoke the Belgian will.

It may be necessary to consider whether the will is validly executed. Section 1 of the Wills Act 1963 provides that a will is to be treated as properly executed if made in accordance with the internal law of a country:

(a)  where the will was executed; or

(b)  where the testator was domiciled or habitually resident; or

(c)  of which the testator was a national at the time the will was executed or at his death.

Section 2 of the Wills Act 1963 provides other ways in which a will may be validated.

Particularly useful is section 2(b) of the Wills Act 1963, which provides that a will is valid 'so far as it disposes of immovable property, if its execution conformed to the internal law in force in the territory which the property was situated'.

## 9.6  Helping clients to deal with local lawyers

In an ideal world, clients would take advice on succession when buying a foreign property and make a will at that point to deal with it. Sadly, this is often not the case.

Where clients have not made a will dealing with the foreign property, they should be advised to consult a lawyer in the local jurisdiction. The best results are achieved if the firm preparing the will for England and Wales has links or contacts with a firm in the local jurisdiction so that both firms can work in unison as part of an overall estate plan.

If this is not possible and the client is going to see a local lawyer 'cold', it will be helpful for the client to have a checklist of issues to work through with the local lawyer. A possible checklist is set out below:

(a)    Clients should tell the lawyer they have a will dealing with all assets except those in the local jurisdiction. They should be prepared to show the will to the foreign lawyer if necessary.

(b)    Clients should tell the lawyer that they want the will limited to the foreign property and without a general revocation clause. They should be prepared to question the local lawyer about the viability of succession concepts (such as a life interest), which although recognised in an English will may not be so in the local jurisdiction.

(c)    Clients should ask the lawyer whether there are any fixed inheritance laws. If so, are there any ways of circumventing those provisions, including dealing with succession outside the terms of a conventional will, such as holding the property in a company or trust or co-owning it? They should also ask the lawyer to explain the tax consequences of owning property in such a way.

(d)    If the state involved is a party to the EU Succession Regulation, clients will normally want a declaration that they want the law of their nationality to apply. They must explain that there is no succession law applying to the United Kingdom as a whole so the declaration must state that the law of England and Wales or Scotland or Northern Ireland is to apply.

(e)    Clients should ask the lawyer who will deal with the transfer of property after death. Is the transfer done by executors or beneficiaries? If the work is done by executors, who could, or should, be appointed? Is it feasible to appoint the same executors as in the 'home' will? Often, however, in civil law jurisdictions the concept of PRs is unknown. Property vests directly in the heir and the formal transfer of legal title is carried out by a notary.

(f)    Clients should ask the lawyer to explain what the tax position is on death in the local jurisdiction. They should be aware that UK domiciliaries are liable to UK inheritance tax on their worldwide assets. Double tax treaties exist which offer some relief from double tax with the following countries: France, Italy, the Netherlands, Sweden, Switzerland, India, Ireland, Pakistan, South Africa and the United States. However, they work in different ways and do not always prevent double tax. If they do not, PRs have to rely on the unilateral relief provisions contained in section 159 of the IHTA 1984, which, broadly, provide that any foreign tax paid in respect of an asset which is also subject to UK inheritance tax may be used as a credit against the UK inheritance tax payable.

(g)   Clients should ask the lawyer whether there any additional costs, such as providing for an English translation, as well as other necessary formalities, such as notarisation or registration, in the local jurisdiction.

Will writers often offer a storage service to clients, usually for a fee. It is important to ask about the cost of storage as there have been stories of very high fees being charged. It is also important to ask where wills are stored and in what conditions as some will writers operate from home and arrangements for storage may be unsatisfactory.

## 10.2   Locating lost wills

If a will cannot be found on death, the answer may be that the testator failed to make one or revoked it, but it is important to make a thorough search of the deceased's papers and make enquiries at the bank to see if there was a safe deposit box.

The probate registry should be contacted to see if the will was deposited and Certainty, the National Will Register (see para 10.1) should be contacted to see if it was registered. If this draws a blank, it is then very much a matter of trial and error. Any solicitors or other professionals who provided legal services or might have prepared a will should be contacted, then firms in areas where the deceased lived.

Certainty, the National Will Register offers not only a search of its own register (currently 7 million wills are registered), but also a 'Combined Search' which also sends a notification request to solicitors and will writers close to the deceased's address and other areas where a will may have been made.

## 10.3   Obtaining probate in absence of the original will

If an original will cannot be found, it may be possible to obtain probate of a draft, copy or even an oral reconstruction based on recollection of its terms. This requires an application for an order under rule 54 of the NCPR 1987 and must be supported by evidence to show the will was duly executed, it has not been revoked and, of course, the terms of the will. Notice may also need to be served on anyone, namely those entitled on intestacy or under an earlier will, who might be prejudiced by the making of an order.

In *Ferneley v Napier* (see para 10.1.2), the High Court confirmed the standard of proof for establishing the terms and execution of a missing will is the usual civil standard of balance of probabilities. There was no binding authority to say the higher criminal standard of beyond reasonable doubt should apply, although previous cases suggested the substitution of oral or other extrinsic evidence in place of the physical evidence usually required by the WA 1837 demanded clear proof and was not to be lightly undertaken.

# 11 Appointment of Executors and Trustees

## 11.1 Why appoint executors?

The ability to appoint one or more executors to obtain a grant of probate to deal with the administration of the estate and then carry out the terms of a will is one reason why it is better to die testate rather than intestate.

If the testator fails to make an effective appointment of an executor, then the administration and implementation of the will must be carried out by one or more administrators appointed by the court. The person(s) able to make application for a grant of administration are determined by rule 20 of the NCPR 1987 with the most likely applicants being amongst those entitled to residue. While such person(s) will have a beneficial interest in the estate and the motivation to see it is administered without delay, it could be such person(s) were not uppermost in the testator's mind as being the right or best people to deal with the estate.

Even if the application of rule 20 is consistent with the testator's choice of person(s) to deal with the estate, there are differences between the offices of executor and administrator (see para 11.2).

## 11.2 Executors distinguished from administrators

It is important to distinguish between the offices of executor and administrator; in particular, it is only an executor who has authority before the grant is issued.

The authority of an executor derives from being appointed by the deceased in the will and it starts at the date of death. The executor will obtain a grant of probate to confirm both the will and the executor's appointment within it are valid. Consequently, the grant acts as the court's confirmation to third parties that the executor's authority exists.

In theory, an executor can exercise all the powers required to deal with the deceased's property without obtaining a grant. The executor can sue or be sued, though if he is bringing an action which depends upon title to act as executor, a grant is necessary before judgment as proof of that title.

In practice, however, the executor will almost always need to obtain a grant as proof of title to collect in the deceased's assets. In addition, no purchasers of estate property are likely to part with their money without proof of the executor's title as seller, whilst any beneficiary in whose favour a transfer or assent of land is made will want sight of the grant to be satisfied as to the executor's authority.

As regards administrators, whether or not there is a will, their title derives from the grant itself. Unlike an executor, they are appointed by the court and not by the deceased. Pending the grant, legal title to the deceased's assets vests in the Public Trustee (section 9 of the Administration of Estates Act 1925 (AEA 1925) (as amended by the Law of Property (Miscellaneous Provisions) Act 1994)). Whilst the estate of an intestate person vests in the Public Trustee until the issue of the grant, if the deceased leaves a will and:

(a)    at the time of death there is no executor with power to obtain a grant; or

(b)    at any time before probate is granted, there ceases to be an executor with power to obtain a grant;

the estate disposed of by the will vests in the Public Trustee.

The person with the best right to take the grant of administration has no right to deal with the estate in the interim period; see, for example, the Court of Appeal decision in *Millburn-Snell and others v Evans* [2011] EWCA Civ 577, upholding the rule that a claim form issued on behalf of an estate before the grant is obtained is a nullity. Further, the grant when made does not relate back to the date of death except for the purpose of allowing the administrator to sue for wrongs done in the period between the death and the grant.

## 11.3    Drafting the executor's appointment

A grant of probate can issue only to an executor who is appointed by the will or a codicil. The most certain way of doing this is by an express appointment clearly:

(a)    identifying by name the person(s) who are the subject of the appointment; and

(b)    stating that they are to be appointed 'executor'.

A suitable form of wording is:

> I appoint [A] of …… and [B] of …… to be my executors.

Sometimes, an appointment might be made by description rather than by name, for example.

> I give my whole estate to my husband and appoint him my sole executor.

Such an appointment of a spouse (or civil partner) is unlikely to give rise to a problem other than the 'husband' in the example needing to identify himself when submitting his application for the grant. However, appointments along similar lines of 'my son, 'my sister', 'my nephew', etc are not recommended because, although the appointment may be valid, there could be difficulties if there is more than one person satisfying the description. If the matter cannot be satisfactorily resolved, the appointment could fail for uncertainty.

It is also possible to appoint an executor who is the holder of an office. If the appointment simply refers to the office without naming anyone, this is treated as an appointment of the person holding that office at the date of *death* (see *In the Estate of Jones* (1927) 43 TLR 324). However, more common is an appointment of the members of a firm (e.g. solicitors) which in the absence of any contrary provision in the will is *prima facie* treated as an appointment of the members of the firm at the date the will is *made* (or the date of any codicil republishing the will containing the appointment) who are entitled to act (see *Re Horgan (Deceased)* [1969] 3 All ER 1570). As to codicils and republication of a will, see para 6.3.

An appointment can still take effect even if the word 'executor' is not used if the appointment is 'according to the tenor of the will'. This means the appointment is implied if the will shows an intention a particular person should perform the functions of an executor, though not expressly so described. A direction to 'pay the testator's debts' has been held sufficient, as has the appointment of a trustee 'to get in all my property'.

However, a simple unqualified appointment of someone as a 'trustee' of property is not enough for that person to be treated as an executor because the office of a PR and trustee are different in nature (see *In the Estate of MacKenzie* (1909) P 305 and see para 11.7 as to the function and appointment of trustees). Similarly, in *Vucicevic v Aleksic* [2017] EWHC 2335 (Ch), a case of a handwritten will made by a British citizen with a poor command of written English, a reference to someone given obligations consistent with being a trustee and who was also asked 'to be in charge' was not sufficiently clear to show the testator intended to appoint him as an executor of the will.

## 11.4   Who can be appointed?

The relative merits of possible appointees must be considered with the testator. The choice will be influenced by a number of factors, such as:

(a)   the availability and willingness of suitable persons to act, bearing in mind the size and nature of the estate, including its geographical location;

(b)   the possibility of a conflict of interest arising, either between potential executors and beneficiaries, or amongst the executors themselves;

(c)   the terms of the proposed will and the likely issues that might arise under it;

(d)   the possibility of the chosen executor(s) predeceasing;

(e)   costs and remuneration.

The main categories of possible appointees (but bear in mind that any combination of the following may be possible) are:

(a)   *Individual – relatives and friends.* Appointing a relative has the advantage that the individual has personal knowledge of the testator and will act without remuneration. The disadvantage may well be a lack of expertise in dealing with financial matters and an unwillingness to cope with the burdens of the office due to inexperience or perhaps immaturity. However, the appointee can always seek professional advice. There is also the risk that the chosen individual may predecease.

Unless there is reason to believe a conflict of interest might arise, there is no reason why a beneficiary cannot also act as an executor and it is quite common for the residuary beneficiary to be appointed, particularly in the case of a spouse or civil partner.

It is clearly desirable to obtain the agreement of an individual to act, particularly if he is not being provided for beneficially in the will. As to giving a legacy to an executor as a reward for acting, see para 11.5.

Some individuals might not be suitable to act in a representative capacity, even if they are family members. They could include persons who live abroad, minors, mentally incapacitated persons, bankrupts, those in prison or others who have shown that they are not good at managing property/money. The courts will not lightly pass over a testator's choice of executor, even if it is an unwise choice. However, the court does have an overriding jurisdiction to pass over any person entitled to a grant if it appears to be necessary or expedient to appoint some other person as administrator (section 116 of the Senior Courts Act 1981).

(b) *Solicitors, accountants or other professionals, etc.* An appointment of a professional person, whether as a member of a firm or an individual, has the obvious advantage of ready expertise coupled with a lack of personal interest which might otherwise have been the basis for conflict. If a firm is appointed, the appointment takes effect as an appointment of the partners at the date the will is made unless a contrary intention is shown in the will. Consequently, the will should expressly provide that it is an appointment of the partners at the date of death (or the members or directors at death if the firm is a limited liability partnership (LLP) or incorporated law firm). Although an appointment will not necessarily be invalidated if the firm changes its trading status, a well-drafted appointment should anticipate such changes by making provision for change of name, becoming an LLP, incorporated practice, amalgamation, etc. The usual practice is then to express the wish that just two of the partners (or as the case may be) should obtain the grant and act initially in the administration, with power being reserved to the others.

A suitable form of wording is:

> I APPOINT the equity partners [including salaried partners] at the date of my death in the firm of [name] of [address] to be the executors [and trustees] of this my will and I express the wish that two and only two of them shall prove my will [and act initially in its trusts] and I DECLARE that if at the date of my death [name] has been succeeded to by another firm, company or limited liability partnership which carries on the practice and business of [name] then this appointment shall take effect and be construed as an appointment of the equity partners [including salaried partners], directors or profit-sharing members of such succeeding firm, company or limited liability partnership as the case may be].

Care must be taken to ensure that the initial appointment is valid since an appointment of 'any two of the partners in ...' will fail for uncertainty. Similarly, care needs to be taken if appointing an incorporated practice so that the individual members or directors are appointed in the first instance, the point being that under the Solicitors Incorporated Practice Rules 2004, the practice is not a trust corporation as such (as to trust corporations, see (c) below). Also, it is wise to add 'including salaried partners' when making an appointment of 'the partners at my death' to ensure that all partners, not just those sharing profits, are within the appointment (see *Re Rogers deceased* [2006] EWHC 753 (Ch)).

Of course, if the testator has a close connection with individuals within a firm, the testator can always decide to appoint individual professionals by name as opposed to appointing the partners, etc at death. However, this runs the risk that such an individual may retire or leave the firm in question.

On 24 July 2018, the Law Society published a Practice Note, *Appointment of a professional executor*. It emphasises the information that should be given to clients when discussing an appointment involving members of the firm with particular emphasis on the alternatives available and costs (see para 11.5 as regards remuneration).

The Practice Note may be viewed at:

> www.lawsociety.org.uk/support-services/advice/practice-notes/appointment-of-a-professional-executor/

See further para 21.1.4.

(c) *Trust corporations, including banks having such status through authorisation made under rules in the Public Trustee Act 1906 to act as a custodian trustee.* The usual practice is to appoint the trustee department of a bank using its own precedent which incorporates its standard terms and conditions (see remuneration, para 11.5). Apart from the fact that a trust corporation is normally unwilling to accept the appointment unless its terms and conditions can apply, this also ensures that the trust corporation is properly appointed because the trustee department may well be a separate trust corporation distinct from the ordinary commercial wing of the bank. The relatively small size of many estates may not justify the additional costs that are often involved in the engagement of a trust corporation.

It is also possible to appoint the Public Trustee who, if accepting the appointment, has a statutory right to remuneration (Public Trustee (Fees) Order 2008 (SI 2008/611)). Such an appointment is rarely made except in cases where there might be difficulty in finding someone able and willing to act. If intending to appoint the Public Trustee, the testator should first obtain consent, which can be done by email: enquiries@offsol.gsi.gov.uk.

## 11.5    Remuneration of executors

Executors and trustees are not entitled to remuneration for their services under the general law, although they can be reimbursed out of the estate for expenses incurred in carrying out their duties.

However, a testator can authorise payment expressly in the will. It is usual to authorise 'reasonable' payment. The test of reasonableness is objective.

In the case of a challenge to the level of remuneration charged, a court will ask what the 'going rate' is for such work (see *Pullan v Wilson* [2014] EWHC 126 (Ch)).

In the absence of express authority to charge, the beneficiaries of the will may agree to payment from the estate (but this is possible only if they are all of full age and capacity).

Lastly, section 29 of the Trustee Act 2000 allows the payment of reasonable remuneration to a trustee (including an executor or administrator) for time spent and work done (even if the work could be done by a lay person) but only if the trustee is either:

(a)     a trust corporation; or

(b)     a trustee 'acting in a professional capacity' who is not a sole trustee and who has obtained the written consent of all his co-trustees. 'Acting in a professional capacity' means acting in the course of a profession or business which provides relevant services to trusts and so will include solicitors, accountants and the like.

However, an express charging provision (or authorisation by the beneficiaries) is still required to allow any trustee not falling within section 29 to charge for time spent. This includes a sole trustee, even if acting in a professional capacity. An express clause may also extend the implied power to charge reasonable remuneration under section 29, for example, by allowing a trust corporation, such as a bank, to charge in accordance with its standard terms and conditions, or by allowing a trustee to retain remuneration received as director of a company in which the estate or trust holds shares. It is usual in an express charging clause to say the trustee may charge for all work, even if it could be done by a non-professional, despite the fact that the Trustee Act 2000 now provides this will be implied into a clause providing for remuneration.

Until the Trustee Act 2000 came into force, a charging clause was treated as a legacy subject to section 15 of the WA 1837 (see para 8.6) and would abate with other legacies if funds were needed for the payment of debts (see para 8.11).

Section 15 provides a beneficiary loses the legacy if he or his spouse or civil partner witnesses the will. In the past, a will containing a charging clause could not be witnessed by the solicitor, or partner in the firm, who was to benefit from it. If it was, the charging clause was void. However, section 28(4)(a) of the Trustee Act 2000 now provides the benefit of a charging clause does not qualify as a legacy for the purpose of section 15 of the WA 1837 if the death occurred after 1 February 2001, regardless of the date the will was made. Similarly, section 28(4)(b) of the Trustee Act 2000 provides a charging clause no longer abates with other legacies.

If a relative or friend is being appointed an executor, it is not uncommon for the testator to give a legacy to the appointee. Is the legacy intended as reward for the services provided as executor, or could the appointee still claim the legacy despite renouncing the executorship on the testator's death? If it is a legacy (as opposed to an interest in residue), the legacy by implication is conditional on the appointee accepting the executorship. If the testator wants the appointee to benefit from the legacy in any event, the will should make this intention clear. A suitable form of wording is:

> I give £5,000 to Edward Jones whether or not he proves my will and acts initially in its trusts.

## 11.6    How many executors?

Any number of executors may be appointed, though only four may take out the grant of probate in respect of the same property. If more than four executors are appointed, the grant will be made to the first four with power reserved to the others in the event of vacancy occurring.

A sole executor has the same powers as two or more, by virtue of section 2(1) of the AEA 1925. In relation to an estate which includes land, a sole executor can give a valid receipt for capital moneys (see section 27 of the LPA 1925). Nevertheless, it makes sense to consider the appointment of more than one executor to cover the possibility of one predeceasing the testator or becoming incapable of acting. Also appointing two executors is sensible if they are also to become trustees because once they act in the latter capacity, two trustees (or a trust corporation) are needed to give a good receipt for capital money when disposing of land.

## 11.7    Executors as trustees

If a trust will, or may, arise, it is usual to appoint the same people as both executors and trustees. The job of executors is to collect in the estate, liquidate funds if necessary and then pay the debts and testamentary expenses before giving effect to the legacies under the will. The task of trustees is essentially one of managing funds for the benefit of those entitled, for example until they satisfy a contingency or during a life interest. Even though the duties and functions attached to each office differ, the criteria for selection of appropriate appointees are much the same because both executors and trustees are fiduciaries who are subject to many of the same statutory and equitable obligations.

Whether or not the trustees are different people, the executors will need to vest the relevant trust property in the trustees once the property in question has been ascertained and is no longer required to satisfy debts and liabilities or other claims against the estate. Typically, in the case of a residuary trust, this will be at the end of the estate administration.

## 11.8    Limited and special appointments

Most appointments are 'unlimited' and confirm authority to deal with the whole estate and without limitation of time.

However, it is possible for an appointment to be limited as to time (e.g. 'until my son X attains his majority'); or as to specific property (e.g. an appointment of an 'executor to deal with the deceased's business or literary affairs'); or even for a particular purpose (such as to conduct litigation).

Any grant issued to such executors will be similarly limited and as such there can be more than one grant current in an estate at any one time.

## 11.9    Conditional, substitute and alternative appointments

Appointments can be made subject to a condition precedent or subsequent. A suitable form of wording is:

> I appoint Edward if he has been admitted to the roll as a solicitor by the date of my death and if not I appoint Freda.

However, care should be taken to avoid an appointment which might fall within a survivorship clause (see para 8.4.2) such as, 'If my wife survives me by 30 days, I give her my whole estate and appoint her my sole executor'. The problem here is that until the condition is satisfied, the spouse cannot apply for a grant and nor has she authority to do any act she might have done if the appointment was unconditional. It is better to keep the appointment separate and if a general survivorship clause is being used in the will (see para 22.2.1, Inconsistent survivorship clauses), it should make it clear it applies only to beneficial interests.

An appointment may be substitutional, for example:

> I appoint as my executor Xaviar but if he is unable or unwilling to act then I appoint Sara.

Sara may prove the will if Xaviar is dead or decides to renounce (see para 11.10).

## **11.10**    Failure of appointment – divorce/ annulment, renunciation and uncertainty

An appointment may not take effect for any of the following reasons:

(a)    *Divorce, dissolution or annulment*: a will may appoint the testator's spouse or civil partner as an executor or trustee. If the marriage or civil partnership is later dissolved or annulled, then such an appointment takes effect as though the former spouse or civil partner had died on the date of such dissolution or annulment (sections 18(A)(1) and 18(C) of the WA 1837). This rule is, however, subject to a contrary intention appearing in the will.

(b)    *Renunciation*: an executor appointed by the will may renounce the office in writing after the death but before doing any act which amounts to intermeddling in the estate and which thus demonstrates acceptance. As to what does or does not amount to intermeddling, see 11.12.2. Once made, a renunciation cannot be retracted unless the court so allows (rule 37 of the NCPR 1987).

There is no process to compel an executor to renounce but, in practice, professional executors and bank trust corporations are sometimes asked to do so by the testator's family (or may even make the suggestion themselves) if the estate is relatively small and uncomplicated and does not justify the additional expense of involving professional executors. In the case of an appointment of a firm, or partners in a firm, a renunciation can be made via two of the profit sharing partners who can renounce on behalf of the others (rule 37(2A) of the NCPR 1987, as amended).

(c)    *Uncertainty*: as with any provision in a will, an appointment may fail if it is uncertain who the testator intended to appoint. So, an appointment of 'any two of my sons', as in *Re Blackwell's Goods* [1877] 2 PD 72, is bad (see, also, para 11.3).

## **11.11**    Protecting executors and trustees

A testator may wish, or be advised, to include a provision exonerating executors or trustees from the consequences of their own negligence resulting in a breach of trust, or to provide them with an indemnity from the estate if held liable for loss caused by a co-executor or co-trustee. Since the decision in *Armitage v Nurse* [1998] Ch 241, such clauses are generally accepted as valid provided the exclusion of liability is limited to acts or omissions in good faith (including negligence) even though the clause affords relief for breach of the duties of exercising due skill, care, prudence and due diligence. However, it is not possible to exclude liability for acts of fraud or bad faith. The exclusion of such liability would make it impossible to give effect to the trust. A clause which is drafted so widely that it purports to exclude liability for all breaches, including fraudulent ones, is likely to be void.

Section 1 of the Trustee Act 2000 contains a statutory duty of care saying a trustee (including a PR) must exercise such care and skill as is reasonable in the circumstances. It is possible to exclude this and it may be appropriate to do so for the benefit of unpaid executors and trustees.

Whilst it is clearly appropriate to exonerate friends and family who are acting out of respect to the testator and for no financial benefit, it is much less so in the case of professional fiduciaries who use the fees received to pay for the benefit of professional negligence policies.

A 2006 Law Commission report on the use of trustee exemption clauses advocated a non-legislative solution by recommending professional and regulatory bodies to adopt rules and guidance, to the effect that any clause in a will or other trust instrument which purports to limit or exclude liability for negligence must be brought to the testator or settlor's notice before execution.

# 11.12    Some other issues relating to executors

## 11.12.1    Chain of representation

If the testator is appointed as an executor of another's estate, there is the possibility that someone who he appoints as his own executor could end up having to administer not only the testator's estate but also the estate of which the testator was executor. This can arise if the so-called chain of representation applies under section 7 of the AEA 1925.

If a *sole or last surviving executor who has proved* the testator's will by obtaining a grant of probate, *dies with a will which appoints an executor* before he has completed the administration of the estate, the estate remaining un-administered is dealt with by the executor's executor, provided the latter proves the executor's will. This chain of representation is created as soon as the executor's executor takes probate of the first executor's will. No further grant is necessary to deal with the un-administered estate; both grants being produced together to complete the administration.

A chain of representation may continue through several sole or last surviving proving executors and will not be broken by a temporary/limited grant. However, the chain is broken (or never starts) if:

(a)   the sole or last surviving proving executor dies intestate;

(b)   the sole or last surviving proving executor fails to appoint an executor in his own will; or

(c)   the sole or last surviving proving executor's executor fails to prove the former's will.

The chain will also be broken if the original grant was taken by one or more of several executors with power reserved to other executors and one or more of those who had power reserved take(s) a grant of double probate.

If the *chain does not apply*, or is broken as above, the un-administered estate must be dealt with by an administrator who takes a special grant known as a grant *de bonis non*, i.e. limited to the un-administered portion of the estate.

## 11.12.2   Executor *de son tort*

The term 'executor *de son tort*', meaning an 'executor as a result of his own wrong', is misleading as it refers to someone who was not appointed as an executor but who has intermeddled in the affairs of the estate after the testator's death in such a way that it is appropriate he incurs liability as though he had been so appointed.

By holding himself out as an executor, for example by doing acts such as selling property, collecting debts and paying bills, he becomes liable to both creditors (including HM Revenue & Customs (HMRC)) and beneficiaries of the estate to the extent that property comes into his hands (section 8 of the AEA 1925). Certain acts of charity, humanity or necessity, including arranging the funeral and moving the deceased's property to protect it, are not enough to amount to intermeddling (see, e.g. *Pollard v Jackson* (1994) 67 P & CR 327).

Acting as an executor *de son tort* confers no authority to act. Anyone having intermeddled should deliver up any assets received to the lawful executor (or administrator), since this will usually bring to an end any liability owed to creditors or beneficiaries.

# 12 Appointment of Testamentary Guardians

## 12.1    Introduction

It is possible for a parent with parental responsibility (see para 12.2) to appoint guardians to look after his minor children after his death. Such appointments can be made in a will and, when they are effective, parental responsibility for the child is conferred on the appointee.

The commonly used term 'testamentary guardian' is simply indicative of a person who has been appointed in a will but an appointment which is intended to take effect on death does not have to be in a will and can be in any document or deed which satisfies the requirements for appointing a guardian in section 5(3)–(5) of the Children Act 1989, as amended by the Adoption and Children Act 2002 (see para 12.3). A document intended to be a will which is dated and satisfies the formalities for execution in section 9 of the WA 1837 (as amended) complies with the requirements of section 5 but a document which does nothing else apart from nominate guardians cannot be admitted to probate as a will, even though it may, in all other respects, comply with the formalities for a will.

It is usually convenient for those with young children to make the appointment of guardians in their will because the will can also deal with other important issues related to the future upbringing and welfare of the children. In particular, the beneficial entitlements of the children must be considered together with the ability to draw on income and capital for the children's maintenance, education and future welfare. This is usually catered for through a trust fund and it may be desirable to include the intended guardians as trustees of the fund as an aid to administration (see para 12.6).

The will may also include directions as to the manner in which the child is to be brought up. For example a direction may be included that the guardians shall bring up the child as a member of a particular religion or attend a particular school. Such a direction is in no way binding and is merely a statement of wishes. It is often more convenient to state such wishes in a separate document which can then be updated without having to make a new will.

In resolving any dispute concerning the upbringing and welfare of the child, a court may have regard to statements of wishes but ultimately will be concerned with what is in the best interests of the child.

A person appointed as a guardian under section 5(3) of the Children Act 1989 may disclaim the appointment by an instrument in writing signed by him and made within a reasonable time of first knowing the appointment has taken effect (section 6(5) of the Children Act 1989). In all cases it is vital for the testator to discuss the implications of the guardianship appointment with the proposed guardians and secure their consent and willingness to act before making the appointment.

## 12.2    Who can appoint a testamentary guardian?

An appointment can be made by a parent having 'parental responsibility' as defined in section 3 of the Children Act 1989. More than one person may have parental responsibility and so each can make an appointment.

If a child's parents were married or in a civil partnership at the time of the child's birth, then both will have parental responsibility. Otherwise, the mother alone has parental responsibility.

A father (or person treated as a father under section 36 of the Human Fertilisation and Embryology Act 2008) who is not married to the child's mother at the time of the child's birth can later acquire it in a number of ways. These include marrying the child's mother, entering into a parental responsibility agreement with the mother, obtaining a parental responsibility order from the court, or having his name as father registered on the child's birth certificate (see, further, sections 2 and 4 of the Children Act 1989, as amended).

Where a woman is treated as a child's second female parent under section 43 of the Human Fertilisation and Embryology Act 2009, she can acquire parental responsibility by entering into a parental responsibility agreement with the mother, obtaining a parental responsibility order from the court, or having her name registered as a parent on the child's birth certificate (see, further, sections 2 and 4ZA of the Children Act 1989, as amended).

If someone is not a child's natural parent but enters into a marriage or civil partnership with one of the natural parents, he or she does not acquire parental responsibility merely by being a step-parent. However, he or she will do so if either the natural parent agrees or the court orders it (section 4A of the Children Act 1989).

## 12.3    Requirements for a valid appointment

Section 5(5) of the Children Act 1989 provides an appointment which is intended to take effect following death must be in writing, dated and signed by the person making the appointment. As long as the appointer signs the document personally there is no requirement the signature is witnessed. Thus an appointment need not be in a will as such – this is sometimes referred to as the 'informal' procedure. Notably, this means if a will is not admitted to probate due to non-compliance with section 9 of the WA 1837 (see para 4.3), an appointment of guardians within it can still be effective as long as the testator signed and the writing is dated.

Alternatively, section 5(5) of the Children Act 1989 provides that if the appointer is a testator who makes a will which he does not sign in person but which is signed at his direction in accordance with the requirements of section 9 of the WA 1837 (see para 4.3.3), then the appointment is effective. Also, in any other case (i.e. if the document is not a will), the appointment is also effective if the writing is signed at the direction of the person making the appointment, in his presence and in the presence of two witnesses who each attest the signature.

The wording of section 5(5) of the Children Act 1989 means an appointment in a will satisfying section 9 of the WA 1837 *which the testator has signed personally* will comply with section 5(5) of the Children Act 1989 *as long as it is dated*. If the date is omitted or overlooked, then the will might be ineffective as an appointment of a guardian despite being admissible to probate (see *Williams on Wills* (LexisNexis, 10th edn, 2014), at 28.1). Similarly, the lack of a date means it does not comply with the 'informal procedure'.

If the testator later revokes his will, then the appointment is also revoked (section 6(4) of the Children Act 1989).

In practice, an appointment is often worded to take effect only if the other parent has predeceased the testator. Of course, there will be cases where the testator or testatrix wants the appointment to take effect on his or her death notwithstanding the survival of the other parent, for example if the parents are divorced or the testator or testatrix has a sole residence order in his or her favour but this is not always possible (see para 12.4).

Section 7(4) of the Children Act 1989 expressly provides an appointee can appoint another person to take his place in the event of his own death. Notwithstanding this statutory authority, it may be desirable to express this fact in a will because the appointee may be unaware of his ability to appoint a successor.

## 12.4     When does an appointment take effect?

Section 5(7)–(9) of the Children Act 1989, as amended, sets out rules to determine when an appointment is effective. The appointee will become the child's guardian if, at the testator's death either:

(a)     no parent with parental responsibility survived the testator; or

(b)     there was a residence order in the testator's *sole* favour in respect of that child.

Otherwise, if neither condition applies, the appointee will only become the guardian when the child no longer has a parent with parental responsibility, for example when the other parent with parental responsibility dies. If the surviving parent with parental responsibility has also made an appointment, then both appointments become effective raising the possibility of different people as appointees.

It is for this reason that some people choose to state that the appointment of a guardian is only to take effect if the other parent is not alive.

## 12.5     Consequences for the guardian

Although an effective appointment of a guardian gives the appointee parental responsibility and with it the duties of looking after the child, there are differences compared to being a parent, notably:

(a)     no succession rights to property arise, for example, on intestacy in favour of the child (or the guardian if it is the child who dies);

(b)     on the guardian's death, the child will not qualify as a child of the deceased under section 1(1)(c) of the I(PFD)A 1975 for the purpose of bringing a claim for reasonable financial provision, assuming the guardian has not adopted the child. However, it seems the child could show eligibility under section 1(1)(d) as someone who is not a child but who has been treated as a child of the marriage or civil partnership to which the guardian was a party. Similarly, eligibility might be established under section 1(1)(e) on the basis the child was being 'maintained' by the deceased immediately before death. As to the meaning of 'maintained' and the I(PFD)A 1975 generally, see para 2.2;

(c)     it is not possible for the court to make any financial order or property provision against the guardian under the terms of the Children Act 1989.

Notwithstanding these differences, it is worth bearing in mind that as long as the guardian was appointed under the Children Act 1989 before the child attained 18, the child will forever count as a 'lineal descendant' for the purpose of a claim for the inheritance tax residence nil rate band on the parent's death (see further para 16.6).

## 12.6     Funding for guardians and trust funds

Apart from having to decide who to appoint as the guardian(s) of minor children, the testator must also consider how best to ensure funds are available for the guardian to carry out his duties.

One possibility is to confer benefits directly on the guardian but this has the inherent risk such funds may be misdirected, either at the instigation of the guardian or otherwise, as where the guardian is later made bankrupt or dies.

A more viable option is to place funds in trust, coupled with wide powers of maintenance and advancement so both income and capital can be made available as required (see Chapter 18 as regards powers to deal with income and capital). This raises an issue of whether the guardian should be made a trustee of the fund and, if so, whether there should also be further trustees. This is not an easy matter on which to advise because much will depend on the circumstances of each situation, including the value of the funds available and the age(s) of the child(ren), as well as the financial position of the proposed guardians themselves.

The following is a non-exhaustive list of points those giving advice may wish to consider with the testator:

(a)     Are the guardians best placed to consider the needs of the child over anyone else?

(b)     Can the guardians be trusted to make the right decisions regarding financial expenditure?

(c)     Would the guardians be happy to make such decisions or would they rather rely on other people?

(d)     To what extent, if any, will the guardians require additional capital from the fund, either to buy a larger house or extend their existing property if having to cope with a larger family? If capital is required, what are the options available, such as lending from the fund or making a new purchase jointly with the fund?

(e)    Would having separate trustees avoid the children putting pressure on the guardians to meet their demands?

(f)    Should the testator be concerned that allowing the guardians to have control of trust funds might place them in a position where their own interests conflict with those of the child? For example, having a larger family might, justifiably, demand a bigger car but the guardians could be tempted into spending extravagantly on a top-of-the-range model rather than using the fund for a more modest purchase to meet actual needs.

(g)    Can the guardians be relied on to exercise their powers as trustees wisely, for example, applying income for the benefit of the child rather than allowing it to accumulate with possible adverse income tax consequences?

(h)    Would the guardians benefit from having one or more co-trustees and if so, should at least one of them be a professional person?

(i)    Can the guardians be relied on to establish an appropriate investment policy for the fund, or should they have a co-trustee with investment knowledge?

(j)    If there is more than one child involved, can the guardians make decisions to ensure each child is treated equally or as the testator might have wished?

(k)    How vital is it to separate guardianship responsibilities from trust fund management?

(l)    Should separate trustees be appointed with a duty to consult with, or seek consent from, the guardians on certain issues?

Ultimately, the testator needs to discuss with the proposed guardians not just their willingness to accept the appointment but also what views they have on the way in which they will bring up the children.

# 13 Legacies

This chapter considers how a will can make provision for gifts of assets other than land (known as 'personalty') which are not part of a residuary gift. However, many of the issues covered in this chapter can also apply to gifts of land covered in Chapter 14 and gifts of residue in Chapter 15.

## 13.1 A word on terminology

Historically, 'legacy' or 'bequest' was used to denote a gift of personalty, whilst a gift of land was referred to as a 'devise'. Similarly, the recipients were referred to as 'legatees' or 'devisees'. These days, as part of the move towards the use of plain English in legal documents, many draftsmen prefer to express legacies, bequests and devises as simply 'gifts' in favour of 'beneficiaries', irrespective of the subject matter.

Since 1925, the distinctions between gifts of personalty and realty have largely disappeared for all practical purposes but the use of the old terminology has not been lost entirely. For example, sections 62–64 of the Taxation of Chargeable Gains Act 1992 refer to 'legatee', and rule 20 of the NCPR 1987 refers to a 'legatee or devisee'.

Technically, a person taking assets as 'legatee' or 'devisee' can be someone doing so as a trustee for someone else rather than as a beneficiary in their own right.

In this chapter, we use the words 'legacy' or 'gift' and unless the recipient is to hold on trust, we use the word 'beneficiary'.

## 13.2 Types of non-residuary legacy

A non-residuary legacy may be classified as specific, general or demonstrative. Any such legacy may also be pecuniary in nature. The classification is not merely relevant for academic purposes, it can also have important practical consequences both for the person drafting a will and also for those administering the will after the testator's death.

## 13.2.1    Specific legacy

This is a gift of a particular item of property *distinguished in the will* from any other property of the same kind owned by the deceased.

EXAMPLES

> I give to Freda my 100 shares in ABC plc.
>
> I give to Charlie the gold watch my mother gave me.

A legacy is not specific just because the testator happens to own an item of property which exactly matches the description; there must be words used in the will which distinguish the property in question from similar property. This may be signified by the use of a possessive word such as 'my' but the item does not necessarily need to exist at the date the will is made. A legacy of 'the car which I own at the date of my death' is a specific legacy even though the car in question may not have been owned by the testator at the date of the will.

A specific legacy will fail if the specific subject matter does not exist as part of the testator's estate at death. In such a case it is said to have adeemed (see para 8.3). However, a specific legacy will rank after a general legacy for the purposes of abatement and so the property given will be at less risk from having to be used to pay the deceased's debts (see para 8.11).

## 13.2.2    General legacy

This is a legacy of property not distinguished in the will from property of a similar kind.

EXAMPLE

> I give to Freda 100 shares in ABC plc.

Contrast the specific legacy in para 13.2.1 which uses 'my'.

A general legacy is often pecuniary in nature.

EXAMPLE

> I give £100 to Michael.

If the testator does not own property answering the description at the date of death, the legacy is not adeemed and the PRs must purchase property of the appropriate description with the estate funds or offer the equivalent cash sum to the beneficiary. If there is insufficient cash in the estate already to fund a general legacy, the PRs must sell estate assets which are not themselves the subject of a specific legacy.

General legacies abate before specific legacies if there are insufficient assets in the estate to fund the payment of debts (see para 8.11).

### 13.2.3  Demonstrative legacy

This is 'in its nature a general legacy but there is a particular fund pointed out to satisfy it' (see *Ashburner v Macguire* [1786] 2 Bro CC 108).

EXAMPLE

> I give £500 to Alex payable out of my Lloyds Classic Bank Account.

Demonstrative legacies can never adeem because to the extent the particular fund does not exist as part of the testator's estate at death, the legacy is still payable, albeit as a normal general legacy. In that sense they are equated with general legacies because if there is not enough in the designated fund, the balance is paid out of the testator's residue.

However, they rank as specific legacies for abatement purposes (see para 8.11) and so will not fail for that reason to the extent the specified fund exists to provide for the legacy.

In practice, there is often no compelling reason to advise in favour of a demonstrative legacy as opposed to a general one. However, demonstrative legacies are frequently encountered in homemade wills because testators often think they must specify the account or fund from which a gift of money is to be paid.

### 13.2.4  Pecuniary legacy

In the sense that a 'pecuniary legacy' is a gift of money, it will usually be expressed as a general legacy as described in para 13.2.2 but it could take other forms. For example, a gift of money can be specific, as where a will gives 'the £1,000 I keep in the top drawer of the desk in my study', or it could be demonstrative as in '£1,000 out of my account at Barclays Bank'. If directed to be paid by instalments, it is usually called an annuity, for example, '£1,000 per annum to my wife' for which a fund will usually be set aside from which each instalment is paid.

The term 'pecuniary legacy' is defined in section 55(1)(ix) of the AEA 1925 as including 'an annuity, a general legacy, a demonstrative legacy so far as it is not discharged out of the designated property, and any other general direction by a testator for the payment of money, including all death duties free from which any devise, bequest, or payment is made to take effect'.

A will should make express provision stating expressly which property in the estate is to be used to pay pecuniary legacies as so defined. Failing to do so can lead to the imposition of the statutory rules contained in the AEA 1925 which are difficult to apply in some circumstances. This issue is considered further in Chapter 15.

## 13.3    Methods of making gifts

Whatever the type of gift, a testator has a number of choices about the terms of the gift.

### 13.3.1    Absolute or otherwise?

The simplest gift is one that is absolute, providing the beneficiary with an immediate vested entitlement on the testator's death. However, a gift may be less than absolute if:

(a)    the will imposes a condition or contingency which must first be satisfied. Typically this might be the attaining of an age or status, such as marriage, but it could be anything as long as it does not conflict with certain recognised restrictions (e.g. the condition must not be contrary to public policy) and is not inconsistent with other provisions in the will. If the condition or contingency is not fulfilled, the gift fails unless the testator has provided for the possibility by making a substitutional gift;

(b)    the will creates one or more successive interests in the same property, as where the will gives a life interest to a particular individual (that is a current right to its income or enjoyment) either for life or a lesser period (such as until remarriage) before the property ultimately vests absolutely in one or more remainder beneficiaries.

If a less than absolute interest is created, the property must be held in trust by trustees until the interest becomes absolute when the property can then be vested in the beneficiary who is entitled.

### 13.3.2    Precatory trusts

A so-called 'precatory trust' arises if a testator makes an outright legacy to X, but also includes an unenforceable direction to X to further dispose of the property in favour of others. Often the direction is expressed as a 'wish', 'hope' or 'desire'. Since no imperative fiduciary duty falls on X, as with a normal trust, X is free to ignore what the testator has said and is under only a moral obligation to dispose of the property in accordance with the testator's direction.

Since the legacy is an absolute one, inheritance tax rules initially apply in the usual way. If the legacy is to the testator's spouse or civil partner, it will be exempt; otherwise it may be chargeable depending on the rest of the estate. However, section 143 of the IHTA 1984 provides that if X transfers the property in compliance with the testator's expressed wishes and within 2 years of the death, the IHTA 1984 has effect as if the property had been given directly to the transferee. Consequently, if X chooses to comply with the testator's precatory direction within the time limit:

(a) it will not utilise X's annual inheritance tax exemption;

(b) X will not make a potentially exempt transfer and so if X dies within 7 years of the transfer, it will not count towards X's own cumulative total and there is no possibility of the transfer giving rise to a charge to inheritance tax for X;

(c) the spouse exemption may become available or be lost depending on the relationship between the eventual transferee and the testator.

EXAMPLE

Shirley's will contains a legacy of her collection of jewellery to her daughter, Polly. Her will says:

> … it is my hope that Polly will see fit to distribute it amongst my family in accordance with any note I may leave her before my death.

Within 2 years of Shirley's death and in accordance with the note she left, Polly distributes some jewellery to Shirley's grandchildren and gives the wedding ring to Shirley's civil partner in accordance with a note left by Shirley. The rest she keeps for herself.

On Shirley's death, all the jewellery is chargeable to inheritance tax since no exemption is available. The effect of section 143 of the IHTA 1984 is that no adjustment of the inheritance tax position is needed as regards the jewellery later transferred to grandchildren. Since Polly has not made a transfer of value herself, there are no inheritance tax consequences if she dies within 7 years. However, the ring passing to Shirley's civil partner now qualifies for the spouse exemption and, if appropriate, inheritance tax is reclaimable.

There is no corresponding provision for capital gains tax and so the jewellery will be treated as left to Polly who will then be treated as making a disposal when she gives effect to the note. However, it is rare for a chattel to have risen substantially in value between the date of death and its subsequent disposal. If there has been an increase and it is less than £6,000, it will fall within the exemption for chattels contained in section 262 of the Taxation of Chargeable Gains Act 1992. Also, the person named in the will may have the annual capital gains tax exemption available.

If the will refers to '… any note *I may leave* …', the note cannot be incorporated into the will because it is not a reference to a document already in existence at the time when the will is made (see para 13.3.4). This is advantageous because it allows Shirley to change her wishes after making the will by simply writing a new note. Had the note been incorporated into the will, she would have had to make a new will or execute a codicil.

(See, also, gifts of personal chattels at para 13.5.1.)

### 13.3.3    Rights of selection or division

A testator owning a collection or several items of property may want the beneficiaries to choose which item(s) they would like to take. This can be done by including a provision allowing several persons in order of preference to select one or more items (possibly up to a maximum value).

The legacy must be carefully drafted to clarify the range from which the selection can be made, who can select and the manner of selection. Selection should be in writing to the executors within a prescribed time period, ideally starting at a point when the executors give notice to the person of their right to select. The time period needs to be long enough to allow for a decision but not so long that awaiting the outcome might delay the progress of the administration, keeping in mind that items selected by a surviving spouse or civil partner will qualify for exemption and so affect the inheritance tax calculation.

As an alternative, the will can provide for division of items amongst potential donees. This task can be entrusted to the executors or a third party, or even to the potential donees themselves. Again, the intention must be clearly expressed and the ground rules established.

Regardless of how the legacy is structured or expressed, it should make provision for failure of the selection or division process. Items not selected will become part of the residue unless there is a specific direction as to what is to happen to them.

In cases where it is left to the pool of donees to divide up items, provision should be made for a disagreement. Commonly the executors are given the final say. For example:

> I give all my personal chattels as defined by section 55(1)(x) of the Administration of Estates Act 1925 to my grandchildren living at my death to be divided between or among them as they shall agree in writing within two months of my death but so that in

> default of such agreement such division shall be made by my
> Executors in their absolute discretion and according to their own
> estimate of the value of each item and such decision shall be final
> and binding on my said grandchildren.

(See, also, gifts of personal chattels at para 13.5.1.)

## 13.3.4   Incorporation of an unexecuted document by reference

A document not executed as a will within section 9 of the WA 1837 cannot be admitted to probate (unless the testator enjoyed privileged status, see para 4.7.1); however, it may become part of the will under the doctrine of incorporation by reference if the following three requirements are satisfied:

(a)   the document must be *dispositive*; and

(b)   the document must be in existence at the date of the will and be clearly identified by the will; and

(c)   the will must state the document *already exists* at the date of execution of the will or a later codicil republishing it.

EXAMPLE

> Mary's validly executed will says:
>
>> I give my collection of china to my nieces as set out in a list
>> headed 'China Collection' which I have written and which will
>> be found with my will.
>
> Following Mary's death, a list is found setting out which niece is to
> have each piece of china. The list is dated the same day as the will
> but not signed by Mary or witnessed. The list satisfies the three
> requirements for incorporation and will be treated as though part of
> the will itself.

If the reference is equivocal or capable of referring to a future document, such as 'any list I may write before I die', the document in question cannot be incorporated.

There are potential problems with incorporation by reference. Quite apart from not fulfilling the three requirements, there is the obvious danger the document may be lost. It is clearly preferable to include all dispositions in the will itself but incorporation may be a useful alternative if disposing of an extensive collection.

If incorporation is intended, the will must be carefully drafted to comply with the rules which must be explained to testators so that they are not tempted to make changes by the apparently simple means of substituting a new document or amending the existing one. Any document substituted or any new words added after executing the will cannot be incorporated unless referred to in a later will or codicil.

Testators must also be told that an incorporated document becomes 'public', like the will itself, once probate is granted. So, it is not a means of keeping dispositions secret.

Care is also needed to avoid incorporation when it is not desired (see precatory trusts, para 13.3.2).

A statement by the testator for the purposes of the I(PFD)A 1975 (see para 2.2) explaining why he is not making provision for a potential applicant, is not incorporated unless testamentary in form. Normally, it need not be produced when applying for a grant, though if mentioned in the will, it is best to lodge a letter or certificate from the solicitor dealing with the matter explaining that the statement is not dispositive.

### 13.3.5    Options to purchase

See para 14.3.4 where options to purchase are considered in relation to gifts of land.

### 13.3.6    Variable gifts

#### Nil rate band formula legacies

As part of inheritance tax planning strategy, considered further in Chapter 16, testators may be advised to leave an amount up to their available nil rate band in favour of their children or other non-exempt beneficiaries with their residue being left to their surviving spouse or civil partner. The nil rate amount may be given outright as a legacy or to trustees to hold on discretionary trusts. The consequence is that the whole of the testator's nil rate is used and no inheritance tax is payable on the death estate.

Although the current nil rate threshold of £325,000 has been frozen until the end of tax year 2020/21, it has in the past increased by an amount linked to inflation. Consequently, draftsmen have devised a means of ensuring that the amount of the nil rate legacy similarly matches the amount of any increase without having to update the will, as well as ensuring it takes account of circumstances which reduce the actual nil rate band available to the particular testator.

A simple formula clause which can achieve this is as follows:

> I give to [such of my children who survive me and if more than one in equal shares] the maximum amount which can be given under this clause without inheritance tax becoming due in respect of the transfer of value of my estate which I am deemed to make immediately before my death [or the sum of £ ...... whichever is smaller].

The amount passing under this clause is calculated by starting with the statutory nil rate figure and then reducing it by other calls on that amount, such as:

(a)    chargeable transfers (including failed potentially exempt transfers) made in the 7 years before death;

(b)    gifts to non-exempt beneficiaries in the will (or as a result of partial intestacy);

(c)    property passing to non-exempt beneficiaries outside the will, for example by survivorship;

(d)    property in a trust treated as part of the testator's estate (i.e. interest in possession or immediate post-death interest);

(e)    property treated as part of the testator's estate under the reservation of benefit rules.

It also contains an option to 'cap' the amount of the legacy (see below).

Longer formula clauses may set out the above in more detail, although this is not necessary if the correct wording is used in the short form. However, care must be taken if using any formula clause because:

(a)    the testator may have a transferable nil rate band from a former spouse or civil partner who has predeceased, so increasing the amount which can be left without inheritance tax becoming due;

(b)    the estate may include property qualifying for business or agricultural property relief which, if not otherwise given away in a separate specific legacy, will increase the amount passing under the nil rate clause as a result of the effect of section 39A of the IHTA 1984. This section provides that where property attracting relief passes as part of the residue of an estate, the benefit of the relief is apportioned so that the inheritance tax value of all the gifts is reduced;

(c)    the testator may be entitled to a downsizing allowance as a result of disposing of a residence completely or moving to a smaller residence on or after 8 July 2015. Such an allowance will increase the amount that can pass to lineal descendants without inheritance tax becoming due. (The residence nil rate band (RNRB) itself is not relevant to the size of a pecuniary legacy as it applies only to the inheritance of a residence or interest in a residence. For further explanation of the RNRB and downsizing allowance, see para 16.6.)

The consequence of any of the above is that the amount passing under the legacy may be considerably higher than the statutory nil rate figure and so the residue for the spouse or civil partner might be much less than anticipated or even reduced to nothing. For this reason, formula clauses are often 'capped' with the insertion of a specific amount by including the words in square brackets.

For the avoidance of doubt it is sensible to state expressly whether or not the legacy is to include the benefit of any transferred nil rate band and downsizing allowance available on death. Where the legacy is to include such amounts, it is also sensible to direct the executors to claim any transferred nil rate band and downsizing allowance available as they will only be obtained if claimed.

### Index linked legacies

When making a pecuniary legacy, a testator can make provision for the initial amount to be increased in line with inflation. This is best achieved by linking the initial sum to a recognised index and providing for a precise and clear means explaining how the index is to be used to calculate the amount due. It is usual for the index linking to cover the period (in terms of months) between the execution of the will and the testator's death.

Most practitioners would say that index linking is no substitute for regular reviews of an existing will and if necessary making fresh provision to cater for changing circumstances.

## 13.4    Particular recipients

### 13.4.1    Gifts to charities, etc

Whenever there is any legacy to a charity or unincorporated association (such as a club or society), it is important to:

(a)    confirm the institution's existence, correct name and registered charity number if relevant;

(b)    confirm its charitable status if wanting to secure inheritance tax exemption;

(c)    include provision for change of name or objects, amalgamation or dissolution;

(d)   include a receipt clause, discharging the PRs by the receipt of the person 'appearing' or 'professing' to be the secretary, treasurer or other officer of the organisation concerned.

(See Appendix 1 and clauses 5 and 8.2 of the Will of James Matthew Appleby.)

The point about including a receipt clause is particularly important if the organisation is an unincorporated association because, since it has no separate legal identity of its own, the PRs would otherwise have to obtain a receipt from each of its individual members.

Most charitable and other organisations have an abundance of information available on their websites for testators contemplating gifts, including precedents for use in the drafting.

If the testator wants to state in the will that the legacy must be used for a particular purpose, it is important to check first with the organisation that it is prepared to accept the legacy on those terms and whether effect can be given to the testator's specific wishes. It is normally preferable to express a wish rather than to impose a condition.

Many charities have local branches and the testator may wish to benefit the local branch rather than the organisation as a whole. If so, check whether the local branch is a separate entity capable of receiving gifts in its own right. Branches of some charities are registered as entities in their own right but others are simply part of the main organisation with a mandate limited to fundraising. Even where a branch can accept gifts, it is necessary to provide for what is to happen to the funds, if they cannot be used for the local branch, for example because it no longer exists.

Often a testator must accept that a request for use of money in a particular way cannot be made binding on the organisation.

## 13.4.2   Gifts to executors

If a lay person, such as relative or friend, is appointed as executor, the testator may wish to give him a legacy.

In the case of a non-residuary gift there is an implied condition that a legacy to a named executor is conditional on that person acting as such. The wording should make it clear whether the legacy is payable in any event or whether it is conditional on the executor obtaining probate and, where relevant, carrying out the terms of any trust created by the will.

A suitable form of wording is:

> I give Vijay £5,000 whether or not he proves my will and acts initially in its trusts.

If a professional executor is appointed, the testator should be reminded of the inclusion of any charging provision allowing the executor to be remunerated for his services. There is no need to provide such a person with a further legacy unless the testator specifically wishes to do so (see, further, para 13.4.4).

### 13.4.3    Gifts to person who has prepared or been instrumental in the making of a will

Where a person has prepared or been instrumental in the making of a will under which he receives a substantial legacy, evidence will be required of the testator's knowledge and approval of the contents of the will (see *Wintle v Nye* [1959] 1 WLR 284). If this is not forthcoming, the legacy will fail.

This is not the case for a charging clause in favour of a professional, nor where the legacy is of a token amount only.

### 13.4.4    Gifts to solicitor drafting will

Special rules of conduct apply to solicitors and others regulated by the SRA.

The SRA Codes of Conduct 2019 for individuals and firms rely on adherence to seven core Principles and maintaining specified standards.

Principles 5 and 7 require those regulated by the SRA 2019 to act with integrity and in the best interests of clients.

Standard 1.2 of both SRA Codes requires, 'You do not abuse your position by taking unfair advantage of clients or others'.

Previous versions of the Codes dealt specifically with gifts to those drafting wills but the current version is much less detailed. The Codes describe the standards of professionalism that the SRA expects of those it regulates, and comprise a framework for ethical and competent practice.

Individuals and firms are expected to exercise judgement in applying the standards. Clearly, it would be unwise to draft a will giving significant amounts to the drafter or the drafter's family as this would raise questions as to whether the drafter was taking unfair advantage of the client.

### 13.4.5    Gifts to minors

The testator needs to decide whether such a legacy should take effect as an absolute one or whether some condition, such as an age contingency, should be attached. A further issue arises in relation to the provision of a receipt before the beneficiary has achieved majority (see Chapter 18 for powers to deal with income and capital and Chapter 19 for administrative powers for PRs and trustees). Parents and guardians can give a receipt on behalf of minors and in some cases testators may not wish this to happen. The will can provide the legacy is to be held on trust for the minor until the contingency is fulfilled.

For other considerations when making legacies to minors, including the meaning of 'children' and class gifts, see Chapter 7.

## 13.4.6 Gifts to employees

If the testator wants to give a legacy to an employee, the will should make clear whether the legacy is to take effect only if that person is still in the testator's employment at the date of death and not under notice to leave. It should also make clear that the legacy is in addition to any sums owing to the employee by way of arrears of salary.

## 13.4.7 Gifts for pets and other animals

Pets and other animals owned by the testator are property and without any specific provision pass as an asset of residue.

People often want to make provision for their pets and other animals after death by suggesting a sum of money is set aside for their maintenance. Doing so creates a trust of imperfect obligation because there is no human beneficiary capable of enforcing it and it is otherwise a purpose trust which is non-charitable. However, these trusts have some legal recognition because whilst the obligation to maintain the animal cannot be compelled, equally the trustees cannot be criticised if they decide to comply with the testator's wishes. If they decide not to carry out the purpose expressed by the testator, then they will hold the fund, and any income derived from it, as part of the residue of the estate.

The main case is *Re Dean* (1889) 41 Ch D 552 where an annuity was given to trustees to maintain animals and their stabling for 50 years 'if any of the said horses and hounds should so long live'. The court said trusts for animals were valid 'although the testator must be careful to limit the time for which it is to last, because, as it is not a charitable trust, unless it is to come to an end within the limits fixed by the rule against perpetuities, it would be illegal'.

The extension of the perpetuity period to 125 years by the Perpetuities and Accumulations Act 2009 does not apply to purpose trusts (section 18) and consequently the duration of such a trust is limited to 21 years. So, any direction to the trustees to use the fund needs to be limited to the animal's natural life or 21 years from the testator's death (whichever is the shorter).

Such a trust is perhaps best suited for substantial sums.

There are the following other options available which will often be more satisfactory:

(a)    Give both the animal and a pecuniary legacy to the executor with a request that the executor deals with both in accordance with an expression of wishes. The testator provides instructions on who he would like to look after the animal. This is a burden for the executor.

(b)    Give the animal and a pecuniary legacy to a named individual with a condition that the legatee must undertake to care for the animal with a gift over to another beneficiary in default of the undertaking. The drawback here is that breach of the undertaking and an attempt to recover the legacy may well be unenforceable, either by the executors or by the default beneficiary.

(c)    Give the animal and a pecuniary legacy to the RSPCA, local rescue centre or similar body subject to a request (or condition) that the legatee finds the animal a suitable home. The RSPCA's national presence means that it can act swiftly and other bodies will usually have good local contacts. The legacy will be exempt from inheritance tax if the legatee has charitable status.

In each case, consider providing that the legacy fails if the animal is not alive at the date of death.

## 13.5    Subject matter of legacies

### 13.5.1    Gifts of personal chattels

Uppermost in the minds of many testators is how and to whom they might dispose of their household contents and other personal items. If the whole estate is going to a single beneficiary, there is no need to deal specifically with such items. However, the testator may wish to use these items to benefit a number of friends and family members, for example by selecting particular items which have previously been 'promised' to certain people or perhaps leaving it up to individuals to select what they would like as a keepsake.

There are a number of ways to approach the giving of chattels including the use of a precatory trust, right of selection or incorporation of an unexecuted list as considered in para 13.3, although none of these options may necessarily achieve the desired consequence if problems arise.

Whichever option is adopted, the drafting must clearly establish the subject matter of the legacy.

If the testator is giving away a single item, being one of several similar items he owns, such as a piece of jewellery or a picture, then it is vital to accurately identify the piece in question. There is no real substitute for a full accurate description, ideally one containing reference to any distinguishing features.

If the legacy is a more general one, personal chattels can be defined by reference to the statutory definition contained in section 55(1)(x) of the AEA 1925 which says:

> 'Personal chattels' means tangible movable property, other than any such property which—
>
> consists of money or securities for money, or
>
> was used at the death of the intestate solely or mainly for business purposes, or
>
> was held at the death of the intestate solely as an investment.

The definition was substituted by the Inheritance and Trustees' Powers Act 2014, for wills executed on or after 1 October 2014. The wording will pass what most people would regard as their personal chattels but notably it excludes money, securities for money or chattels used mainly for business purposes. Where the deceased used items such as cars or personal computers partly for business purposes and partly for personal use, it may be difficult to decide what the main purpose was. It is, therefore, advisable to add words such as 'including any car or office equipment kept at my home' if these are intended to pass. Items bought partly for enjoyment but with an eye to investment potential such as art or jewellery will be within the definition but an item bought only for investment, such as fine wine, to be kept in store and then sold, will not.

A common problem occurs if a life interest in the home is contemplated, perhaps in favour of a surviving spouse or civil partner (see Chapter 14). Should the contents be settled with the house? Normally, the answer is that they should not because of the practical and legal difficulties which can result. Almost invariably, an absolute legacy of the contents is preferable.

Of course, in many situations, the contents of a co-owned house will be jointly held anyway and so any provision dealing with them in the will of the first to die will have no relevance.

If any chattel is the subject of a credit sale or loan agreement and at death there is an outstanding financial liability, the amount due is an ordinary debt payable out of general residue, unless the testator imposes an obligation on the beneficiary taking the item to pay it. In the case of a chattel subject to a hire purchase agreement, the testator does not own the item and so it will not pass under a legacy of 'my personal chattels', although if the testator has rights under the agreement which are capable of being transferred to the beneficiary, then these can be made the subject of a specific legacy.

## 13.5.2    Gifts of business interests

A testator with business interests may be a sole trader, a partner or a shareholder in a company. Whilst it is possible to deal with succession issues in a will, it is usually preferable to make such provision in the testator's lifetime, the point being that not only can succession to the interest be considered, but steps can be taken to involve the successor in the day-to-day management of the business. It is also the case that with a partnership or a company, there may be very limited scope, if any, for dealing with succession on death anyway.

In all cases involving the 'handing down' of a business or its assets, whether during lifetime or on death, the tax implications must be considered. As regards inheritance tax, the availability of business property relief is considered at para 16.3 (for power to carry on a business, see, also, para 19.15).

### *Sole trader*

A testator who runs his own business may have in mind a successor within the family. The testator can leave the business to the successor by way of a specific legacy which needs to be very clearly drafted to show what is intended to pass. It should make express reference to (as appropriate) the business premises, plant, machinery, tooling, stock, vehicles, the goodwill, the benefit of all contracts, book debts and also the cash held by the business, including amounts standing to the credit of business bank accounts. The legacy should also make clear whether (as is usual) the beneficiary is to take the business subject to its liabilities.

As well as the legacy itself, consideration needs to be given to the powers of the executors, and indeed the appointment of special executors to handle the business pending it being vested in the beneficiary or, perhaps preferably, the appointment of the beneficiary as special executor.

Implied powers for executors are very limited and it is usual to include express powers allowing the executors to carry on the business, appoint a manager with a salary (perhaps from within their own number) and look to other capital in the estate to fund the business. It is also usual to provide the executors with a personal indemnity out of the other estate assets in respect of any loss or liability when carrying on the business during the administration period.

One common problem is that the business often constitutes a substantial part of the estate and so leaves relatively little to satisfy the provision the testator would like to make to other members of the family. One solution is to give the successor an option to purchase the business at a reduced price so that the proceeds can then fund legacies to other beneficiaries. Options to purchase are considered further in para 14.3.4.

## Partnership interests

Most partnership agreements are set up so that when a partner dies, the remaining partners have an option to buy out the deceased partner's share at a valuation, the means of which is pre-determined by the agreement. It is structured in this way to preserve the availability of inheritance tax business property relief which would be unavailable if the deceased died with a binding contract for sale already in place. Partners usually implement life cover to provide the sum necessary to buy out the deceased partner and so enable the price to be paid to the PRs.

If there is no such provision in a partnership agreement, or perhaps no agreement at all, the Partnership Act 1890 provides for the automatic dissolution of the partnership, with the result that a sum will ultimately be payable to the deceased's PRs in respect of the interest once the assets have been sold.

It follows from the above that a testator with a partnership interest can at best give away only his share of the proceeds, resulting from either a purchase by the other partners or the dissolution of the partnership and realisation of assets. It is very unusual to find a partnership agreement which allows a partner to give away his interest in the partnership. Of course, if the surviving partners are willing to admit the testator's successor into the partnership, they can agree to do so and the successor can use the testator's capital as a means of buying in.

When drafting a will for a partner, it is sensible to check that the provisions dealing with valuation of a deceased partner's interest are clear and satisfactory. Ambiguity can lead to expensive litigation. For examples, see *White v Minnis* [2001] Ch 393 and *Drake v Harvey* [2011] EWCA Civ 838.

## Incorporated business

In form, a legacy of the testator's shares in a company in which he has a personal interest is no different to a specific legacy of shares in any company. However, unlike a legacy of shares in a quoted company, it is likely that an unquoted company may well contain pre-emption rights in favour of other members in the articles of association. If so, any legacy of the shares will be subject to the pre-emption rights. It is important for the testator to consider both the articles of association and also the impact of any shareholders' agreement when considering a legacy of his shares by will.

Another factor to consider is that gifting shares to an existing shareholder may increase the beneficiary's holding to the extent it alters the balance of power within the company.

The precise wording of the gift requires thought. For example, a gift of 'my 3,000 shares in XYZ Ltd' will not pass any additional shares resulting from bonus shares or rights issues. Instead, the additional shares would pass with residue. It is likely to be preferable to say 'my shares in XYZ Ltd' so that all shares answering the description at the date of death will pass under the gift (see para 7.5.1).

### Gifts releasing a debt

The right to enforce payment of a debt is an item of property which the testator owns. A will can make provision for the release of the debt.

The testator should be advised that if the debtor predeceases, then the release, just like any other legacy, will lapse. That being so, the testator's executors can still enforce payment against the debtor's estate and if they refuse to do so, may risk a claim of breach of duty from the other beneficiaries. It is therefore necessary to provide expressly that the release extends to the debtor's PRs. It is also prudent to make clear that the release extends to all interest owing, as well as the outstanding capital. If the debt is secured, its discharge will also require release of the security and the testator may wish to make clear that any associated costs in achieving this are met as a testamentary expense from residue.

If a testator wishes to release multiple debts, each should be dealt with separately. A general release of 'all debts owing to my estate' could be construed as relieving banks and other financial institutions from an obligation to account for what they owe to the estate!

## 13.6     Relieving provisions and other qualifications attached to gifts

### 13.6.1     Inheritance tax

A legacy of UK property which is not held in trust, including a pecuniary legacy payable out of such property, is automatically treated as being 'free of tax', subject to any contrary intention (section 211 of the IHTA 1984). This means any inheritance tax attracted by the legacy is not borne by the beneficiary taking the legacy but instead is payable out of residue along with other testamentary expenses. The same is true of any legacy that is expressly stated to be 'free of tax' for additional clarity.

In either case, since the tax is paid from residue, it will reduce the amount the residuary beneficiary ultimately receives. If this is not what a testator wants, he can express the legacy as being 'subject to tax'. This alters the incidence of tax and so casts the burden on the beneficiary taking the legacy rather than the residuary beneficiary. Both options need to be explained before the testator decides.

A further issue concerns the need to 'gross up' if legacies are being made to non-exempt beneficiaries and the residue is being left to an exempt beneficiary.

Suppose Ted wants to give a legacy to his child that exceeds the amount of his available nil rate band and leaves residue to his spouse; the value of the 'free of tax' legacy must be grossed up in order to work out the amount of inheritance tax that must be taken from the exempt residue passing to the spouse.

Expressing the legacy as 'subject to tax' will avoid grossing up and will result in less tax being paid and the tax will not reduce the amount of residue going to the spouse – but against that, the net amount of the legacy received by the child after tax will be less than if it had been 'free of tax'. Once the issues have been explained to Ted, he will have to decide how to deal with the tax.

### 13.6.2   Debts and charges secured on property

If a legacy is made of property which has been charged in the testator's lifetime with a mortgage or other debt, section 35 of the AEA 1925 provides that the property is taken by the beneficiary subject to the debt or charge unless there is evidence of a contrary intention. This rule probably has more relevance to legacies of land and is considered further in Chapter 14.

As regards personalty, the most likely instance of something being charged with a debt is a gift of shares (see para 13.5.2, Incorporated business, and see, also, para 13.5.1 as regards chattels which may be subject to an outstanding financial liability, albeit not secured on the property itself).

### 13.6.3   Costs of transfer and insurance

A testator should be asked if he wishes a specific beneficiary to bear the expenses relating to the transfer of the subject matter to the beneficiary. These could include the cost of carriage and insurance and unless the will provides otherwise, such costs have to be met by the specific beneficiary once an assent of the property has been made. The circumstances may result in high costs of carriage which the beneficiary may have difficulty meeting, for example if a valuable painting is given to a relative who lives abroad. In such situations, provision can be included to place the burden on residue.

### **13.6.4**    Gifts in priority

A testator may add provisions to a legacy saying that it is to be paid immediately on death and/or that it will rank in priority to all other legacies in the will. Such a provision is usually added to a legacy in favour of a dependant whom the testator wishes to benefit in preference to anyone else.

A suitable form of wording is:

> I give £20,000 to my husband to be paid immediately after my death and I declare that this legacy shall be paid in priority to all other gifts in my will and shall not abate with them.

The first part of the clause requires the executor to pay the legacy as soon as sufficient funds are available and results in interest being payable from death rather than from the first anniversary of the death.

The second part ensures that the legacy will be paid in priority to other legacies in the event of insufficient assets to pay all legacies in full. Without this provision, the legacy would abate proportionately with other legacies of the same kind (see para 8.11).

# 14 Dealing with the Home and Land

## 14.1 Initial considerations before advising the testator

The nature of land and the possible interests in it make it essential to check the exact extent of the testator's claim to ownership by reference to the official copy entries and/or title deeds. Apart from knowing about the value of the property and any potential for claiming inheritance tax agricultural or business property relief, there are certain key questions about the title which must be considered before advice is offered on how the land should be dealt with in the will. These questions include (but may not be limited to) the following:

(a)  Is the testator the sole legal and beneficial owner? A testator may hold the legal title as trustee for someone else. Is what the testator thinks is his property actually vested in a company, albeit one he controls (see, also, para 21.1.10)?

(b)  Is the testator a co-owner and if so, with whom and are the beneficial interests owned as joint tenants or tenants in common? If the latter, what is the extent of the testator's share, since it should not be assumed it is equal to that of the other co-owner(s)?

(c)  Is the tenure freehold or leasehold?

(d)  Does the testator have vacant possession or is the land subject to a lease or tenancy or right of occupation which would be binding on a successor?

(e)  Is the land encumbered in any way and if subject to a mortgage or charge, how much is outstanding? Is any mortgage or charge on the property supported by any form of life or mortgage protection assurance to cover repayment of the debt? If so, does the policy pay out on the first death or that of the survivor if there is co-ownership?

Above all, it is vital to ascertain whether the testator has power to dispose of the land and if enquiries reveal the testator is an equitable joint tenant, it is important for the person taking instructions to advise on the need to sever a joint tenancy so there is an interest the will can dispose of. Failure to do so is likely to lead to liability in negligence to the disappointed beneficiary in the will. According to *Carr-Glynn v Frearsons* [1998] 4 All ER 225, it is necessary to go even further and advise on the possibility of serving a *precautionary* notice of severance if the testator is uncertain of the nature of the co-ownership and it is not possible to clarify the position quickly.

In the case of spouses and civil partners, it is important to consider whether the provision made by will makes 'reasonable financial provision' for the survivor. The court has power under the I(PFD)A 1975 to make an order redistributing the deceased's estate (see para 2.2). The survivor is entitled to reasonable financial provision irrespective of whether or not it is required for maintenance. A life interest or other occupation right (see para 14.3.2) may not be regarded as reasonable (see *Iqbal v Ahmed* [2011] EWCA Civ 900, *Berger v Berger* [2013] EWCA Civ 1305).

## 14.2   Points relevant to all testamentary gifts of land

Typically, the family home represents a major asset in most estates and is probably the asset carrying most value. Whilst in many wills it may not need to be dealt with as a separate gift because the whole estate is being given to one person or a class of people, in others it may be the subject of specific provision. Exactly what type of provision will depend on the circumstances and this is considered at para 14.3, but all gifts of land, and particularly the family home, share some common features.

### 14.2.1   Description

As with any specific gift it is important to describe the property with sufficient certainty. In the case of residential property, the full postal address usually suffices supported by the registered title number (though by no means essential) if there is one. In the case of other property, again the property address and any title number should suffice but sometimes more might be needed. For example, the gift might be of agricultural land with an unregistered title but described in the title deeds by Ordnance Survey numbers and/or a statement of its area.

Whatever the nature of the property, there is no need to recite any rights, covenants and the like which may be mentioned on the title documents since these will pass with the property in any event. Similarly, there is no need to say a property is subject to an existing tenancy because it will be in any event.

## 14.2.2 Ademption

A specific gift fails by ademption if the subject matter is no longer part of the estate at death (see para 8.3).

A specific gift of land is at risk from ademption, whether it is the family home or an investment property, due to the likelihood of it being sold after the date of the will and replaced with a different property. Should this happen, the problem can obviously be dealt with by putting in place a codicil or making a new will which refers to the new acquisition but a better solution is to draft the initial gift in such a way that it is ademption proof.

The common way of doing this is to express the gift in the alternative.

A suitable form of wording is:

> I give my freehold property Tall Trees, 56 Kings Drive, Addleton, Surrey or such property which is my principal private residence at the date of my death to …

Of course, the testator may own more than one property and spend periods of time in each during the year. Consequently, it is usual to add words to the effect that if there is more than one such residence, or doubt as to which is the principal one, the executors have the right to choose. If the testator has a residence outside the United Kingdom as well as one within, the will should make clear it is a gift of the UK residence if such is his intention.

Ademption of a specific gift will occur if the property is subject to a binding contract for sale at the date of death and this includes a compulsory acquisition under statute or an option that has been exercised. The testator may wish to include a provision entitling the beneficiary to the net proceeds of sale or compensation due to the estate. A testator can extend this to the case where the sale is completed before death but no replacement property is acquired which would otherwise have passed under an appropriately worded gift as in the example above. This can happen if an elderly testator moves into residential care and sells his home. It is possible to give the beneficiary a pecuniary legacy equivalent to the net proceeds of sale (as clearly defined) of the house. This can work satisfactorily if the death is shortly after the sale but with the passage of time the estate can be diminished, for example, through application to care fees, and so the beneficiary's legacy may then be out of proportion to the rest of the death estate.

## 14.2.3 Charges, mortgages and life assurance

If a legacy is made of property charged in the testator's lifetime with a mortgage or other debt, section 35 of the AEA 1925 provides that the property is taken by the beneficiary subject to the debt or charge unless there is evidence of a contrary intention. Consequently, a gift of a house which has an outstanding mortgage means that the beneficiary who takes the property, must do so subject to the burden of paying off the capital and any interest that is due. In practice, this could mean the beneficiary has to sell the house. The charge need not be created by the testator and so section 35 will apply to an HMRC charge for unpaid tax or a charge imposed by the court in favour of a judgment creditor.

The testator can easily shift the burden to residue along with ordinary unsecured debts but care is needed when drafting because a simple direction to 'pay my debts from my residuary estate' is not enough. Such a direction is construed as referring only to unsecured debts. There must be:

(a)   a specific reference to the actual debt if payment is to be made from a general fund such as residue, such as:

> … to pay from my Residuary Estate all my debts funeral and testamentary expenses including any outstanding capital and interest owing on any mortgage or charge subsisting on any freehold or leasehold property at the date of my death …

or:

(b)   a general direction to pay all debts from a specific fund other than residue, such as:

> I direct that any monies owing on any debts subsisting at my death shall be paid by my Executors out of the proceeds of my Aviva life assurance policy No …

or:

(c)   a specific relieving provision attached to the gift, such as:

> I give Redwood to my brother James free of any mortgage or any charge subsisting at my death.

Section 35 of the AEA 1925 allows a contrary intention by 'will, deed or other document'. This allows a contrary intention to be established outside the will itself, although doing so can create difficulties. In *Ross v Perrin-Hughes* [2004] EWHC 2559 (Ch), the testator mortgaged his property before he made his will and the mortgage was supported by an endowment policy which he contemporaneously assigned to his lender. Shortly before his death the testator was told that the policy was likely at maturity to be insufficient to pay off the mortgage. He agreed to increase the monthly premiums but died before the new policy came into effect. The court held that it was clear the testator had intended the property in the will to be free of the mortgage because he had provided for its discharge via the assignment of the policy and increased the premiums he was paying.

The above case concerned a homemade will but it highlights the need for a practitioner, faced with a gift of mortgaged property, to find out what arrangements, if any, are in place to discharge the debt. This information will assist in advising what directions should be given in the will. An interest only mortgage is often linked to one or more endowment policies, so arranged to produce a sum to pay off the debt on maturity or on the mortgagor's death if earlier. Capital repayment mortgages may be similarly supported by a mortgage protection policy on the mortgagor's life, which pays an amount to discharge the mortgage debt at death if it occurs within the term of the mortgage. The amount may be geared to the original loan or may reduce over time by being linked to the balance outstanding at death.

If the policy proceeds are payable to the estate, they increase its size for inheritance tax purposes to the extent the proceeds might exceed the outstanding mortgage debt at death. Also, there is no compulsion on the PRs to use the proceeds to pay off the mortgage. In other words, if the mortgaged property is left to X and section 35 of the AEA 1925 applies in the usual way, X must take the property subject to the burden of the mortgage debt even though the residuary estate has the policy proceeds. If the will shows a contrary intention, for example by making the gift expressly free of mortgage, then the burden of course falls on residue. However, it is probably better for the testator to leave X the property subject to the mortgage and to assign the policy to X so that X can use the proceeds to pay off the mortgage.

If the proceeds of a life policy are assigned to a third party, they will not increase the size of the estate for inheritance tax purposes and this applies regardless of whether or not the policy was effected for mortgage purposes. Any assignment of a policy will be a potentially exempt transfer (see para 16.2) of the value of the policy at the date of assignment. Of course, the assignment means that the testator loses all rights over the policy so should be done only if the testator is certain the assignee should benefit.

Where the property is co-owned, a policy (or policies) will usually cover both lives and pay out on the first death. Typically, payment is made outside the estate to the surviving joint tenant, either under the terms of the policy or because separate policies have been written in trust for the other.

### 14.2.4    Inheritance tax and its mitigation

A gift of land in the United Kingdom, which is not held in trust, is automatically treated as being 'free of tax', subject to any contrary intention (section 211 of the IHTA 1984). So, any inheritance tax attributable to the land is payable out of residue rather than the beneficiary taking the land. The same consequence follows if the gift is expressly stated to be 'free of tax' for additional clarity.

The testator can vary the statutory rule by making a gift of land 'subject to tax'. If this is considered, thought should then be given to whether the beneficiary is also to bear the burden of any mortgage on the land, which will automatically be the case unless anything is said to the contrary (see para 14.2.3). If it is decided to place the burden of the mortgage on residue but make the gift subject to tax, an issue might arise as to whether the beneficiary is burdened with tax on the full value he receives or merely such value reduced by the mortgage. The point should be clarified in the drafting of the gift.

Of course, the burden of inheritance tax is not an issue if the property is being given to an exempt beneficiary (spouse, civil partner or charity), either absolutely or by way of an immediate post-death interest, or if the value of the estate is such that inheritance tax is not payable.

However, where spouses or civil partners leave everything to the other, although there may be no tax on the first death, the relatively high value of houses means that the estate of the survivor is likely to exceed the nil rate threshold. Until 2007, married couples and civil partners had to employ quite complex strategies by transferring the house, or the testator's interest in it, to a discretionary trust on the first death to ensure that the nil rate band of the first to die was not wasted. However, since the introduction of the transferable nil rate band if the survivor dies on or after 9 October 2007, there is no need for such schemes. If desired, the whole interest in the home can now be left to the surviving spouse or civil partner, either outright or by way of a limited interest qualifying for exemption and full use of both nil rate bands will still be available (see, further, Chapter 16).

A further inheritance tax consideration is the introduction of the RNRB for deaths on or after 6 April 2017 (see sections 8D–8M of the IHTA 1984) and the discussion at para 16.6. This gives an additional nil rate sum where a residence or interest in a residence is left to a lineal descendant. The value of the additional nil rate band was £100,000 for tax year 2017/18 rising by £25,000 each tax year until 2020/21 when it will be £175,000. Thereafter, it will rise in accordance with the Consumer Prices Index. Estates will not necessarily benefit from the whole amount. The allowance is capped at the value of the residence after deducting any debts charged on the property.

Unused RNRB can be transferred to a surviving spouse or civil partner in the same way as the ordinary nil rate band.

The RNRB is gradually withdrawn if the deceased's estate at death exceeds the taper threshold of £2 million. This is something for spouses and civil partners to be aware of. Individually, their estates may be well under the taper threshold but if the first to die leaves everything to the other, the threshold may be exceeded.

It is not necessary for the will to refer expressly to the residence. A gift of 'my estate' or 'my residue' where the estate or residue includes a residence or interest in a residence will be sufficient. If the gift is to be divided between lineal descendants and others, the value of the house is apportioned.

EXAMPLE

Tanya leaves her £1 million estate which includes a mortgage-free residence worth £300,000 equally to her nephew and grandson.

The grandson and nephew are each treated as inheriting 50% of the value of the house.

If Tanya dies in 2019/20 when the allowance is £150,000, the estate will benefit from a full RNRB but if she dies in 2020/21 when the allowance is £175,000, the estate's allowance will be capped at £150,000 being the value of the grandson's share in the residence.

In that case the grandson and nephew should consider entering into a post-death variation so that the grandson receives a bigger share of the house and the nephew more of the other assets. A post-death variation is treated as the deceased's disposition for all inheritance tax purposes (see para 8.2.2).

The RNRB is considered in more detail at para 16.6.

Ideally, the home should not be used as part of a tax planning scheme and the will should, instead, make proper practical provision to ensure the necessary occupational rights for the family. Choices are considered at para 14.3.

## **14.2.5** Costs of transfer

In the absence of any expression of intention, the cost of making an assent to a specific beneficiary is an expense payable out of general residue but the usual rule is that any costs thereafter must be borne by the beneficiary, perhaps casting doubt on who should bear the cost of first registration if this is necessary to perfect the title. Ideally, the will should clarify whether or not the specific beneficiary has to pay for the costs of transferring title including the costs of first registration (see the example at para 14.3.1).

### 14.2.6    Trusts of land

The choices for a testator considered at para 14.3 may involve land being held on trust. Since the Trusts of Land and Appointment of Trustees Act 1996 (TLATA 1996) came into force on 1 January 1997, any trust which consists of, or includes, land is now a trust of land with the legal estate held by the trustees. No new strict settlements under the Settled Land Act 1925 can be created and all trusts for sale of land became trusts of land, whether they were created before or after the commencement of the TLATA 1996. Trusts for sale have not been abolished by the TLATA 1996 and can still be created, although the trust for sale has no effect in relation to land. Section 4 of the TLATA 1996 provides that if a will contains an express trust for the sale of land, there is an implied power for trustees to postpone sale despite any provision to the contrary. Note, however, that this implied power does not apply to personalty (see, further, para 15.4).

The TLATA 1996 and also the Trustee Act 2000 provide for extensive powers in favour of the trustees of a trust of land including powers of management and delegation to beneficiaries. Additionally, they are under a duty to consult with beneficiaries in some circumstances before exercising particular powers, and the TLATA 1996 also makes provision for a right of occupation for certain beneficiaries having an interest in possession in the land (see, further, para 19.18).

### 14.2.7    Minorities

A gift of realty can be made in a will to someone who is a minor but if the beneficiary is still a minor when the testator dies, the property will be subject to a trust of land (see para 14.2.6) for the minor until the age of 18. A minor cannot hold a legal estate in land.

## 14.3    Choices for the testator

### 14.3.1    Simple outright gift

This will be the choice if the testator has no need to provide for a limited right of occupation, for example, in favour of a surviving spouse for life, but instead can simply make an absolute gift to someone who is to take the property immediately and unconditionally.

A suitable form of wording is:

> I give to my daughter Louise my freehold property Whitehaven, 53 Barrington Lane, Lipstock, Somerset TA12 2HJ or such other property that constitutes my principal private residence at the date of my death and I direct that this gift shall be free of

> inheritance tax, free of any mortgage or charge subsisting at the date of my death and free of costs of transfer and registration.

If the gift is to two or more people, they take as beneficial joint tenants in the absence of words of severance such as 'equally' or 'divided between' or a division in unequal proportions which indicates a tenancy in common. If the gift is such that a beneficial joint tenancy is created, then if one joint tenant predeceases, the surviving joint tenant(s) will acquire the whole interest – in other words there will be no lapse of a share as there would have been had the gift been on terms creating a tenancy in common.

Where the testator owns land with another person, he can dispose of his interest by will if he is a tenant in common in equity to anyone he chooses. For example:

> I give to my son George all my share and interest in my freehold property 41 High Road, Shelton, West Sussex BN18 4BM and all my share and interest in the proceeds of sale thereof and any income arising from the property whether before or after the sale absolutely.

If he is a beneficial joint tenant, however, he can only dispose of his interest by will if he first severs the joint tenancy.

## 14.3.2    Rights of occupation without outright ownership

*Life interest*

One method of giving a spouse, partner, relative, employee or friend, etc a home without making an outright gift is to create a life interest in a property. This confers on the beneficiary not only a right to occupy the property but also a right to the net rents and profits from the property and, if it is sold, the right to receive the income from any investment of the proceeds of sale. Once the life interest ends, the property or its proceeds will pass to the remainder beneficiaries as determined by the testator. These may be the same people as those taking the residue under the will, in which case the remainder can be expressed to pass as an accretion to the residuary estate.

A life interest is appropriate if the testator is not only content to allow the beneficiary to occupy for as long as the beneficiary wishes, but also happy for the beneficiary to take the income from any sale proceeds, either in part of the trust property if the house is traded down for something smaller, or in the whole fund if a house is no longer required, as where the beneficiary moves into a care home or sheltered accommodation. The life interest does not only serve the purpose of providing a roof for so long as the beneficiary requires, but is also a means of generating income to help fund the provision of alternative accommodation. It is often desirable to include a power for the trustees to advance capital to the life beneficiary if it is thought additional funds might be needed, for example to supplement the income which might otherwise be insufficient to pay for care fees.

The life interest will be a trust of land with the legal estate in the property being held by the trustees. Under the TLATA 1996 (see para 14.2.6), the trustees may impose reasonable conditions on the beneficiary's occupancy of the land, such as requiring the beneficiary to bear the cost of insurance, repairs and other outgoings. If the testator intends these costs to be borne by another fund rather than the life tenant, the will should expressly say so.

Section 12 of the TLATA 1996 gives the life tenant a right to occupy but even so, it is usual to make express provision for the occupancy and also to say that the trustees shall not sell without the life tenant's consent. By section 11, the trustees must consult with the life tenant and act in accordance with his wishes insofar as they are consistent with the general interest of the trust (although this power can be excluded). However, it is usual to give the life tenant an express right to require the trustees to sell an existing property and use the proceeds towards the purchase of a suitable replacement.

A life interest does not have to be 'for life' and can be for a lesser period, for example, until remarriage. However, any attempt to foreshorten a life interest must be clearly stated to avoid a dispute as to when it has ended. Consequently, saying something like 'for life or until X ceases to reside in the property' should be avoided unless additional provision is included allowing the trustees to make the final determination if, for example, there has been non-occupation through illness, work placement, etc.

The effect of creating a life interest will be to give the occupier an immediate post-death interest for inheritance tax purposes (see para 16.2). Consequently, when the interest ends there will be a charge to inheritance tax because the property will be treated as part of the occupier's estate. However, if the occupier is the testator's surviving spouse or civil partner, the creation of the interest will have attracted the spouse exemption and despite the fact the value of the property will later be included in the survivor's estate for inheritance tax, there may well be transferable nil rate band and RNRB available to mitigate any charge (see paras 16.5 and 16.6.5).

### Right to occupy

This is an alternative to a life interest where the testator merely wants the beneficiary to have the right to occupy a house for as long as the beneficiary wishes. Subject to that, the property will devolve as instructed, perhaps going to residue. This type of arrangement is often appropriate if the testator has more than one child, one of whom is living in the home and the testator wants to ensure that child still has somewhere to live. Once the beneficiary decides to leave, the house can be sold and the proceeds shared among all the children as part of residue.

Unlike a life interest, such a gift does not entitle the beneficiary to receive income from the property or income from any sale proceeds. The testator may allow the trustees to sell the house and buy one that might be more suited to the occupant but without them being compelled to do so.

In other respects, creating a mere right to occupy can be similar to a full life interest and so provision may be made as to the terms of the occupancy such as by stipulating whether or not the occupant is personally liable for any outgoings. Also, the duration of any permitted occupancy can be expressed to terminate on the happening of an event such as marriage or entering into a civil partnership.

Similarly, as in the case of a full life interest, the effect of creating a right to occupy will be to give the occupier an immediate post-death interest for inheritance tax purposes (see para 14.3.2, Life interest).

A suitable form of wording is:

> 1 I give my house known as St Isaac, 65 Boldmere, Drive, Sutton Coldfield, Warwickshire B72 3DC ('the House' which includes any house or flat acquired pursuant to paragraph 1.1.2 below) to my Trustees to hold on trust as follows:
>
> 1.1 My Trustees must allow my civil partner Hazel ('the Occupier') to live in the House and use it as her main place of residence for so long as she wishes and without any charge provided that:
>
> 1.1.1 The Occupier pays all rates and outgoings and keeps the House in the same state of repair as at the date of my death and insured to the satisfaction of my Trustees;
>
> 1.1.2 Subject to her compliance with paragraph 1.1.1 above my Trustees must not sell the House without the consent of the Occupier (unless my Trustees are of the reasonable opinion that she is unable to give such consent though lack of capacity) but my Trustees may sell the House at the request of the Occupier and buy another house or flat to which the provisions of this clause X shall then apply.
>
> 1.2 On paragraph 1.1 ceasing to apply the House or any proceeds of sale of the same shall form part of my Residuary Estate.

The fact that the trustees 'must' allow the occupier to live in the property means the occupier has an enforceable right to do so, subject to compliance with the conditions in paragraph 1.1.1. As currently expressed, this right is not ended by the occupier subsequently entering into a marriage or civil partnership but it could be made to do so if the testator wished.

Paragraph 1.1.2 currently leaves it to the trustees to decide whether to buy a substitute residence, although they cannot sell without the occupier's consent. If required, the wording can be changed so that the trustees *must* lay out the proceeds in the purchase of a substitute property but it is then usually desirable to make further provision, for example limiting the location of such property to the United Kingdom and requiring the trustees to be satisfied on appropriate evidence, such as a surveyor's report, that the replacement is a suitable property for them to acquire.

There is an inheritance tax drawback with this type of interest. Because the occupier has an immediate post-death interest, if he moves out his interest comes to an end and he is deemed to make a transfer of value. Usually, the property will pass to other beneficiaries absolutely so the transfer will be a potentially exempt transfer. While there is no immediate tax liability, if the former occupier dies within 7 years, the transfer uses up some or all of his nil rate band. If any tax is payable on the transfer, the former trustees will be liable so they should be careful to retain sufficient trust assets to meet the liability until the 7-year period has elapsed.

### Permission to occupy

A further choice for the testator is to give his trustees the power to *permit* a beneficiary to occupy a house. This is not the same thing as giving the beneficiary *a right* to occupy because it depends on the trustees deciding to exercise the power in the beneficiary's favour.

Giving such a power is best dealt with through the creation of a discretionary trust with the intended occupier being amongst the class of beneficiaries. Since simply allowing the occupier to live in the property affords the beneficiary little or no comfort in terms of security, the main motivation for this type of arrangement is usually to avoid an inheritance tax charge when the occupier dies, the point being that the occupier does not have an immediate post-death interest as with the case of a full life interest or right to occupy. However, trustees need to be careful to ensure they do not, perhaps unintentionally, grant a *right* to occupy (as opposed to simply allowing the occupier to live in the property by way of a licence) within the first 2 years after the death. If they do so, the writing-back effect of section 144 of the IHTA 1984 produces an immediate post-death interest which may not be what is wanted (see para 17.2.1).

### 14.3.3 Family home as part of residue or separate gift?

One consideration is whether the family home (or the deceased's interest in it) should be dealt with specifically or as part of residue. It may be that the spouse or civil partner, for example, is to take an absolute interest in the house but a life interest in residue, or vice versa. In these cases, the house will obviously be the subject of separate provision.

However, even if the spouse or civil partner is to take a life interest in both the house and residue, it may still be prudent to deal with the house separately, not least because all the provisions relating to the house, particularly those relating to payment of outgoings and maintenance obligations, can then be packaged together in one clause where they can more easily be brought to the spouse's or civil partner's attention (see, also, para 15.5.2).

### 14.3.4 Option to buy

A dilemma for some testators is that a house or land they own represents a substantial part of the estate and giving it to one beneficiary often means there is insufficient elsewhere to fund similar provision in terms of value for other beneficiaries. This is typically the case if the testator is a farmer and wants to pass on the farm to one of his children but there is not enough in the rest of the estate to make provision for his other children.

A testamentary option in favour of one individual, allowing them to buy the property at an undervalue, can produce the necessary liquid funds to provide for other beneficiaries. The difference in price between the full market value and the option price represents a legacy in favour of the grantee and any inheritance tax applicable to it will be paid from residue unless a contrary intention is expressed in the will.

Great care is needed, both in determining the terms of the option and then in drafting those terms in the will. Factors that must be considered include:

(a) What property is the subject of the option?

(b) Is the price to be fixed by the testator in the will, by the trustees or by a valuer?

(c) If the valuation is to be by a named person or made in a specific way, is that to be of the essence? If it is and it fails (as where the named person predeceases), then the option cannot take effect. If not of the essence, the court can always order an appropriate method of fixing the price.

(d)    If the price is to be determined after death, what is the basis for the valuation? Is it to be based on the agreed probate value for inheritance tax purposes (assuming there is one) or on an 'open market valuation' which might not necessarily produce the same figure? Should it take account of any existing right of occupation?

(e)    Within what time period must the option be exercised and in what manner? The problem here is in establishing whether any time limits are of the essence, i.e. they must be adhered to strictly as part of the offer. When setting a time limit, care must be taken in seeing that it is one the grantee can comply with. It is not recommended that time starts to run from the date of death because there may be delay in obtaining a grant or the will may be challenged. Ideally, time should not start to run until the price has been determined. Also, it is desirable to provide that the executors must give notice to the grantee of the option to ensure the grantee has the chance to exercise it and that his right to do so does not lapse through ignorance.

So many problems can arise in relation to any option (not just one given by will) that it is essential to use an established precedent or to instruct counsel to draft an appropriate clause.

# 15 Residuary Gifts Including Residuary Trusts

## 15.1 Need for an effective gift of residue

Often testators seem to give less thought as to who should take the residue of their estate than to pecuniary legacies and specific gifts. However, an effective gift of residue is essential to avoid a partial intestacy. Not only must testators have one or more beneficiaries in mind to take what is left of their disposable property after all other gifts, liabilities and testamentary expenses have been satisfied, but practitioners taking instructions should also push testators further to find out who they want to take in default should any of the initial residuary provisions fail for any reason.

## 15.2 Value of residue uncertain

The decision as to who benefits from residue will be dictated quite often by the potential value that residue has to offer. Whilst this can be estimated at the time the will is made, it is vital the testator understands that matters may change in the future. Once testators realise this, they may wish to structure the will differently.

EXAMPLE

Uncle Ted (a widower) has an estate worth £450,000. He has a niece, Linda and a nephew, Raj.

He makes a will leaving £100,000 to Linda and his residue to Raj. He calculates that after paying the legacy of £100,000, it will leave Raj with £350,000 subject to taking out what is needed to pay for his funeral, any debts and lawyer's fees for administering the estate. Ted is happy with that because he thinks Raj is much more deserving than Linda, having helped him since his wife died. Ted's wife's transferable nil rate band ensures there will be no inheritance tax liability when Ted dies.

Uncle Ted dies 5 years after making his will and in the intermediate period:

(a)    he has made some charitable gifts totalling £40,000;

(b)    he has spent £250,000, mainly on residential care;

(c)    since he had to sell his house and invest the proceeds, the value of his investments has decreased, giving rise to a loss of £10,000 against the value of his estate when he made the will.

Consequently, his death estate is worth just £150,000.

The legacy to Linda will be paid in full, leaving £50,000 in residue for Raj subject to the payment of funeral and administration costs.

Obviously, Uncle Ted could have reviewed his will in light of his changing financial position, assuming he had capacity to do so, but it might have been better if Uncle Ted had structured his will differently by either:

(a)    doing away with a legacy to Linda and instead dividing residue (in effect his whole estate) so that Linda takes, say, a one-fifth share and Raj takes four-fifths. Doing this would have preserved the relative amounts received by each beneficiary in keeping with his wishes despite any fluctuation in the value of his estate; or

(b)    giving a pecuniary legacy of, say, £350,000 to Raj and then leaving the residue to Linda. Of course, should Uncle Ted subsequently win the lottery, Linda as residuary beneficiary would reap the benefit of the increase in his estate.

Whilst not every change in estate valuation is predictable, some might be. In Uncle Ted's case, whilst the fall in investment values may only have been a possibility, his future expenditure on residential care was probably foreseeable. Similarly, his intention to make charitable gifts might have been in his mind when he made the will and so questions about future plans for his money might have alerted his adviser.

## 15.3    Calls on residue

In determining the size of residue, testators should consider calls on their residuary property which can arise on death. Often, these arise from legal rules about which the lay client may have no knowledge so the will drafter must explain them. In other cases the calls may result from the way the will is drafted – in which case the will drafter must check that the result accords with the testator's expectations and wishes.

### 15.3.1 Payment of unsecured debts and pecuniary legacies

Usually, the testator wants any unsecured debts and pecuniary legacies (see definition in section 55(1)(ix) of the AEA 1925 at para 13.2.4) paid out of residue and in many cases will make that assumption anyway. So, there should be either a gift of residue 'subject to' or 'after' payment of debts and legacies, or a gift of residue on an express trust with a direction to the executors and trustees to pay debts and legacies out of the proceeds of sale before the net amount is paid to or divided amongst the residuary beneficiaries.

A suitable form of wording is:

> I give all the rest of my estate to my Trustees upon trust to sell or retain for so long as they in their absolute discretion think fit without being liable for loss and after payment thereout of my debts funeral and testamentary expenses and any legacies given by this will to hold the residue ('my Residuary Estate') as follows
> …

The term 'testamentary expenses' includes any inheritance tax payable out of residue (see, also, para 15.3.3).

If no provision is made expressly in the will, unsecured debts and pecuniary legacies are paid from residue anyway under rules in the AEA 1925. However, the application of these rules can sometimes cause uncertainty, particularly if a partial intestacy arises and so it is always better to make express provision.

### 15.3.2 Payment of mortgages and charges secured on specific property

Under section 35 of the AEA 1925 a mortgage or other debt charged on property which is the subject of a specific gift is borne by the beneficiary taking that property. However, this rule is displaced by a contrary intention and so the testator may require discharge to be made from residue (see para 14.2.3).

### 15.3.3 Payment of inheritance tax

Under section 211 of the IHTA 1984, any inheritance tax attracted by a gift of UK property not held on trust, or a pecuniary legacy payable out of such property, is payable as a general testamentary expense out of residue rather than by the beneficiary taking the gift. The same consequence follows if the legacy is expressly stated to be 'free of tax' for additional clarity.

The burden of tax on other chargeable property (e.g. foreign property, property passing by survivorship, lifetime gifts) falls on the property in question or the beneficiary acquiring it. However, this rule can always be reversed by a testator so that even this tax is payable out of residue as well. However, care is needed in ascertaining precisely which tax the testator intends being paid from residue and then drafting the residuary provision accordingly (see para 22.3.1, Burden of inheritance tax).

### 15.3.4   Relieving provisions

The testator may make it clear that costs and expenses of transfer that might otherwise have fallen on a specific legatee are to be paid from residue (see paras 13.6.3 and 14.2.5).

### 15.3.5   Unexpected legal costs and claims

Most testators know that as well as their funeral costs, their existing liabilities at death and the costs of administering the estate will come out of residue. What may not be expected are additional legal costs arising from litigation over the validity of the will, or its interpretation.

## 15.4   Is a trust of residue always necessary?

Prior to 1 January 1997, it was usual to include a trust for sale to avoid a strict settlement if there was land involved. Since then, strict settlements of land cannot be created (see para 14.2.6). However, an express trust for sale with power to postpone sale, or alternatively a trust to sell or retain is often still included:

(a)   whenever successive interests are created; or

(b)   whenever there is the possibility that any beneficiary will either be under the age of 18 or still subject to a contingency when the testator dies; or

(c)   to facilitate a testator's understanding of what will in any event probably happen if residue is split between more than one beneficiary; or

(d)   to emphasise a testator's intention where he anticipates property being sold and the proceeds divided.

If a trust for sale is created, section 4 of the TLATA 1996 automatically implies a power to postpone sale but this is only if the trust consists of or includes land. Consequently, a trust for sale ought to be expressed for the sake of personalty, because once the estate administration has finished, there is no longer a power of sale over personalty (section 39 of the AEA 1925).

A trust for sale imposes a duty on the trustees to sell, subject to any power, express or implied, to postpone sale. An alternative is to give the trustees a *power* of sale which may accord more with the client's expectations.

## 15.5    Residuary provision

There are various choices available to a testator when it comes to making residuary provision. One testator may be happy to leave property to someone absolutely, while another may wish to retain some degree of control over the property after death.

### 15.5.1    Absolute gifts

If making a gift to named beneficiaries in pre-determined shares, it is important to deal with any lapsed share(s), for example by directing that they accrue to the shares of the surviving beneficiaries and/or by including substitutional gifts, perhaps to the children of the beneficiary whose share has lapsed. If no such direction is included, the lapsed share of residue will pass under the intestacy rules.

A suitable form of wording is:

> 1.1    My Trustees shall divide my Residuary Estate equally between my daughters Alesha and Binesh.
>
> 1.2    If either of my daughters dies before me leaving children living at my death, such children shall on attaining 21 take (equally if more than one) the share of my Residuary Estate which their mother would have taken had she survived me to attain a vested interest.
>
> 1.3    If the trusts of one half of my Residuary Estate fail, that half is to be added to the other half and if both halves fail then my Residuary Estate is to be held for ...

In the case of a class gift, the class must be clearly defined and the effect of the class closing rules considered and explained to the testator (see para 7.7). Consider including substitutional gifts in favour of the issue of any members of the class who predecease the testator or who survive then die later before satisfying any expressed contingency (see para 15.5.3).

The question of lapse in this case will only arise if all members of the class predecease the testator or fail to obtain a vested interest.

## **15.5.2**   Successive interests in property (including the home)

Successive interests are usually suggested if the testator wants to control where property goes after the death of the main beneficiary and this intention is best achieved behind a trust, for example, by leaving residue to the testator's spouse or civil partner for life and remainder to the children.

If the life tenant is the surviving spouse or civil partner, the testator may want to ensure the right to occupy the family home. This can be achieved in a number of ways, as considered at para 14.3.

In a full life interest, if the life tenant moves out of the house, the trustees can sell it and invest the proceeds, either in a new house for the life tenant to live in, or in cash investments, the income from which is payable to the life tenant. The remainder beneficiary receives nothing until either the life tenant dies or his interest ends in some other way as provided for in the will, such as where the life interest is expressed to be terminable by the trustees having power to appoint the residuary fund (see below).

When creating a life interest, it is necessary to consider whether the subsequent interests of the remainder beneficiaries should depend on being alive at the life tenant's death, or whether it is sufficient for them to be alive when the testator dies.

One school of thought says it should suffice if the remainder beneficiaries simply survive the testator. The advantage is that if the remainder beneficiaries are defined as a class, for example, 'my nephews', the extent of the class is known at the testator's death. This makes administration easier, as well as allowing the life tenant and the remainder beneficiaries to vary the residuary gift if they are all in a position to do so and are in agreement. The disadvantage is that the remainder beneficiaries have vested interests in the remainder (subject to satisfying any expressed contingency) and so, if one of them should die before the life tenant, their entitlement devolves as an asset of their own estate and its ultimate destination will be determined by their own will or application of the intestacy rules.

EXAMPLE

>Mum leaves her estate to Dad for life remainder to such of their two children, Sam and Donna, as are living at her death.

>When Mum dies, both children are alive. During Dad's lifetime, Donna dies with a will which leaves everything to her husband, Harry. She has a daughter, Grace. When Dad dies, Donna's estate is entitled to half of the trust fund and Harry will inherit it.

>This may not be what Mum and Dad would have wanted.

The alternative is to make the interests of the remainder beneficiaries dependent on being alive when the life tenant dies so that if any die before the life tenant nothing passes to their estate. Instead, the will can provide either for substitution, perhaps to their issue, or accrual to those remainder beneficiaries who do survive the life tenant.

A suitable clause requiring beneficiaries to be alive at the death of the life tenant is as follows:

> 1.1 to pay the income of my Residuary Estate to my husband Simon during his lifetime and then
>
> 1.2 to pay my Residuary Estate to such of my children Elsie, Frances and Gordon as shall be living at the death of the survivor of myself and my husband and if more than one in equal shares provided that if any of my said children shall die before me or before attaining a vested interest leaving children living at the death of the survivor of myself and my husband then such children shall on attaining the age of 18 take by substitution and if more than one in equal shares the share of my Residuary Estate which his, her or their parent would have taken if he or she had attained a vested interest.

> In this example, the children's interests do not vest until the death of the husband, assuming he is the surviving spouse. Consequently, a child who dies before the husband has no interest. Instead, the interest the child would have taken will devolve under the substitution provision to the dead child's issue living at the husband's death rather than devolving as part of that child's estate.

Particularly in husband and wife or civil partner cases, the testator may have in mind that the life interest, and with it the right to occupy any house, shall end if the life tenant remarries or enters into a civil partnership. This can be accommodated by a provision in the will. Similarly, such an interest could be stated to end if the life tenant 'cohabits'. However, the draftsman must advise a testator of the difficulties this can cause in establishing, as a matter of fact, whether cohabitation as a state of affairs exists or not. Rather than express this limitation of the interest in the will, it may be better giving the trustees an overriding power to determine the interest as they think fit by appointing the fund to the remainder beneficiaries. The fact that a life interest is terminable at the instance of the trustees does not of itself prevent the life tenant's interest qualifying as an immediate post-death interest for inheritance tax purposes (see para 17.2.2).

The following clause could be used in conjunction with clauses 1.1 and 1.2 in the previous example so as to give the trustees the option of terminating the husband's life interest in whole or in part. The 'discretionary beneficiaries' would need to be defined and might typically include the children, present and future grandchildren, etc:

> 1.3    Notwithstanding the provisions of clause 1.1 my Trustees shall have power to appoint the whole or any part of my Residuary Estate upon trust for or for the benefit of such of the Discretionary Beneficiaries, at such ages or times, in such shares, upon such trusts (which may include discretionary or protective powers or trusts) and in such manner generally as my Trustees shall in their discretion think fit and any such appointment may include such powers and provisions for the maintenance, education or other benefit of the Discretionary Beneficiaries or for the accumulation of income, and such administrative powers and provisions as my Trustees think fit.

An alternative approach to creating a terminable life interest is initially to draft the gift as a discretionary trust and provide for a right to income for the life tenant until such time as the trustees decide to exercise their discretionary powers. Notwithstanding the discretionary trust, the provision of an immediate right to income means that the life tenant's interest still qualifies as an immediate post-death interest (see para 17.2.2).

### 15.5.3    Contingent interests

Just as with any gift in a will, the testator may wish to impose a contingency on any residuary entitlement.

Regardless of whether contingent interests are to take effect immediately or following the ending of a prior life interest, consider the following two matters:

(a)    What is to happen to income pending fulfilment of the contingency? If the beneficiary's entitlement to residue is immediate or contingent, then the gifts carry the intermediate income. Section 31 of the Trustee Act 1925 will apply in the absence of any direction to the contrary (see, further, Chapter 18 as to powers to deal with income and capital).

(b)    What is to happen if the contingency is not satisfied? In the absence of contrary intention (e.g. a substitutional gift or accruer provision), the capital will pass under the intestacy rules as undisposed of residue.

The introduction of the RNRB means there is another consideration. If a residence or interest in a residence is held on trust for a beneficiary with a qualifying interest in possession (such as an immediate post-death interest), the residential interest is part of the beneficiary's estate for inheritance tax purposes. Section 8J(5) of the IHTA 1984 provides that the residential interest held in the trust can benefit from the RNRB but only if lineal descendants of the beneficiary with the qualifying interest in possession are beneficially *entitled* to the residence. This means that the RNRB is not available if the lineal descendants take contingently or with limited interests; they must take absolutely.

EXAMPLE

> Mum leaves the matrimonial home which is in her sole name to her second husband, Sid, for life remainder to her daughter from her first marriage, Dolly. Dolly's interest is contingent on reaching 18.
>
> Dolly is a step-child of Sid so is a lineal descendant of Sid for the purposes of the RNRB. If Dolly is over 18 when Sid dies, she will be beneficially entitled to the residence but if she is below 18 she is only contingently entitled and the RNRB will not be available against the residence held in the trust.

Unless there is another residence available to benefit from the RNRB, it is preferable to make the remainder interest absolute rather than contingent. For a fuller discussion of the RNRB, see para 16.6.

## 15.5.4 Substitutional gifts

These should be contemplated in relation to any gift, but are especially important in the context of a residuary gift. In the absence of such a provision, a non-residuary gift which fails will fall into residue; if a residuary gift fails, there is a partial intestacy.

Section 33 of the WA 1837 (see para 8.4.3) may effect an 'implied substitution' if the gift was to the *testator's* child or remoter issue. However, express provision is desirable for clarity even in this case and essential where the gift is to anyone else.

When drafting a will containing substitutional gifts, it is best practice to say:

> If [the beneficiary] predeceases me or does not survive me for [a specified period] or if the gift fails for any reason then …

The final words ensure that if the gift fails, the substitutional gift is effective, not only if the main beneficiary dies but also as a result of something else such as a beneficiary witnessing the will (other reasons for failure of legacies are dealt with in Chapter 8).

## 15.5.5   Survivorship clauses

These may be considered in relation to any gift, but will be especially important in respect of residuary gifts. The idea is that the 'primary gift' is made contingent upon the beneficiary surviving for a specified period, with a substitutional gift to take effect if this does not happen. Without such a clause, the beneficiary would take the gift even if surviving for just a few seconds and so the property would pass to the beneficiary's estate for ultimate distribution under his or her own will or intestacy.

In practice, such clauses should not (for tax reasons) require survival for longer than 6 months, but since distribution cannot begin until the primary beneficiary dies within the period (when the substitutional gift takes effect) or survives to attain a vested interest, it is often for a much shorter period, such as 28 days.

The inclusion of a survivorship clause enables the testator to control the ultimate destination of the estate should the beneficiary die shortly after him, for example, if the testator and beneficiary die shortly after one another in a road accident. It will also save the expense and inconvenience in such circumstances of a 'double administration' of the assets passing otherwise through two estates in rapid succession (see para 22.1).

Including a survivorship clause also negates the effect of the '*commorientes* rule' (section 184 of the LPA 1925) that the elder is presumed to have died before the younger. Consequently, the younger beneficiary will not take the gift under the will just because he was presumed to have survived the testator.

From an inheritance tax point of view, the inclusion of a survivorship clause can prevent a double charge or 'bunching'.

EXAMPLE

> Suppose that Faheem and Sara are both the victims of a road traffic accident. They are not spouses or civil partners. Faheem dies instantly leaving all his estate of £325,000 to Sara. Sara dies 2 days later leaving Tom her own estate, also worth £325,000, together with the property inherited 2 days ago from Faheem.
>
> If there was no survivorship clause in Faheem's will, his property is taxed once on his death and then again on Sara's death 2 days later. On Faheem's death, the charge is covered by his available nil rate band. However, Sara's estate is now worth £650,000 in total and whilst the first £325,000 of that is covered by her available nil rate band, the balance is taxed at 40% (£130,000).
>
> If Faheem's will included a suitable survivorship clause, Sara would not inherit his property and instead it would pass to the substitute

beneficiary named in Faheem's will. Sara's taxable estate now consists of just her own property and so, like Faheem's estate, is covered by his nil rate band – so no tax is paid at all.

Including a survivorship clause in Faheem's will has the additional benefit that he controls where his property goes by a substitute provision in his own will, rather than it passing eventually to Tom as the beneficiary named in Sara's will. It also means that Faheem's property is administered just once, whereas if allowed to pass to Sara and then on to Tom, it is administered twice.

Until recently, a survivorship clause was often used when making a gift to a spouse or civil partner due to the interaction of the nil rate band and the effect of the spouse or civil partner exemption. However, this is no longer an issue for spouses or civil partners if the survivor dies on or after 9 October 2007 because of the transferable nil rate band (see para 16.5). Notwithstanding this change, a survivorship clause may still be recommended for the non-tax reasons mentioned earlier.

However, if there is a transferable nil rate band available, the presence of a survivorship clause can have inheritance tax disadvantages:

(a) If property passes from the estate of an elder spouse or civil partner to the estate of the younger under the *commorientes* rule in section 184 of the LPA 1925, the effect of section 4(2) of the IHTA 1984 is that the property which passes is not taxable as part of the younger's estate. However, the property passing to the younger still qualifies for the spouse or civil partner exemption in the elder's estate.

This means that whatever the value of the estate passing to the younger spouse or civil partner, it suffers no tax in the elder's estate and then when it is passed on under the younger's will, say, to the children, it also suffers no tax because it is not treated as part of the younger's estate *for inheritance tax purposes*. Furthermore, the younger's own estate will still benefit from any transferable nil rate band in respect of property already belonging to the younger and which is taxed as part of that estate.

If a survivorship clause had been in operation which has the effect of passing the elder's estate directly to the children, the elder's nil rate band will be used to cover such property and so there will be less (and perhaps none at all) available to transfer to the younger's estate.

For this reason, some will drafters like to say that the survivorship condition is not to apply if the deaths of testator and beneficiary occur in circumstances where the *commorientes* rule applies so as to secure the tax advantage in the event such situation arises. Such a provision should be included only in the will of the elder spouse or civil partner.

A suitable form of wording is:

> I give my Residuary Estate to my [husband] if he survives me by 28 days but if my [husband] fails to survive me by 28 days or if the gift of my Residuary Estate to my [husband] fails for any other reason then I give my Residuary Estate to ...... PROVIDED THAT if my [husband] and I shall die in circumstances where it cannot be known which of us survived the other then the foregoing survival condition shall not apply and the gift of my Residuary Estate in his favour shall take effect.

(b)    If the estate of the first spouse to die is above the nil rate band but the estate of the second is below, it is preferable for the first estate to pass to the surviving spouse with the benefit of the spouse exemption. The combined assets will then pass with the benefit of the transferred two full nil rate bands.

## 15.5.6    Discretionary trusts

As an alternative to leaving residue absolutely or on fixed successive interests, it may be appropriate to leave it on terms allowing trustees complete discretion over capital and income. Since no immediate post-death interest is created on the testator's death, if a discretionary beneficiary dies no part of the trust fund is treated as part of his estate, as in the case of the death of a life tenant.

A discretionary trust may be advised if it is desirable to ring fence residuary assets in such a way that they do not form part of any beneficiary's estate, both for tax and succession purposes. Not only will the residuary fund escape tax on a beneficiary's death but since no beneficiary has a claim on the residuary fund, other than being amongst the class of potential beneficiaries, it should mean the fund is not taken into account when assessing beneficiaries for any means-tested benefits, such as those in connection with residential care.

Similarly, the estate is put out of reach of creditors, should a beneficiary run into financial problems leading to bankruptcy and in the same way it is less likely to be taken into account in the event of financial claims stemming from a breakdown in a relationship.

Discretionary trusts are particularly useful where the family includes children who may not yet have reached financial independence or 'maturity'. The drawback is that the parental control that would otherwise have been exercised by the testator now falls to the trustees. It is important to provide the trustees with a letter of wishes setting out matters such as how the fund should be used for the future upbringing, welfare, education and so on of the children. The testator should provide as much detail as possible, particularly if the needs and requirements of each child may not be identical or where one of the children may have a disability which might need to be catered for. In fact, it is often the case that a testator with a child having special needs will set aside a specific non-residuary fund for the purpose of meeting the child's requirements but will include other potential beneficiaries, perhaps the child's siblings, to provide flexibility.

Even if the testator's spouse or civil partner is one of the potential beneficiaries of a discretionary trust, the spouse or civil partner exemption will not apply on the testator's death. However, if the trustees of a testamentary discretionary trust exercise their powers within 2 years of death, under section 144 of the IHTA 1984, their actions are automatically read back to the date of death for the purposes of inheritance tax (see para 17.2.1). So if the trustees appoint assets from the discretionary trust to the surviving spouse or civil partner, either absolutely or by way of a life interest, then the gift is treated as having been effected directly by the testator's will and so the spouse or civil partner exemption will apply.

Similarly, if a residence or interest in a residence is left on discretionary trusts, the RNRB is not available even if all the potential beneficiaries are lineal descendants of the deceased. However, if the trustees appoint the residence to lineal descendants within 2 years (either absolutely or on immediate post-death interest trusts), there will be reading back under section 144 and the RNRB will be retrospectively available.

There is a pitfall attaching to section 144. The section applies automatically and cannot be dis-applied. For example, if trustees give a beneficiary a right to income within 2 years of death, they will create an immediate post-death interest. Creating an immediate post-death interest can have adverse tax consequences as the underlying fund supporting the life interest will be treated as part of the life tenant's estate for inheritance tax purposes.

It should also be kept in mind that any trust created in a will, whether containing discretionary, or fixed interests will invariably carry with it the imposition of ongoing costs in the form of trustees' remuneration and other professional fees, and also compliance obligations, including registering the trust with HMRC's Trust Registration Service.

# 16 Principles of Inheritance Tax

## 16.1    Importance of inheritance tax

Although inheritance tax can sometimes be payable on lifetime transfers at the time they are made, this is relatively unusual. Generally, taxpayers only encounter inheritance tax when someone dies. It is a very unpopular tax. In May 2018, the government's Intergenerational Commission produced a report, *Passing On: Options for reforming inheritance taxation,* which said that the current system 'manages the uniquely bad twin feat of being both wildly unpopular and raising very little revenue'.

Only 4% of estates actually pay inheritance tax. This is partly because of a generous system of exemptions and reliefs but also because lifetime giving can significantly reduce exposure to the tax.

This chapter considers the basics of the tax, and the implications for will drafting are looked at in Chapter 17.

## 16.2    Death estate

When a person dies, they are treated as making a transfer of value of all the assets to which they were beneficially entitled immediately before death less any debts and funeral expenses (section 5 of the IHTA 1984). Some property is excluded from inheritance tax but this statement is broadly correct.

Where a person is entitled to the income from a trust or has the right to occupy or enjoy settled property they are said to have an interest in possession. If the interest is a 'qualifying' interest in possession their estate will include the capital value of the trust assets.

EXAMPLE

> Ted leaves £100,000 to Luna for life, remainder to Raoul absolutely. When Luna dies her estate includes the value of the settled property. While Luna's interest continues, Raoul's interest has no value for inheritance tax purposes so he can give away his right to inherit without any tax consequences.

Before 22 March 2006 it was possible to create a qualifying interest in possession by lifetime transfer. Since that date qualifying interests in possession can generally only be created on death and must take effect immediately. They are called 'immediate post-death interests'.

EXAMPLE

> Tom leaves £400,000 by will to his wife for life and then to his daughter for life. Tom's wife has an immediate post-death interest and will be treated as the owner of the trust assets for the purpose of inheritance tax. When the wife dies, Tom's daughter will not have an immediate post-death interest. Instead the trust will be classified as a relevant property trust and will be subject to a different tax regime (see Chapter 17).

Qualifying interests in possession created before 22 March 2006 retain that status regardless of the method of creation.

The only type of lifetime transfer to a trust which creates a qualifying interest in possession on or after 22 March 2006 is a lifetime transfer to a trust which qualifies as a disabled person's trust (see sections 89–89C of the IHTA 1984). The details of these trusts are beyond the scope of this book.

Lifetime transfers to individuals do not attract any tax at the date they are made; they are treated as potentially exempt.

Lifetime transfers to most types of trust are initially chargeable to tax at half the death rates.

In both cases, if the transferor dies within 7 years of the transfer, it becomes chargeable at the full death rates (unless an exemption or relief applies). Credit is given for any tax paid at the date of a chargeable transfer and once the transferor has survived 3 years, tapering relief is available to reduce the amount of any tax payable.

An obvious way of saving tax is to make lifetime gifts but, of course, the moderately wealthy often have no surplus assets which they can spare.

A lifetime transfer to a trust which qualifies as a disabled person's trust (see sections 89–89C of the IHTA 1984) is not an immediately chargeable transfer. It is a potentially exempt transfer. The details of these trusts are beyond the scope of this book.

## 16.3    Exemptions and reliefs

Some transfers are completely exempt from inheritance tax. These include:

(a)  *Transfers between spouses or civil partners*: all transfers between spouses and civil partners are exempt from inheritance tax, provided the gift has immediate effect (section 18 of the IHTA 1984). Such gifts include gifts into trust for a spouse or civil partner for life made on death.

Since 2006 lifetime transfers into trust for a spouse or civil partner for life are not treated as a transfer to the spouse and so do not attract the spouse exemption. They are treated as a transfer to a relevant property trust and therefore are immediately chargeable at half the death rates.

There is a limitation on the spouse exemption where the transferring spouse or civil partner is domiciled in the United Kingdom but the recipient is not.

Section 18(2) then limits the amount of the exemption to the level of the nil rate band. It is possible for the surviving spouse or civil partner to elect to be treated as domiciled in the United Kingdom for inheritance tax purposes (see sections 267ZA and 267ZB of the IHTA 1984) but this has a significant drawback: the worldwide assets of the foreign spouse or civil partner become subject to UK inheritance tax. Normally, a person who is not domiciled in the United Kingdom is liable to inheritance tax only on his UK assets.

(b)  *Gifts to political parties*: section 24 of the IHTA 1984, as amended by the Finance Act 1988, makes all gifts to political parties wholly exempt from inheritance tax.

(c)  *Gifts to charities and national institutions*: gifts to charities are totally exempt from inheritance tax whenever made and regardless of amount (section 23 of the IHTA 1984). Gifts to certain named institutions, for example certain museums, the National Trust, government departments, local authorities and universities in the United Kingdom, are similarly exempt.

(d)  *Death on active service*: under section 154 of the IHTA 1984, no inheritance tax is chargeable on the death of a person from a wound inflicted or a disease contracted while a member of the armed forces if that person was on active service at the time, or on service of a warlike nature or involving the same risks (see *Barty-King v Ministry of Defence* [1979] 2 All ER 80, QBD).

(e)  *Death of emergency service personnel*: under section 153A of the IHTA 1984, no inheritance tax is chargeable on the death of a member of the emergency services from an injury sustained, accident occurring or disease contracted at a time when that person was responding to emergency circumstances. 'Emergency circumstances' means circumstances which are causing or likely to cause death, serious injury to, or serious illness of a person or animal, serious harm to the environment or to any building or other property, or a worsening of any such injury, illness or harm.

(f)    *Death of constables and service personnel targeted because of their status*: under section 155A of the IHTA 1984, no inheritance tax is chargeable on the death of a person from an injury sustained or disease contracted in circumstances where the person was deliberately targeted by reason of his status as a constable or former constable.

Some property attracts relief from inheritance tax. Which property is basically a policy matter; currently certain businesses and agricultural property attract relief:

(a)    *Business property relief*: the details of this relief are found in sections 103–114 of the IHTA 1984.

Relief is not available if the business consists, wholly or mainly, of one or more of the following:

(i)     dealing in securities, shares, land or buildings; or

(ii)    making or holding investments.

Businesses which take an income from land are regarded as holding investments so relief is not available on them. Examples of businesses which take an income from land are those letting residential or commercial property and self-catering holiday accommodation.

The relief is available or unavailable on the whole of the business. So, where a business has a mixture of activities, the question is whether it consists 'mainly' of one of the ineligible activities. If it does, no relief at all is available. If it does not, property relating to all the activities is eligible for relief.

The effect of the relief is to reduce the market value of the property transferred by a given percentage when assessing the tax chargeable. In the case of partly exempt estates, section 39A of the IHTA 1984 provides that any available business property relief (or agricultural property relief – see (b) below) available on assets which are specifically bequeathed attaches only to the specific gift.

The reduction is 100% on the value of businesses run as a sole trader, in partnership or through an unquoted company.

There is a 50% reduction available on land, machinery or plant owned by an individual and used in a partnership of which he is a member or in a company which he controls.

A 50% reduction is also available on quoted shares but only if the transferor controls the company.

In general, property must have been owned by the transferor for at least 2 years before the transfer (section 106 of the IHTA 1984). If a transfer of a business has been made from one spouse or civil partner to another on death, the ownership period of the deceased spouse or civil partner is treated as that of the recipient spouse or civil partner, but this is not the case for lifetime transfers (section 108).

Section 110(b) of the IHTA 1984 provides that only the value of assets used in the business is eligible for relief. It is not, therefore, possible to shelter large amounts of cash within a business unless the taxpayer can demonstrate that the cash was being accumulated for a legitimate business purpose such as the acquisition of assets to be used in the business.

(b)    *Agricultural property relief*: the details of this relief are found in sections 115–124 of the IHTA 1984.

Relief is given on transfers of value of agricultural property as defined in section 115(2) of the IHTA 1984. There are three parts to the definition:

(i)    agricultural land or pasture;

(ii)   woodland and any building used in connection with the intensive rearing of livestock or fish if the woodland or building is occupied with agricultural land or pasture and the occupation is ancillary to that of the agricultural land or pasture;

(iii)  such cottages, farm buildings and farmhouses, together with the land occupied with them, as are of a character appropriate to the property.

To qualify as agricultural land, the land must be reasonably substantial and used for agricultural purposes; an extended garden does not qualify.

The level of relief is 100% of the agricultural value where the interest of the transferor in the property immediately before the transfer carries the right to vacant possession, or the right to obtain vacant possession within 12 months.

No relief is available, however, unless the further requirements of section 117 of the IHTA 1984 are satisfied. These are that the property was:

(i)     occupied by the transferor for the purposes of agriculture throughout the period of 2 years ending with the date of the transfer; or

(ii)    owned by the transferor throughout the period of 7 years ending with that date and occupied by the transferor or another for the purposes of agriculture throughout that period.

Other reliefs:

(a)    *Timber growing and 'heritage' property*: relief is available on the value of growing timber (sections 125–130 of the IHTA 1984) and on 'heritage' property (sections 30–35).

To qualify as heritage property, the Treasury must designate it as pre-eminent or outstanding and the owner must undertake to provide reasonable public access falling into one of the categories set out in section 31(1) of the IHTA 1984.

(b)    *Quick succession relief* (section 141 of the IHTA 1984): this relief is designed to mitigate the effect of a double charge to inheritance tax where property passes through two estates due to the death of a donee shortly after a previous transfer made to the donee. The relief is based on a sliding scale depending on the time between the first transfer and the second, which must be a transfer on death.

## 16.4     The rate of tax

The rate of tax is determined by the value of the chargeable estate plus the value of lifetime chargeable transfers. A portion (the nil rate band) is taxed at 0% and the balance at 40%. The nil rate band generally increases with inflation but has been frozen at £325,000 since the tax year 2009/10 and will remain so until, at least, the end of the tax year 2020/21.

EXAMPLES

Fred, who is divorced, dies with an estate of £325,000 which he leaves to his two children:

(a)    If he has made no lifetime chargeable transfers, his whole estate is within the nil rate band and no inheritance tax is payable.

(b)    If in the 7 years before death he made chargeable transfers to his children of £400,000, no nil rate band is available to his death estate which will all be taxed at 40%. In addition, the last £75,000 of the lifetime gifts will be taxed at 40% subject to the taper relief once Fred has survived 3 years.

The Finance Act 2012 inserted a new Schedule 1A into the IHTA 1984 which introduces a special reduced rate of inheritance tax (36% instead of 40%). The reduced rate is available where 10% or more of a deceased's net estate is given to charity. The net estate for this purpose is the deceased's estate less the available nil rate band, exemptions and reliefs and is referred to as 'the baseline amount' in the legislation.

To make it easier to qualify for the reduced rate, the estate is divided into three components as follows:

(a)   *The survivorship component*: this is any of the deceased's property which passes by survivorship

(b)   *The settled property component*: this is any settled property in which the deceased had a qualifying interest in possession so that he is treated as owning the underlying trust property for inheritance tax purposes.

(c)   *The general component*: this is all the rest of the deceased's assets. It is therefore made up of what is often called the 'free estate': i.e. property capable of passing under the deceased's will.

If the 10% test is met for any one of the three statutory components of the estate, that component is taxed at the reduced rate. The test is 'all or nothing' so that a gift of 9% of the component to charity will not give rise to any relief. It is most likely that the test will be met in respect of the general component.

It is possible to elect to merge components. This will be attractive if, for example, a substantial charitable gift is made by the deceased's will which exceeds 10% of the baseline amount for the general component and the deceased also either had a qualifying life interest in settled property (the settled property component) or owned joint property (the survivorship component). After an election the merged components become one and the 10% test is then applied to the merged components.

The election must be made by the 'appropriate persons', who are the PRs (for the free estate), the surviving joint owners (for the joint property component) and the trustees (for the settled property component).

Because the amount required to meet the 10% requirement will depend on matters which cannot be known before death, some testators will want a formula clause included in their will. HMRC has included a clause in its *Inheritance Tax Manual*, IHTM45008 (available at www.gov.uk/hmrc-internal-manuals/inheritance-tax-manual/ihtm45008), which is worded to ensure that a specific legacy to charity will always meet the 10% test:

> I give to [name of charity] such a sum as shall constitute a donated amount equal to 10 (or larger figure) per cent (%) of the baseline amount in relation to the [general component] [aggregate of the general, [survivorship], [settled property] components and [reservation of benefit property]] of my estate.
>
> The legacy given by this clause shall in no event:
>
> (i)     be less than £nn whether or not the lower rate of tax shall be applicable; and
>
> (ii)    exceed £nn (the upper limit) even if in consequence of this restriction in the value of the legacy the lower rate shall not apply. [If this proviso shall apply and in consequence the lower rate of tax shall not be payable, the amount of this legacy shall [be equal to the amount of the upper limit] [be reduced to £nn] [lapse]].

The clause may include other administrative provisions. The Society of Trust and Estate Practitioners has developed a model clause for wills. It may be viewed at:

> www.step.org/sites/default/files/Policy/Model_Clause_August_2 013_updated_8.8.2013.pdf

Beneficiaries will always take less if gifts are made to charity than if no gifts at all are made but where the reduced rate of tax applies, the cost of giving is reduced. Where charitable gifts are below but close to the 10%, beneficiaries will receive more by varying the disposition of the estate to increase the level of charitable gifts to 10%. For the reading back effect of variations, see para 8.2.2.

# 16.5     Transferable nil rate band

Where a spouse or civil partner dies with some or all of their nil rate band unused, the personal representatives of the survivor can make a claim to have the unused proportion of that nil rate band transferred.

EXAMPLE

> Tom died in 2002/03 when the nil rate band was £250,000. He had made lifetime chargeable transfers of £100,000 and so 60% of his nil rate band was unused. He left everything to his wife, Sarah.
>
> Sarah dies in a tax year when the nil rate band has increased to £400,000. Her PRs will be able to claim an additional nil rate band of 60% of £400,000 which amounts to £240,000.

Note that, although it is possible to inherit portions of unused nil rate band from any number of deceased former spouses and civil partners, no one can inherit more than one full additional nil rate band (section 8A of the IHTA 1984).

EXAMPLE

> Suppose that in the previous example after Tom's death, Sarah married Ted who died in 2005/06 with 20% of his nil rate band unused, leaving her everything.
>
> She then marries Tim who died in 2008/09 with 50% of his nil rate band unused, leaving her everything.
>
> Sarah's three husbands between them had 130% of unused nil rate band but she cannot inherit more than 100%.

Where it is clear that nil rate band will be wasted if everything is left to the surviving spouse or civil partner, the parties should consider leaving some assets to a discretionary trust created for the benefit of close family members, including the spouse (see Appendix 3, Case study B).

# 16.6    Residence nil rate band

## 16.6.1    When is it available?

An additional nil-rate band can be claimed for deaths on or after 6 April 2017 when a residence or interest in a residence is inherited by a lineal descendant or the spouse or civil partner of a lineal descendant.

A lineal descendant is a straight line descendant; therefore, children, grandchildren, great grandchildren are included, but nephews and nieces are not. The definition of a child in section 8K of the IHTA 1984 is very wide. It includes adopted and illegitimate children, persons who have ever been a step-child or foster child, a child of whom the deceased had been appointed special guardian or guardian under section 5 of the Children Act 1989, and natural children of the deceased who have been adopted by a third party.

To be 'inherited' there must be a disposition effected by will, by the intestacy rules or by survivorship (see section 8J of the IHTA 1984). Where the disposition of an estate is varied under section 142 of the IHTA 1984, the variation is treated as the deceased's disposition for all inheritance tax purposes (see para 8.2.2) so the RNRB can be obtained retrospectively.

Note that the lineal descendants do not have to keep the residence. They can sell it or the PRs can sell it on their behalf. All that matters is that they will be entitled to the proceeds of sale.

Property settled on death for the benefit of the lineal descendant can be treated as 'inherited' but only if the trust creates one of the following interests:

(a)    an immediate post-death interest, or

(b)    a disabled person's interest (as defined in sections 89–89C of the IHTA 1984), or

(c)    a bereaved minor's or bereaved young person's interest. A bereaved minor's interest is contingent on reaching 18 and a bereaved young person's interest is contingent on reaching an age no greater than 25. These interests can only be created by parents for their children or step-children (see sections 71A and 71D of the IHTA 1984). If grandparents leave property on the same terms, the trusts created are relevant property trusts.

Note how few trusts qualify. A discretionary trust does not qualify even if all the beneficiaries are lineal descendants; nor will a trust created by a grandparent, 'for such of my grandchildren as reach 18' if the grandchildren are under 18 when the grandparent dies. In both cases, the trust created is a relevant property trust. However, having the 'wrong' sort of trust at death is not a disaster. As explained in para 17.2, if trustees take action within 2 years of death to modify the terms of the trust, the changes will be read back to the date of death under section 144 of the IHTA 1984 making it possible to secure the RNRB retrospectively.

## 16.6.2    What is a residence?

The IHTA 1984 defines a residence as a dwelling which has been the deceased's residence at some time during his period of ownership. There is no requirement that it be the deceased's main residence or a UK property. A holiday home can qualify. A property which was never a residence of the deceased, such as a buy-to-let property, will not qualify. However, the property does not have to have been a residence for the whole period of ownership. It is sufficient that it was the deceased's residence at some point in his ownership.

EXAMPLE

The RNRB will be available if, shortly before death, the deceased moves into a property originally bought as a buy-to-let investment; or if, on his going into care, the family rent out the former residence to provide funds to pay the care fees.

### 16.6.3    Amount of residence nil rate band

The value of the residence nil rate amount was £100,000 in 2017/18, rising by £25,000 each tax year until it reaches £175,000 in 2020/21. It will then increase in line with the Consumer Prices Index. Note, however, that the figures are *maxima*. The amount of the allowance is 'capped' at the value of one residential interest. PRs can nominate which residential property should qualify if there is more than one in the estate. Debts charged on a residence reduce its value. A person who is diagnosed with a terminal illness, and who wishes to reduce his inheritance tax liability, should consider paying off some of a mortgage if the equity in the residence is insufficient to obtain the full residential allowance.

### 16.6.4    The taper threshold

The allowance is subject to a taper threshold of £2 million. When the net value of an estate exceeds this threshold, the residential allowance is withdrawn by £1 for every £2 that the value of the estate exceeds the taper threshold.

The 'estate' is everything in the beneficial entitlement of the deceased at the date of death. There is, therefore, an inheritance tax benefit in making lifetime gifts before death to reduce the estate below the threshold.

Reliefs and exemptions do not reduce the estate for this purpose.

EXAMPLE

> Fay, a wealthy entrepreneur, dies with assets valued at £5 million. Business property relief at 100% is available on £4 million of the assets. Although Fay's chargeable estate is reduced to £1 million, her estate remains at £5 million for the purposes of the taper threshold. Hence, her RNRB is lost.

### 16.6.5    Transferred residence nil rate band

If a person dies without having made use of the whole or part of the RNRB, the unused proportion can be transferred to a surviving spouse/civil partner. So, a spouse who dies having used none of their residential allowance will pass 100% to the survivor. As with the ordinary nil rate band, the PRs of the surviving spouse or civil partner must make a claim for the transfer.

The transferred allowance is subject to taper.

> Gamil dies in May 2017 and leaves everything to his wife, Abida. He, therefore, uses none of his RNRB. However his estate is worth £2.1 million. In 2017/18 the RNRB was £100,000 so the allowance available for transfer is reduced by 50%.

> If Abida dies in 2019/20 when the allowance is £150,000, her allowance is increased by 50% to £225,000. If her estate exceeds the taper threshold of £2 million her increased allowance will be tapered.

Obviously, a spouse or civil partner who dies at any time before 6 April 2016 cannot have had the benefit of a residential allowance and so it is available for transfer to surviving spouses and civil partners who die after that date. For taper purposes there is a deemed RNRB of £100,000 for anyone dying before 6 April 2017. Hence, if Gamil in the previous example had died in 2015 with an estate of £2.1 million, his deemed allowance of £100,000 would have been reduced to 50%.

## 16.6.6 Downsizing allowance

To prevent people clinging on to residences which are no longer suitable, an allowance (called a downsizing allowance) is available when, on or after 8 July 2015, a person:

(a)   disposes of a residence completely; or

(b)   moves to a cheaper residence.

The calculation is complex but, in outline, the value of the former residence is expressed as a percentage of the RNRB available at the time of the disposal (or £100,000 if the disposal was before 6 April 2017). That percentage is then carried forward and applied to the RNRB available at the date of death. However, no more than 100% can be carried forward. The downsizing allowance calculated is merely the maximum available. The actual allowance is capped at the value of assets inherited by lineal descendants.

> Dan, who is divorced and moving to residential care, sells his residence for £250,000 in 2017/18 when the RNRB is £100,000. The value of the residence is 250% of the 2017/18 RNRB so Dan is treated as entitled to 100% of the RNRB available on death.

> However, the downsizing allowance actually allocated to Dan's estate is limited to the value of assets he leaves to lineal descendants.

## **16.6.7**    Residential interest held on trust for deceased

A residence that was held in trust for the deceased can qualify for the residential allowance if the settled property is treated as part of the deceased's estate for inheritance tax purposes (i.e. the deceased must have a qualifying interest in possession, such as a pre-March 2006 interest in possession or an immediate post-death interest).

On the death of the beneficiary with the qualifying interest in possession, the RNRB will be available provided, a lineal descendant of that beneficiary becomes beneficially entitled to the residence (section 8J(5) of the IHTA 1984). It is helpful that a step-child is a lineal descendant but the requirement that the lineal descendant is '*entitled to the residence*' can cause problems. The entitlement on the death of the beneficiary must be absolute; if any sort of trust arises, the requirement is not satisfied.

EXAMPLE

> Wanda leaves her estate, which includes a residence, on trust for her husband for life and following his death to their daughter contingent on reaching 18.
>
> If the daughter has reached 18 when the husband dies, she is absolutely entitled and the RNRB can be set against the residence held in the trust.
>
> If the daughter is 12 when the husband dies, her interest is merely contingent and the RNRB cannot be set against the residence held in the trust.
>
> In such a case the trustees should use any powers of appointment they have available under the terms of the trust to modify the gift over during the husband's lifetime to create an absolute entitlement for the daughter on his death. For trustee powers, see Chapters 18 and 19.

## **16.6.8**    Will drafting points

To obtain the RNRB it is not necessary to refer to a residence specifically. A gift of the whole estate or of the residue will be sufficient provided the estate or residue includes a residence.

If the residue is divided between lineal descendants and third parties the value of a residence is similarly divided (see HMRC, *Inheritance Tax Manual*, IHTM46027 (available at www.gov.uk/hmrc-internal-manuals/inheritance-tax-manual/ihtm46027)). For example, if the estate is left 60% to son, 40% to nephew and the estate includes a residence, the son will be treated as inheriting 60% of the value of the house.

If 60% of the value of the residence is not enough to secure the full RNRB, the son and nephew should vary the disposition of the estate so that the son takes more of the residence and the nephew takes more of the other assets.

See also para 17.3 for further planning points making use of the RNRB.

# 17 Planning a Tax-efficient Will

## 17.1    Introduction

For most people, the overwhelming priority when planning a will is to make the best provision possible for close family members, typically their spouse, civil partner, cohabitee, children and grandchildren.

Finding ways of reducing the inheritance tax payable on the estate is important because it increases the amount available to the family. However, few people want to get involved in complicated or costly tax planning exercises. There are some relatively simple tax strategies which can help when planning wills and this chapter looks at the most important. These commonly involve the use of trusts or planning to make best use of the RNRB.

There are some case studies in Appendix 3 which put those strategies into effect.

## 17.2    Using trusts

When property is settled we often talk about a 'trust' of the settled property but, strictly speaking, property is held in a 'settlement'; the particular terms on which it is held are the trusts. However, we use the term 'trust' as it is rather more user friendly.

Many people dislike the idea of trusts regarding them as complicated and expensive. However, they can be exceptionally useful. They provide flexibility where testators are not sure precisely how to leave their property and, in some cases, they can achieve tax advantages.

There are four main types of trust that can be created on death:

(a)    discretionary trusts (and other trusts where no one has a present entitlement, such as trusts creating contingent interests);

(b)    trusts with an immediate post-death interest;

(c)    trusts for a bereaved minor;

(d)    trusts for a bereaved young person.

In a book of this length we can do no more than give an outline of the key features of each trust and its possible uses.

## 17.2.1    Discretionary trusts

### *Distinguishing feature*

These are the most flexible type of trust. The trustees hold the assets for the benefit of a class of beneficiaries, for example 'my grandchildren', and have power to apply income and capital amongst the beneficiaries at their discretion.

The trust can last for up to 125 years at which point any remaining assets must be distributed. In general, trusts will come to an end much more quickly.

Testators will normally leave a letter of wishes setting out their hopes and expectations and the matters they would like the trustees to take into account when exercising their discretions. The letter of wishes is in no way binding but conscientious trustees will take such wishes into account.

Discretionary trusts are very useful where the deceased wants funds to be used for the benefit of those in a class who turn out to have particular needs. Trusts with a contingent interest, for example for 'my grandchild, Gabrielle, if she reaches 21', are similar in that Gabrielle is not entitled to the trust property while she is under 21. However, once she fulfils the contingency, she becomes entitled. The will must provide for what is to happen to the property if Gabrielle dies under 21.

### *Inheritance tax treatment*

From an inheritance tax perspective a discretionary trust is a relevant property trust; the funds held within the trust do not 'belong' to the beneficiaries and so the death of a beneficiary does not trigger a tax charge. The trust is a taxable entity in its own right. A trust with contingent interests like the trust for Gabrielle considered above is also a relevant property trust.

Every 10 years there is an anniversary charge on the value of the trust property. The maximum rate of tax is 6% and will often be much less. The rate is calculated by looking at the value of the settled property in the trust at the anniversary, at the settlor's (i.e. the creator's) cumulative total immediately before creation of the trust, which is inherited by the trust, and at the total of transfers from the trust in the previous 10 years.

There are also exit charges as property leaves the trust. These are calculated, using the rate from the previous anniversary, on the basis of the time that has elapsed since the previous anniversary. So an exit half way through a 10-year period would attract half a full charge.

In the first 10 years, exit charges are calculated only by reference to the settlor's cumulative total and the value of the settled property put into the trust when it was created.

EXAMPLES

*(a) Anniversary and exit charges*

In June 2011, Dave died and left £300,000 to a discretionary trust for the benefit of his grandchildren and everything else to his wife. He had never made any lifetime transfers and so a full nil rate band is available to the trust.

In the first 10 years of the trust's life, the trustees make income payments but no capital payments.

On the first 10-year anniversary, the value of the trust assets is £420,000 and the nil rate band has increased to £450,000.

There will be no charge to tax as the assets fall within the nil rate band.

If, in the following 10 years, the trustees start to make capital payments, the exit charge will be at 0% because the rate calculated on the previous anniversary was 0%.

*(b) Transfers in the first 10 years*

Maxine settled £300,000 on discretionary trusts for her children and grandchildren in June 2011. She had a full nil rate band available.

By June 2020, due to very successful investments, the assets have increased to £900,000; the nil rate band has risen to £420,000.

Where trustees distribute assets before the first 10-year anniversary, the rate is calculated on the value of the property originally put into the trust so, with the benefit of Maxine's full nil rate band, all transfers will be taxed at 0%. If Maxine's trustees wait until after the first 10-year anniversary, there will be an anniversary charge and subsequent exit charges.

The moral is always review the value of trust assets before the first 10-year anniversary.

Discretionary trusts are clearly attractive from the point of view of flexibility and can be used to shelter funds for young beneficiaries from inheritance tax. However, they are unattractive from an inheritance tax point of view once the assets held exceed the nil rate band.

In example (a), if Dave had left £925,000 to the trust, there would have been a charge on death on the amount in excess of his nil rate band

(£600,000) and on the first anniversary a charge at 6% on everything in excess of the available nil rate band.

It is not possible for Dave to save anniversary and exit charges by fragmenting assets into a number of small discretionary trusts created on death. If Dave spread his £925,000 of assets between three discretionary trusts created on death, they would be added together for the purposes of calculating charges. This is because an anti-avoidance provision, section 66(4) of the IHTA 1984, provides that trusts created on the same day are 'related' trusts for inheritance tax purposes and the rate of tax charged on anniversaries and exits will take into account the total value initially settled.

It used to be possible to escape the related trusts problem by creating lifetime pilot trusts on different days and transferring nominal amounts within the annual exemption to the trusts. Each trust inherited the available nil rate band of the settlor and, provided funds were left to the trusts on the same day, for example by will, the nil rate bands were not affected.

Sadly, the Finance (No 2) Act 2015 put a stop to this. It does so by providing that when working out the rate of tax on each of the trusts, account is taken of the value of property added by the same settlor on the same day to another relevant property trust (as well as to the trust being taxed). The new rule applies to trusts created on or after 10 December 2014.

There is still some advantage to using pilot trusts: only the original value of property put into trust on the same day is added. Increases in value are ignored.

EXAMPLE

In January 2014, Sam created three pilot trusts on consecutive days each receiving £10. Sam had a full nil rate band available. At the same time he made a will leaving £250,000 to each trust.

Sam dies in January 2018 with his will unchanged and £250,000 is transferred to each trust. In January 2024, the first anniversary charge has to be calculated. The value of the property in each trust at that date is £325,000 and the nil rate band has remained at £325,000.

When valuing the assets in each trust for the purpose of calculating the anniversary charge, it is necessary to add in the value of the assets transferred to the other trusts on the same day but only at their value at that date.

The value for each trust is £325,000 + £250,000 + £250,000 = £825,000.

There is a full nil rate band available to each trust.

Had the will left everything to one trust, the value on the first anniversary would have been £325,000 x 3 = £975,000.

## Section 144 of the Inheritance Tax Act 1984 and discretionary trusts

Many testators are attracted by the flexibility of discretionary trusts but dislike the idea of being stuck with a vehicle which might be unnecessary by the time they die. Section 144 of the IHTA 1984 allows trustees to make appointments from discretionary (and other relevant property) trusts within 2 years from death which are read back into the will, thus enabling unwanted trusts to be dismantled without cost.

EXAMPLE

> Madge leaves everything to a discretionary trust for the benefit of her husband and young children. By the time she dies the children are adults. Six months after Madge's death, the trustees pay capital up to the level of the nil rate band to the children and pay the rest of the capital to her husband.
>
> Madge's estate is treated for inheritance tax purposes as if she had left it in this way.

Section 144 of the IHTA 1984 is very useful as it allows testators to leave property on discretionary trust knowing that, if not needed, the trust can be unscrambled at little cost.

An additional benefit is that the section can be used to amend gifts on trust which as left in the will do not attract the RNRB. Only a limited range of trusts attract the RNRB (see para 16.6.1) and discretionary trusts do not. However, trustees can use their discretionary powers to appoint a residence to lineal descendants either absolutely or on immediate post-death interest trusts. This will retrospectively obtain the benefit of the RNRB.

Note that although the trigger for reading back under section 144 is normally an appointment by trustees, the section is not limited to such appointments. Any event which changes the terms on which the property is held within 2 years of death will suffice.

EXAMPLE

> Property is left on trust for a grandchild contingent on reaching 25. The trust directs that the grandchild is to become entitled to income at 21. At the date of death the grandchild is 20 and with no right to income, this is a relevant property trust at that time within the ambit of section 144. However, since the grandchild becomes entitled to income within 2 years of death, the reading back effect of section 144 gives the grandchild a retrospective immediate post-death interest.

## **17.2.2**    Immediate post-death interests

An interest in possession arises where a beneficiary is given a *right* to the income of trust assets or the *right* to use them. It may be for life or for a shorter period and may be terminable early by the trustees. It is common to give the trustees power to make capital available to the income beneficiary in case of need. Unless such a power is included the trustees have no such power.

As explained in Chapter 16, when a person has a qualifying interest in possession his estate includes the capital value of the trust property. Since 2006 a qualifying interest in possession can only be created on death and must take effect immediately as an 'immediate post-death interest' (unless it qualifies as a disabled person's trust). The rest of this paragraph therefore deals only with the effects of creating immediate post-death interests.

The inheritance tax treatment of these trusts is, therefore, very different from that of relevant property trusts. The fact that the beneficiary is treated as the beneficial owner of the trust assets has the following consequences:

(a)    If the beneficiary is the spouse or civil partner of the deceased, the transfer on the testator's death is exempt under section 18 of the IHTA 1984.

   Hence, if the first spouse or civil partner to die has an unused nil rate band and leaves everything to the survivor for life, no tax is payable as the whole transfer is exempt; on the death of the survivor, there will be a full transferable nil rate band available.

(b)    If the beneficiary still has the immediate post-death interest at death, the trust assets are aggregated with the beneficiary's own free estate and inheritance tax is calculated on the aggregate value. The tax is then apportioned between the trust and the free estate.

(c)    If the immediate post-death interest terminates before death (e.g. because the trustees exercise a power of termination or the beneficiary surrenders or assigns the interest), the beneficiary is treated as making a transfer of value of the settled property held in the trust. The transfer will be potentially exempt if a beneficiary takes absolutely on termination and immediately chargeable at half the death rates if the trust continues. The trustees are liable for the tax and this is something they need to bear in mind. If the beneficiary with the former interest in possession dies within 7 years of the termination, there will be a charge to tax and the trustees will have to find assets with which to meet the liability. Therefore, they should not release all of the trust assets to the new beneficiary until satisfied that there will not be a tax liability.

(d)    If the trustees exercise a power to transfer trust capital to the beneficiary who has the immediate post-death interest, there are no inheritance tax consequences. The beneficiary was treated as entitled to the trust assets for inheritance tax purposes before the advancement and is actually entitled afterwards. Hence, there is no difference in inheritance tax terms.

Creating an immediate post-death interest for a surviving spouse or civil partner with a power to terminate it at a later stage is a useful tax planning tool offering a variety of advantages which are not all tax related:

(a)    The spouse or civil partner exemption will be available to the property subject to the interest when the first spouse or civil partner dies.

(b)    If the trust continues until the death of the survivor, the transferable nil rate band will be available on the survivor's death, as will transferred RNRB.

(c)    The fact that the property is in trust gives the first spouse or civil partner to die control over the ultimate destination of the capital (particularly helpful in the case of second marriages) and protection of the capital against nursing home fees should the survivor go into care.

(d)    The power to terminate the interest gives flexibility and allows the trustees to stop paying income to the survivor when it is no longer required, for example if the survivor goes into care and the care fees are met from other sources. They can then make capital available to the remainder beneficiaries early.

Immediate post-death interests can be created for anyone. They are not limited to surviving spouses or civil partners. There are advantages to creating them for children or grandchildren as a way of deferring their capital entitlement without incurring anniversary and exit charges and keeping the property settled while obtaining the RNRB (see, also, para 15.5.2).

If the trust also fulfils the requirements for a trust for a bereaved minor or a trust for the disabled, it takes effect as a trust of that type and the beneficiary is not treated as having an immediate post-death interest (see section 49A of the IHTA 1984). Trusts for a bereaved minor are dealt with at para 17.2.3, but trusts for the disabled are a specialist topic beyond the scope of this book.

If the trust fulfils the requirements for an immediate post-death interest and a trust for a bereaved young person (dealt with at para 17.2.3), it takes effect as an immediate post-death interest.

Common examples of immediate post-death interests are gifts by will leaving a beneficiary a life interest in a trust fund or a right to occupy a property. It is rare to create 'fixed' life interests. Modern trusts virtually always include power for the trustees to end the interest either by advancing capital to those entitled after the death or by transferring trust assets to the life tenant. This flexibility allows trustees to respond to changes in the life tenant's circumstances.

## 17.2.3    Trusts for bereaved minors and bereaved young people

Parents and grandparents often want to settle property contingent on children or grandchildren reaching a certain age. In the case of parents, there are two types of trust which qualify for special inheritance tax treatment. There are no special provisions for grandparents so if they create a trust which is contingent on reaching a stated age, like the one for Gabrielle in para 17.2.1, the trust is a relevant property trust.

### Trusts for bereaved minors

Trusts for bereaved minors are defined in section 71A of the IHTA 1984.

They are trusts created under the will of a deceased parent for his own minor child. (They may also arise on intestacy or under the criminal injuries compensation scheme.)

They must comply with the following conditions:

(a)    the bereaved minor, B, must become entitled to the capital by 18; and

(b)    pending entitlement to capital, either B must be entitled to the income, or the income must be accumulated for B's benefit; and

(c)    there must be no power to apply income for the benefit of any other person.

Provided the conditions are complied with, there is no charge to tax when:

(a)    B becomes absolutely entitled to capital at or below the age of 18; or

(b)    B dies under that age; or

(c)    capital is paid or applied for the advancement or benefit of B.

The existence of a power to advance capital for the benefit of the minor does not prevent the trust from fulfilling the capital condition. This is important because, at first sight, section 71A of the IHTA 1984 trusts look very inflexible.

However, in appropriate cases, trustees may use their power of advancement to settle capital for the benefit of the beneficiary on new trusts. The existence of that power does not prejudice the status of the trust but, once exercised, the new trust created will not be a bereaved minor trust and will be subject to anniversary and exit charges. This is very useful where, as the age of 18 approaches, it is obvious that the beneficiary cannot be trusted with capital.

## Trusts for bereaved young people

Trusts for bereaved young people are defined in section 71D of the IHTA 1984.

These trusts were introduced to counter criticisms that the age of 18 was too early an age to allow children access to capital. Section 71D of the IHTA 1984 trusts can only be created by will and only for the deceased's own children, but instead of the children having to become entitled to capital at the age of 18, the children can become entitled to capital at any age before 25. The other conditions are the same as for section 71A trusts.

As with section 71A of the IHTA 1984 trusts, the existence of the section 32 of the Trustee Act 1925 power to advance capital to the beneficiary (or an express power in similar terms) does not prejudice the status of the trust.

While the beneficiary is under the age of 18 there are no anniversary or exit charges.

Once the beneficiary reaches the age of 18, if the property remains in trust, a special charging regime set out in section 71F of the IHTA 1984 applies. Tax is calculated in broadly the same way as the exit charge discussed at para 17.2.1, Inheritance tax treatment.

As with section 71A trusts, the power of advancement can be used to make a settled advance deferring entitlement beyond the age of 25. At that point the trust will cease to qualify as a section 71D trust and will enter the 'relevant property' regime, and will suffer anniversary and exit charges. However, it is not subject to anniversary charges.

Most people will prefer to leave their property on section 71D of the IHTA 1984 trusts rather than on section 71A trusts. With section 71D trusts, the trustees are free to advance the trust property to the beneficiaries at the age of 18 if that seems appropriate, in which case no inheritance tax is payable. If, however, it seems appropriate to defer entitlement to the age of 25 or beyond, they can do so at the cost of a charge to tax for the period following the beneficiary's 18th birthday.

## 17.3    Making best use of the residence nil rate band

Unless the testator wants to make a simple outright gift of a residence or interest in a residence to lineal descendants, there are a number of potential pitfalls to be aware of:

(a)    The child of one cohabitee is not a step-child of the other. This is often a trap, for example where a residence or interest in a residence is left to a cohabitee for life and then to the deceased's own children absolutely. The RNRB is only available on properties held in trust if lineal descendants of the trust beneficiary are inheriting. In addition, the value of the residence will be included in the surviving cohabitee's estate, increasing the inheritance tax payable on death. It may be worth considering leaving the residential interest to a discretionary trust for the benefit of the cohabitee and the deceased's lineal descendants. Less tax will be paid on the surviving cohabitee's death but this must be weighed against the anniversary and exit charges payable on the trust. An alternative which will suit some (but not all) couples is to leave an interest in the residence equal to the value of the RNRB directly to the lineal descendants. This risks family tensions and possible loss of the property if one of the lineal descendants becomes bankrupt.

(b)    A residence is defined as a dwelling which has been the deceased's residence at some time during his period of ownership. A problem arises where, for example, one spouse is the sole owner of the matrimonial home and dies first leaving everything to the survivor who at that date is in residential care. If the survivor leaves the residence to lineal descendants, no RNRB is available because the dwelling has not been the survivor's residence during his period of ownership. This is a good example of the need to keep wills under review. When the spouse went into care, the spouse owning the residence should have changed the terms of the will to leave the residence, or an interest in the residence, to the lineal descendants.

(c)    A grandparent who wants to leave property by will to young grandchildren will often want to include a trust but, as explained at para 16.6.1, only a limited range of trusts qualify for the RNRB. Unless a grandchild is disabled for the purposes of inheritance tax so that a disabled person's interest can be created, the only option is to leave the residence to the grandchildren on immediate post-death interest trusts. The grandchildren will have a right to income, although as shown in the clause below, it is possible to direct that the trustees can accumulate income for the benefit of the beneficiary without affecting the status of the trust. Either the beneficiaries can be given the capital contingent on reaching a certain age or the trustees can be given a power to make capital available at their discretion.

A suitable form of wording to create an immediate post-death interest is as follows:

Clause 1

1.1   My trustees shall hold my Residuary Estate for such of my grandchildren as survive me, and equally if more than one.

1.2   However the share in my Residuary Estate of any grandchild ('My Grandchild') shall not vest in him absolutely but shall be retained and invested by my Trustees and held upon the following trusts.

Clause 2

2.1   The share of the Trust Fund held upon trust for My Grandchild under clause 1 is called 'The Share' and that one of my grandchildren who is primarily interested in the Share is called the 'Life Tenant'.

2.2   The income of the Share shall be paid to the Life Tenant during his lifetime. If and so long as the Life Tenant is under the age of 18, the Trustees may pay or apply any income of the Share to him or for his maintenance or education or otherwise for his benefit as they shall in their discretion think fit. Any balance of the income shall be retained by the Trustees upon trust for the Life Tenant absolutely. Section 31 of the Trustee Act 1925 shall not apply to the Share.

2.3   The Trustees may, at any time or times, during the Trust Period, pay or apply the whole or any part of the Share in which the Life Tenant is then entitled to an interest in possession to him or for his advancement or otherwise for his benefit in such manner as the Trustees shall in their discretion think fit. In exercising the powers conferred by this sub-clause the Trustees shall be entitled to have regard solely to the interests of the Life Tenant and to disregard all other interests or potential interests under this Deed.

2.4   Subject as above, the capital and income of the Share shall be held upon trust for such of the children of the Life Tenant as attain the age of 25 before the end of the Trust Period or are living and are under that age at the end of the

Trust Period; and if more than one, in equal shares absolutely.

Clause 3

Subject as above, the Share, together with any accrual to it,

3.1    shall accrue equally to such of my grandchildren as are living at my death, and if more than one, equally between them. An accrual under this clause shall be held upon, with and subject to the same trusts, powers and provisions as the Share to which it accrues.

3.2    and in default of accrual shall be held for [ ].

Drafting such a clause is relatively complex and many testators will prefer an absolute gift to the grandchildren.

The same problem will arise for testators who are leaving property including a residence to their own children with a substitutional gift for children of a child who predeceases them. The substituted beneficiary is a grandchild of the testator. The same choice, therefore has to be made: is the residence to be left absolutely or on immediate post-death interest trusts?

(d)    RNRB is withdrawn at the rate of £1 for every £2 the estate exceeds the taper threshold of £2 million. Married couples and civil partners should consider the impact of the taper threshold on the way in which they leave their property. A husband and wife may each own assets of £1.2 million but if the first to die leaves everything to the survivor (whether absolutely or on life interest trusts, the effect is identical for inheritance tax purposes), the survivor's estate will be £2.4 million and most of the RNRB available will be lost through taper. A possible solution is for the first to die to leave assets equal to the nil rate band to a discretionary trust for the spouse and lineal descendants. In cases where this is not sufficient, the first to die may leave an interest in a residence to the lineal descendants (this may not be popular with the survivor) or leave other assets to the lineal descendants to reduce the estate of the survivor (again, this may not be popular).

Appendix 3 provides case study illustrations of some of the points made in this chapter.

# 18 Powers to Deal with Income and Capital

When trustees hold assets for beneficiaries, it is important that they should be able to apply income and capital early if beneficiaries are in need of funds.

There are statutory powers implied under sections 31 and 32 of the Trustee Act 1925 which are often modified by express provisions.

## 18.1 Power to apply income – section 31 of the Trustee Act 1925

Under this section, trustees can apply any available income towards the maintenance, education or benefit of any minor beneficiary, whether his interest is vested or contingent. Any income that is not applied for maintenance, education or benefit must be accumulated.

### 18.1.1 When is income available?

Income is not 'available' if it has been expressly given to someone.

EXAMPLE

> Sam leaves a trust fund of £500,000 'to my daughter if she reaches 25 and in the meantime to my mother'. The effect of this gift is that Mother is entitled to the income from the trust fund until the daughter reaches 25 so no income is available for the daughter.

Income is also not available if, as a matter of general law, the gift does not carry the right to intermediate income. Under section 175 of the LPA 1925, most gifts do carry the right to intermediate income, but contingent pecuniary legacies do not unless one of the following applies:

(a) There is a direction to set aside a legacy fund for the benefit of the legatee (see *Kidman v Kidman* (1871) 40 LJ Ch 359).

(b) The legacy is payable to a minor child of the testator or to a minor to whom the testator is *in loco parentis* and no other fund is designated for the minor's maintenance. The court will infer an intention to provide maintenance for the child in such a case. It is more difficult (although not impossible) to infer such an intention where the contingency is something other than reaching the age of majority (see *Re Jones* [1932] 1 Ch 642).

(c)    The legacy is payable to a minor who is not the child of the testator nor a child to whom the testator is *in loco parentis*, but the will shows an intention that the income shall be used for the child's maintenance.

These rules can be displaced by contrary intention in the will. Where there is no contrary provision, the intermediate income will be paid to the person entitled to the residue of the estate and the contingent pecuniary legatee will receive only the capital sum.

It is advisable to make express provision for intermediate income to avoid uncertainty (see *Beard v Shadler* [2011] EWHC 114 (Ch) for an example of uncertainty).

### 18.1.2    Matters the trustees are to consider when exercising their discretion to apply income

As originally drawn, the section required trustees to apply such income 'as may, in all the circumstances, be reasonable' which was an objective test. It also set out various matters that the trustees had to consider when exercising their discretion. Trust instruments commonly removed these requirements leaving the trustees with an unfettered discretion.

Section 8 of the Inheritance and Trustees' Powers Act 2014 which came into force on 1 October 2014 amended section 31 to remove the objective test and give trustees an unfettered discretion when deciding on whether and how much income to apply. The amendment applies for trusts 'created or arising after the Act comes into force', subject to amendment or exclusion of the power by the terms of the will. According to Explanatory Note 51, a will trust is created at the date of death not execution.

### 18.1.3    Power to use accumulated income

Any income that has been accumulated may be applied during the minority of the beneficiary as if it were the income of the current year. This power enables the trustees to make up for any deficiency in income in the current year from accumulated income of previous years.

### 18.1.4    When a minor beneficiary reaches the age of 18

Once a minor beneficiary reaches the age of 18 then, if the gift remains contingent, section 31(1) of the Trustee Act 1925 requires the trustees to pay the income of the trust fund to the beneficiary until the contingency is met or the gift fails.

Any accumulations arising during the minority of the beneficiary are normally added to the capital of the fund and pass with it.

If, however, the beneficiary has a life interest in the fund, then that beneficiary becomes entitled to all the accumulated income on attaining the age of 18. If the beneficiary dies under that age, the accumulations are added to capital and pass with it accordingly (section 31(2) of the Trustee Act 1925).

Obtaining the right to income at the age of 18 is significant for income tax purposes. It means that the trust will be subject to the simpler income tax regime that applies to trusts where the beneficiary has a right to income instead of the more complex regime that applies when beneficiaries have no such right.

For inheritance tax purposes, obtaining the right is not normally significant. The beneficiary is not treated as entitled to the underlying trust capital for inheritance tax purposes, because the interest is not an immediate post-death interest (see paras 16.2 and 17.2.2).

Exceptionally, if the minor reaches the age of 18 within 2 years of the death of the testator, the minor will be treated as having been entitled to an immediate post-death interest from the date of death as a result of the reading back effect of section 144 of the IHTA 1984 (see para 17.2.1,).

It is common to exclude the right to income at the age of 18 and to allow the trustees' discretion to continue to a later age or even to exclude the right entirely unless and until the trustees decide to give the beneficiary a right to income. This gives more flexibility and allows the trustees to make decisions based on the needs of the beneficiary and the tax rules in force at the time. (See Appendix 1 and clause 9 of the Will of James Matthew Appleby, which defers entitlement to income to the age of 21. Consequently, the trustees' discretionary power to apply income lasts until the beneficiary reaches the age of 21 and from then on the beneficiary is entitled to the income as of right until the interest vests (at the age of 25 in the case of his children) or fails.)

## 18.2 Power to advance capital – section 32 of the Trustee Act 1925

Subject to certain statutory limitations, trustees have an absolute discretion to apply capital for the advancement or benefit of any person who has either a vested or a contingent interest in capital (section 32 of the Trustee Act 1925). The section is subject to contrary intention.

The statutory power is wide enough to allow property to be advanced to new trustees under new trusts which may contain powers and discretions not given under the original trust instrument.

Any advance given to a contingently interested beneficiary cannot be recovered from that beneficiary's estate should he die before the contingency is met.

### 18.2.1    Limitations on the statutory power

As originally drafted, there were three limitations on the power, as follows:

(a)    the trustees may advance up to one half only of the beneficiary's vested or presumptive share;

(b)    any advance made must be brought into account when the beneficiary becomes absolutely entitled;

(c)    any person with a prior interest, such as a life tenant, must consent to the advance.

It was common to remove or amend one or more of the statutory limitations and leave the exercise of the power to the trustees' discretion.

The Inheritance and Trustees' Powers Act 2014 has removed the first limitation so that, subject to contrary intention, trustees now have statutory power to advance up to the whole of the beneficiary's vested or presumptive share. The amendment applies for trusts 'created or arising after the Act comes into force' subject to amendment or exclusion of the power by the terms of the will. According to Explanatory Note 51, a will trust is created at the date of death not execution.

The other limitations remain unless varied by the will. (See Appendix 1 and clause 9 of the Will of James Matthew Appleby, which allows the terms of an advance to be at the trustees' discretion.)

### 18.2.2    Express power to apply capital for beneficiaries with no interest in capital

The statutory power applies only to those with a vested or contingent entitlement *in capital*. Hence, under the statutory power there is no power to advance capital to a beneficiary who is entitled only to income. Yet this will often be beneficial.

EXAMPLE

Harvey and Wanda have just married. It is a second marriage for both of them and they each have children from their first marriage. Harvey is 70 and Wanda is 66. They want to ensure that the survivor is adequately provided for but also want as much of their own capital as possible to go to their own children. They have bought a house together for £400,000 as beneficial tenants in common and each has £100,000 in investments. They each want to leave the other a life interest in their estate, remainder to their own children.

If Wanda dies first, Harvey will have a life interest and so continue in occupation of the house and have the income from the investments. If Harvey has a sudden need for capital expenditure (perhaps for medical treatment), it might well be helpful for the trustees to be able to advance capital from the trust.

It is possible to include in the will an express power authorising trustees to advance capital to a life tenant.

## 18.2.3 Power to lend capital

An additional power which it is useful to give the trustees in the will is a power to lend trust assets to a beneficiary. They can then allow the beneficiary the use of trust assets while retaining the right to recover the assets from the estate of the beneficiary at a later date. The debt owing to the trust will be deductible from the beneficiary's estate for inheritance tax purposes on death.

# 19  Administrative Powers for Personal Representatives and Trustees

## 19.1    Introduction

Both PRs and trustees are in a fiduciary position, and, in the absence of express provision in the will, are subject to a number of restrictions and obligations. It is common to remove some of these to facilitate the administration of estates and trusts.

When administering the estate or managing a trust created in the will, PRs and trustees need various administrative powers. The will can confer such powers expressly. If it is silent, various statutory powers are implied. The most important statutes are the AEA 1925, the Trustee Act 1925 and the Trustee Act 2000.

For the purposes of the legislation, and for this chapter, the term 'trustee' includes a PR.

Although the statutory powers are very useful, they are not ideal for all situations. Some are subject to limitations which the testator may wish to remove or vary in order to give greater freedom to the trustees.

## 19.2    STEP standard provisions

The Society of Trust and Estate Practitioners (STEP) publishes a set of standard administrative provisions which can be incorporated into a will by reference by using the words:

> The standard provisions of the Society of Trust and Estate Practitioners shall apply to this will.

Many practitioners like to use the standard provisions as they provide relatively full coverage of the needs of a standard estate or trust. In 2011 a second edition of the provisions was published, and no doubt further editions will be published to take account of changing circumstances. Therefore, practitioners must specify which edition is to be incorporated.

## 19.3    Legacies to minors

As a result of sections 3 and 5 of the Children Act 1989, a guardian or person with parental responsibility for a minor can provide a receipt for a legacy on behalf of the minor.

In the case of a small legacy, a testator may prefer to provide that the PRs can accept the receipt of the minor.

Alternatively, the testator may consider appointing trustees to take the legacy on behalf of the minor, in which case it is normally appropriate to make the legacy contingent on reaching a specified age.

It is advisable to provide expressly whether or not a legacy carries intermediate income as contingent pecuniary legacies do not normally carry the right to intermediate income (see para 18.1).

## 19.4    Power to invest

The statutory powers of investment are contained in the Trustee Act 2000. The general power of investment is contained in section 3, and authorises trustees to make any kind of investment that they could make if they were absolutely entitled to the trust assets. It does not authorise trustees to buy land, which is dealt with expressly under section 8. Trustees can, however, invest in loans secured on land.

The statutory power is in addition to any express power contained in the will or trust instrument, but subject to any restrictions imposed there. It applies to trusts and wills whenever created.

When exercising any power of investment (express or statutory), section 4(1) of the Trustee Act 2000 requires the trustees to have regard to the 'standard investment criteria' which are set out in section 4(3). Section 4(2) requires them to review the trust investments from time to time and decide whether, in the light of those criteria, the investments should be varied. The criteria are:

(a)    the suitability to the trust of investments of the kind proposed and the suitability of the particular investment as an example of that type;

(b)    the need for diversification of investments of the trust, insofar as is appropriate to the circumstances of the trust.

The duty to consider the criteria cannot be excluded. However, in cases where a testator intends the trust to be a vehicle for holding a particular asset, such as land or shares in a family business, the testator should leave a statement of wishes by way of guidance on the extent to which diversification is appropriate. In *Gregson v HAE Trustees Ltd and Others* [2008] EWHC 1006 (Ch), [2009] 1 All ER (Comm) 457, the court pointed out that the qualification in section 4(3)(b) of the Trustee Act 2000 that the trustees must consider diversification 'in so far as is appropriate to the circumstances of the trust' means that the trustees can properly take into account matters such as the nature and purposes of the trust, its provisions, any letter of wishes and the feelings of beneficiaries at this point. The court also stated that a trust instrument can go so far as to provide that the original trust investments are not to be sold (although the particular instrument under consideration had not done so). It is unlikely that any sensible testator would want to include a blanket prohibition on sale.

Before investing, or when reviewing investments, section 5 of the Trustee Act 2000 requires the trustees to obtain and consider 'proper advice'. Proper advice is the advice of a person reasonably believed by the trustees to be qualified to advise, by reason of having ability in and practical experience of financial and other matters relating to the proposed investment. Trustees are relieved of the obligation to take advice if they reasonably conclude 'that in all the circumstances it is unnecessary or inappropriate to do so' (section 5(3)). Matters which might justify a decision not to take advice are:

(a)   the expertise of individual trustees;

(b)   the fact that the amount to be invested is small in relation to the trust as a whole.

When exercising any duties in relation to investment, section 1 of the Trustee Act 2000 requires trustees to exercise such care and skill as is reasonable in the circumstances, having regard in particular:

(a)   to any special knowledge or experience a trustee has or holds himself out as having; or

(b)   to any special knowledge or experience it is reasonable to expect of a person, when acting in the course of a business or profession.

Express provision is required in the following cases:

(a)   to permit an ethical investment policy;

(b)   to permit borrowing for the purposes of investment; or

(c)   to permit the retention of non-income-producing assets.

## **19.5** Power to acquire land

Section 8 of the Trustee Act 2000 gives trustees power to acquire freehold or leasehold land in the United Kingdom:

(a)    as an investment;

(b)    for occupation by a beneficiary;

(c)    for any other reason.

If they are acquiring land for investment, the trustees must have regard to the standard investment criteria (see para 19.4) and must acquire and consider proper investment advice. They must also have regard to the statutory duty of care in section 1 of the Trustee Act 2000 unless it is amended by express provision.

If they are acquiring land for non-investment purposes, the standard investment criteria and need for proper investment advice are not relevant.

Section 8 of the Trustee Act 2000 does not give trustees power to acquire property abroad or to acquire an interest in land as a co-owner. It is often beneficial for trustees to have power to acquire property abroad or to invest jointly with a beneficiary, but these powers must be conferred expressly.

Trustees have wide statutory powers to manage land in the United Kingdom, extending to such matters as sale, insurance, repair, improvement, mortgaging and leasing (see section 6 of the TLATA 1996 and section 8(3) of the Trustee Act 2000). Express powers are needed to deal with foreign land or with interests in land such as arise through co-ownership.

It is no longer necessary to provide expressly that land acquired by trustees is to be held on trust for sale. All land held on trust, in a trust created after 1 January 1997, is a 'trust of land' and is governed by the provisions of the TLATA 1996 which includes a power of sale.

PRs have a statutory power of sale over all assets of the estate (section 39 of the AEA 1925) but it may be sensible to include an express power of sale in a will in case a continuing trust of personalty arises.

## **19.6** Power to act though personally interested and to buy trust property ('self-dealing')

Because of the fiduciary nature of the trustees' position, they cannot act when they have a personal interest unless authorised by the trust instrument. This has two aspects.

### 19.6.1 Exercising a discretion when personally interested

There may be circumstances in which trustees are unable to exercise a discretion because of having a personal interest but this is to the detriment of the estate or trust. It is, therefore, sensible to authorise a trustee to act despite having an interest.

However, some sort of control is often appropriate and so it is common to provide that a trustee can exercise powers despite having an interest but only if there is at least one other trustee to whom any such personal interest has been disclosed.

### 19.6.2 Buying assets from the trust

Trustees are prohibited from purchasing trust assets without authorisation from the trust instrument as they would effectively be buying from themselves. If they do purchase property, the purchase is voidable at the instance of the beneficiaries no matter how fair the price paid. *Kane v Radley-Kane* [1999] Ch 274, discussed at para 19.7.3 suggests that there is an exception where an asset has a fixed value, for example shares which are quoted on the stock market.

There are some circumstances in which a court may authorise such a purchase (see *Holder v Holder* [1968] Ch 353, CA and *Ex parte Lacey* (1802) 6 Ves 625). It is also possible for beneficiaries to authorise a purchase.

PRs should be particularly careful if appropriating assets to themselves. An appropriation of assets in or towards satisfaction of a pecuniary legacy or entitlement to residue is equivalent to a sale and so is voidable.

It is often helpful for trustees to buy trust or estate property as they may have particular reasons for wanting to buy assets; for example, where they are the surviving partners or co-shareholders of the deceased. A clause allowing such a purchase is often included. It may also be necessary to include in the will provisions to govern the method of ascertaining an appropriate purchase price.

## 19.7 Appropriation of assets

Under section 41 of the AEA 1925, PRs may, with the relevant consents, appropriate assets in or towards satisfaction of a pecuniary or residuary legacy in the will, either in whole or in part.

Section 41 of the AEA 1925 does not apply to trusts and it is common to include an express power for trustees to appropriate assets in or towards satisfaction of any interest in the trust without the consent of any person and irrespective of whether one or more of the trustees may be beneficially interested in the exercise of the power.

### 19.7.1    Consent and section 41 of the Administration of Estates Act 1925

If an adult beneficiary is absolutely and beneficially entitled and has full mental capacity, then his consent is all that is required. If the beneficiary, though absolutely and beneficially entitled, is a minor or is mentally incapable of dealing with his own affairs, then the consent of a parent, guardian or deputy, as appropriate, must be obtained.

In the case of a settled legacy left in trust, the consent required is normally that of the trustees.

The requirement for consent is frequently varied by will to allow the PRs to appropriate without a formal consent. This is administratively convenient but does contain a possible inheritance tax downside in relation to claims for inheritance tax loss relief.

Inheritance tax loss relief is available where PRs sell land or quoted shares within certain periods after death (12 months for quoted shares and 4 years for land) for less than their value at the date of death.

They can substitute the sale proceeds for the death value thereby reducing the inheritance tax payable on the estate.

HMRC regards an appropriation made with consent in or towards satisfaction of a pecuniary legacy under section 41 of the AEA 1925 as a sale for this purpose but it does not accept it as a sale if the will has removed the need for consent (see HMRC, *Inheritance Tax Manual*, IHTM34153 (available at www.hmrc.gov.uk/manuals/ ihtmanual/IHTM34153.htm)).

### 19.7.2    Value of assets appropriated

When calculating the value of the asset(s) a beneficiary is entitled to, the value at the date of the appropriation is used, not the value at the date of death (see *Re Collins* [1975] 1 WLR 309). This can make a great difference to the amount a beneficiary takes.

A will may give the PRs discretion as to whether they appropriate assets at the death value rather than at the later value. This is useful as it could allow them, for example, to channel more assets to a non-exempt beneficiary in satisfaction of a nil rate band legacy. Including such a power allows for the possibility of making such an appropriation if circumstances after the date of death warrant it.

The STEP Standard Provisions 2nd edition includes such a power but as a special condition which has to be positively selected.

### 19.7.3    Appropriations and self-dealing

If the PR is also a legatee, an appropriation of assets in his own favour will be voidable by the beneficiaries as self-dealing unless:

(a)    the will contains a provision authorising the self-dealing; or

(b)    the PR obtains the consent of the other beneficiaries; or

(c)    the PR obtains authorisation from the court; or

(d)    the assets appropriated have a fixed value, for example quoted shares, and can, therefore, be regarded as equivalent to cash.

In *Kane v Radley-Kane* [1999] Ch 274, an appropriation on intestacy by a surviving spouse without any consent from the other beneficiaries or the court was held to be voidable.

## 19.8    Power to charge

The equitable rule that trustees may not profit from their trust applies to both trustees and executors. Its effect is that an executor or trustee may claim only out-of-pocket expenses and may not charge for time spent in performing his office unless expressly authorised.

Sections 28–31 of the Trustee Act 2000 have made various changes to the general rule of law governing the remuneration of 'professional' trustees (see para 11.5).

However, it is still desirable to include a charging clause as, without one, a sole trustee will be unable to charge and a co-trustee can do so only with the permission of co-trustees.

Once a professional person has retired, he is not able to benefit under a standard charging clause which authorises a person 'engaged in a profession' to charge. According to *Glenister v Moody* [2003] EWHC 3155 (Ch), however, a professional trustee who is winding down his practice is still engaged in a profession while finalising the last few trusts.

A charging clause often authorises a professional to make 'reasonable charges'. The question of what is reasonable is an objective one. It is not sufficient for professionals to say that they are charging at their normal rate (see *Pullan v Wilson* [2014] EWHC 126 (Ch)).

Clients may want non-professionals to be able to charge for time spent on the administration. An express power will have to be included. Sometimes this is dealt with by way of a legacy (see para 11.5).

## 19.9    Retention of directors' remuneration

A major asset of a trust may be shares in a company. Often, the person who sets up a company transfers the shares to trustees to hold for members of the family. To protect the value of the trust's investment, the trustees may require the company to appoint one or more of them as directors of the company.

In the absence of a provision to the contrary, a trustee/director would be liable to account for all director's fees received.

Given that the trustee may invest a great deal of time and energy working for the company, it will often be appropriate to authorise the trustee to retain director's fees.

## 19.10    Power to employ agents

Under section 11 of the Trustee Act 2000 PRs or trustees may employ an agent to exercise any or all of their 'delegable functions'. These are all functions except those relating to:

(a)    whether or how trust assets are to be distributed;

(b)    whether fees or payments should be made out of capital or income;

(c)    the appointment of trustees;

(d)    any power (statutory or express) to delegate or appoint nominees or custodians.

They can also appoint nominees or custodians to hold trust assets (sections 16 and 17 of the Trustee Act 2000). When appointing agents, etc trustees are subject to the statutory duty of care in section 1, unless the will excludes it.

It is increasingly common for trustees to delegate certain functions, such as the investment of funds to a fund manager who makes investment decisions without reference to the trustees but in accordance with an investment policy chosen by the trustees and periodically reviewed by them.

Sections 11–27 of the Trustee Act 2000 allow trustees and PRs to delegate investment functions to such managers and to vest trust assets in nominees. The statutory powers are extensive but do not allow delegation to a beneficiary and include some requirements which may be regarded as unduly burdensome.

These limitations can be avoided by including express powers which replace the statutory ones.

## 19.11 Appointment of new trustees

The number of executors who may take a grant in respect of any particular part of any estate is limited to four (section 114(1) of the Senior Courts Act 1981). The number of trustees of a trust of pure personalty is not limited but the number of trustees of a trust of land is also limited to four. It is not usual, therefore, to appoint more than four trustees in a private trust.

Where only one trustee is appointed, that trustee is able to perform most acts of joint trustees, except that a single trustee cannot give a valid receipt for capital moneys arising on the disposition of land unless the trustee is a trust corporation.

Sections 36(1) and 41 of the Trustee Act 1925 detail the circumstances in which new trustees may be appointed either by the persons specified in section 36 (the person nominated in the instrument, the continuing trustees or the PRs of the last trustee) or by the court (section 41).

## 19.12 Power to act on counsel's opinion

Legal issues may arise concerning the interpretation of the will, the terms of its trusts, or the estate itself. The trustees may apply to the court for directions in any such case, but this would be an expense to the estate.

The High Court has power under section 48 of the Administration of Justice Act 1985 to authorise trustees to take action in reliance on counsel's opinion in relation to any question of construction of the terms of a will or a trust. Counsel must have at least a 10-year High Court qualification.

It is beneficial for trustees to have a power to rely on counsel's opinion which does not require them to apply to court. The trustees or the beneficiaries may still apply to the court if they think fit. It is also helpful to reduce the years of qualification required.

## 19.13 Indemnity clauses

Trustee 'indemnity' clauses are clauses which are intended to absolve trustees or executors from liability in the event of their own negligence or the negligence or fraud of their co-trustees or agents. It is clearly appropriate to include such a clause where the trustees are friends or family who take office as a favour and are unprotected by insurance. It is less appropriate in the case of professionally paid trustees who have the benefit of professional negligence policies. Nevertheless, liability can be excluded in such cases (see *Armitage v Nurse* [1998] Ch 241).

The existence and effect of such a clause should be drawn to the attention of the testator, before the creation of the trust (see para 11.11).

## 19.14    Insurance

Section 19 of the Trustee Act 1925 (as substituted by section 34 of the Trustee Act 2000) gives PRs and trustees the power to insure trust assets against any risks, to their full value, and to pay premiums out of either capital or income. Before the Trustee Act 2000, the statutory power of insurance was inadequate, and so it was normal to extend it by including an express power. However, this is no longer necessary, although many practitioners prefer not to rely on implied powers but to include a comprehensive list of powers in the will or trust instrument.

The Trustee Act 2000 only provides trustees with a power to insure trust *assets*. If trustees want to insure the *life* of a beneficiary or of the settlor (e.g. where there is a risk of a charge to inheritance tax if death occurs within 7 years) they will require an express power.

## 19.15    Power to carry on a business

Where the deceased was running a business as a sole trader, the PRs have an implied power (in the absence of any express provision) to continue the business in order to sell it as a going concern. That power is limited to realising the value of the business and does not continue indefinitely. In case market conditions are unfavourable, it is wise to give the PRs power to carry on any business for so long as they think fit. Unless otherwise provided, the PRs may employ only those assets already used in the business at the date of the testator's death.

PRs running the business are liable for any debts they incur. If the business is being carried on only for the purposes of realisation, then the PRs have a right to an indemnity from the estate in priority to the testator's creditors and to the beneficiaries. If, however, the PRs are given express authority to carry on the business, their indemnity gives them priority over the beneficiaries only, not the creditors.

It is often appropriate to appoint separate PRs to deal with the running of the business after the death of a sole trader.

In the case of partnerships or limited companies, the PRs cannot normally take over any management functions on behalf of the testator. Unless the partnership deed states otherwise, the death of one partner terminates a partnership.

In the case of companies, the articles of association should be consulted for the position on the death of a shareholder. It may be possible to sell the shares, transfer them to a beneficiary, subject to the company's agreement to register the transfer. However, the articles of association may confer pre-emption rights on the other shareholders. It is important that any relevant partnership agreement, or the articles of association of any relevant company, are available to and considered by the draftsman preparing a will.

(See, also, para 13.5.2 as regards gifts of business interests.)

## 19.16    Power to borrow

PRs have power to borrow on the security of the personal estate for the purposes of the administration (section 39 of the AEA 1925).

Trustees have limited powers to borrow. Testators often wish to extend the trustees' powers of borrowing, for example to allow unsecured borrowing or borrowing on the security of land to finance the purchase of other investments.

## 19.17    Exclusion of the apportionment rules

One of the duties of trustees is to ensure that a fair balance is kept between the interests of the beneficiaries. This is particularly important where different beneficiaries are entitled to income and capital, for example where property is left on trust for X for life with remainder to Y. The trustees must ensure that the investments they choose produce a reasonable income for X, the life tenant, and preserve the capital reasonably safely for Y, the remainder beneficiary.

Complicated equitable rules requiring apportionment of income and the proceeds of sale of capital, designed to achieve fairness between different classes of beneficiaries, were developed. They are now regarded as unduly complex and were always excluded.

After 1 October 2013 (the date on which the Trusts (Capital and Income) Act 2013 came into force, this is no longer necessary as the equitable rules are abolished.

### 19.17.1    Equitable rules

The equitable rules to preserve a fair balance between a life tenant and a remainder beneficiary derive from *Howe v Dartmouth* (1820) 7 Ves 137 and *Allhusen v Whittell* (1867) LR 4 Eq 295.

They have been routinely excluded for many years because of their complexity. For trusts created or arising on or after 1 October 2013 exclusion is no longer necessary as section 1(2) of the Trusts (Capital and Income) Act 2013 disapplies the rules.

### 19.17.2    Apportionment Act 1870

Section 2 of the Apportionment Act 1870 provides that income such as rent and dividends is to be treated as accruing from day to day and apportioned accordingly. Section 1(1) of the Trusts (Capital and Income) Act 2013 disapplies the Act for trusts created or arising on or after 1 October 2013.

Where assets in the estate produce income (such as dividends on shares) which is received after death but relates to a period partly before and partly after death, the Apportionment Act 1870 will still apply unless excluded. Apportionment would be required where an income-producing asset is left to one person and residue to another, unless excluded.

EXAMPLE

>    I give my shares to X and my residue to Y.

>    Unless the Act is excluded, dividend income attributable to the pre-death period is Y's and income attributable to the post-death period belongs to X.

## 19.18    Trusts of Land and Appointment of Trustees Act 1996

The TLATA 1996 includes various provisions which testators may wish to exclude in order to give trustees more power.

### 19.18.1    Control of trustees by beneficiaries

Section 19 of the TLATA 1996 provides that where beneficiaries are of full age and capacity and together entitled to the whole fund, they may direct the trustees to retire and appoint new trustees of the beneficiaries' choice. This means that in a case where the beneficiaries could by agreement end the trust under the rule in *Saunders v Vautier* (1841) 4 Beav 115, they now have the option of allowing the trust to continue with trustees of their own choice.

## 19.18.2 Beneficiaries of a trust of land with an interest in possession

The TLATA 1996 does not define 'interest in possession', so it presumably has its usual meaning; a beneficiary has an interest in possession if entitled to claim the income of the fund as it arises. Such beneficiaries are given two special rights.

### Right to be consulted

Trustees exercising any function relating to the land must consult any beneficiary who is of full age and beneficially entitled to an interest in possession in the land and, so far as consistent with the 'general interest of the trust', give effect to the wishes of any such beneficiary (section 11 of the TLATA 1996). The duty to consult may be excluded by the will.

### Rights of occupation

A beneficiary with a beneficial interest in possession, even if not of full age, has the right to occupy land subject to the trust if the purposes of the trust include making the land available for his occupation, or if the trustees acquired the land in order to make it so available (section 12 of the TLATA 1996). There is no power to exclude section 12, but a declaration that the occupation of land is not a purpose of the trust may be included in the will.

# 20 Funeral and Other Requests

## 20.1 Funeral arrangements

Many people have strong views about the sort of funeral they want. Is an expression of their wishes binding?

Any wishes expressed in the will by the deceased are not binding, although they are important (see para 20.1.2).

There is no proprietary interest in a dead body (see *Williams v Williams* (1881–82) LR 20 Ch D 659 and *R v Sharpe* (1857) 26 LJMC 47). However, various people have rights and duties in relation to it.

### 20.1.1 Who has rights and duties in relation to a dead body?

The deceased's PRs have the common law duty to arrange for the proper disposal of the deceased's remains. Where PRs have not yet been appointed, the person with the best right to the grant of administration takes precedence. Where two or more persons rank equally, then the dispute will be decided on a practical basis (see Paul Matthews (ed), *Jervis on Coroners* (Sweet & Maxwell, 12th edn, 2002), para 7–03, n.40; 7–05, n.41).

As the executors' authority derives from the will and not from the grant, they are entitled to obtain possession of the body for the purposes of burial prior to the grant (by injunction under section 37 of the Senior Courts Act 1981, if necessary).

Administrators also have a common law duty to dispose of the body but as their authority derives from the grant, they may not be able to obtain an injunction for delivery of the body prior to obtaining the grant.

The order of priority for taking a grant is set out in rules 20 and 22 of the NCPR 1987. However, the court has power under section 116 of the Senior Courts Act 1981 to pass over the person with the best right if by reason of any special circumstances it appears to be necessary or expedient to appoint someone else. In *Buchanan v Milton* [1999] 2 FLR 844, Hale J said in relation to an application to pass over those entitled because of a dispute over the appropriate funeral arrangements that 'the courts should be slow to entertain proceedings such as these … They delay the proper disposal of the body and the normal processes of grieving while bringing further grief in themselves'.

A householder has a common law duty to dispose of a body situate under his roof. Where the deceased lived alone, the duty passes to the local authority (section 46(1) of the Public Health (Control of Disease) Act 1984). Local authorities will not pay if there are assets and may trace relatives to authorise the cost of the funeral.

If the deceased died in hospital, the hospital authorities are treated as 'the householder'. In *Lewisham NHS Hospital Trust v Hamuth* [2006] EWHC 1669 (Ch), [2006] All ER (D) 145, there was a dispute as to the validity of the will and, therefore, as to the validity of the appointment of the executor. The executor wished to follow the deceased's wishes and cremate the body. The family wanted to bury the body in the family plot. There was no possibility of resolving the dispute over the will within an acceptable period. The court, therefore, declared that the hospital, being in lawful possession of the body, was entitled to decide the appropriate means for the disposal of the body.

## 20.1.2    Effect of the deceased's wishes

According to *Williams v Williams* (1881–82) LR 20 Ch D 659, the wishes of the deceased are not binding. However, the European Convention for the Protection of Human Rights and Fundamental Freedoms 1950 (European Convention on Human Rights) may have an impact on domestic law in this area.

Article 8(1) of the European Convention on Human Rights provides that 'Everyone has a right to respect for his private and family life'; Article 8(2) continues that there should be:

> no interference by a public authority with the exercise of this right except such as in accordance with law is necessary in a democratic society … for the prevention of disorder … the protection of … morals, or for the protection of the rights and freedoms of others.

*Burrows v HM Coroner for Preston* [2008] EWHC 1387 (Admin) considered the effect of the European Convention on Human Rights and stated that in as much as domestic law says that the views of a deceased person can be ignored, it is no longer good law (see *X v Germany* (8741/79), unreported, 10 March 1981 and *Dodsbo v Sweden* (2007) 45 EHRR 22). The views of a deceased person as to funeral arrangements and the disposal of his body must be taken into account. However, this was doubted in *Ibuna v Arroyo* [2012] EWHC 428 (Ch), where Peter Smith J said that the established law in England and Wales was set out in *Buchanan v Milton* [1999] 2 FLR 844 and was that the executor has the primary duty to dispose of the body. The executor is entitled to have regard to any expression of wishes made by the deceased but is not bound by them, There is no room for any post-mortem application of human rights in relation to a body as if it had some independent right to be heard. He doubted *Burrows v HM Coroner for Preston* [2008] EWHC 1387 (Admin).

In any event it is relatively easy to fit the deceased's wishes within domestic law as, in this type of case, a person's wishes can be regarded as a special circumstance for the purposes of section 116 of the Senior Courts Act 1981, justifying passing over a person entitled to take a grant who is unwilling to respect the deceased's wishes.

In *Burrows v HM Coroner for Preston*, the court did pass over the person with the best right to a grant in part to allow the deceased's funeral wishes to be carried out.

### 20.1.3    Should the deceased's wishes be included in the will?

It may be helpful to do so. However, it is even more helpful for individuals to discuss their wishes with their family so that there are no surprises after the death.

## 20.2    Donation of the body and body parts

Many people are happy that their organs should be taken after their death and used as transplants to help others. A rather smaller number are willing to donate their bodies to be used for anatomical examination and research.

The Human Tissue Act 2004 (HTA 2004) came fully into force on 1 September 2006 and replaces all previous legislation in this area. It introduces a new legislative framework making consent the fundamental principle underpinning the lawful storage and use of human bodies and the removal, storage and use of relevant material from the bodies of deceased persons. The type of consent and the requirements in relation to it vary according to the purpose for which the relevant material is used or stored. The possible purposes listed in Schedule 1 to the HTA 2004 include, amongst others, anatomical examination, public display, research in connection with the functioning of the human body, transplantation, and education or training relating to human health.

## 20.2.1   Anatomical examination and public display

Anatomical examination is defined in section 54(1) of the HTA 2004 as 'macroscopic examination by dissection for anatomical purposes' and 'anatomical purposes' as 'purposes of teaching or studying, or researching into, the gross structure of the human body'.

Consent for the donation of a body or relevant material for anatomical examination or public display differs from that required for transplantation. It can only be given by the individual who has chosen to donate. It cannot be given by anyone else on the individual's behalf (section 3 of the HTA 2004).

The consent must be in writing and is valid only if it is:

(a)   signed by the person concerned in the presence of at least one witness who attests the signature;

(b)   signed at the direction of the person concerned, in his presence and in the presence of at least one witness who attests the signature; or

(c)   contained in a will of the person concerned made in accordance with the requirements of section 9 of the WA 1837, or Article 5 of the Wills and Administration Proceedings (Northern Ireland) Order 1994 (SI 1994/1899 (NI 13)).

If the consent is contained in a will, someone else can sign the will on behalf of the testator in accordance with section 9(a) of the WA 1837 (see para 4.3.3).

The Human Tissue Authority (HTA) has produced a model bequeathal booklet and a model body donation consent form to help anatomy establishments. The intention is that they will provide the form to prospective donors.

The HTA accepts that it may not always be possible to obtain written consent from the individual who has chosen to donate his body or part of his body for anatomical examination, for example when a person with sufficient mental capacity to consent is physically unable to write. The HTA has therefore produced a model form for a person to sign on behalf of a donor. In these circumstances, the HTA advises that:

(a)   the potential donor must have sufficient mental capacity to make the decision to donate his body for anatomical examination and must be able to indicate his wish verbally or physically;

(b)   the person should sign his own name, state that he has signed at the direction of the donor and explain the circumstances of this direction;

(c)     the form should then be signed by the witness before being submitted to the receiving institution. This procedure must occur prior to the donor's death. The consent form cannot be signed by the third party after death has occurred.

There are various Codes of Practice which supplement the HTA 2004. Code C deals with anatomy. Paragraphs 27 and 28 provide as follows:

> 27. Anyone wishing to donate their body, or part of their body, for anatomical examination should preferably use a consent form from the facility of their choice, which should be kept as part of the donation records. The HTA has produced a model body donation consent form, which can be modified and adopted by HTA-licensed establishments.

> 28. Individuals may also indicate their choice to donate their bodies for anatomical examination in their will. In this case, an individual should be encouraged to complete and return a consent form from the facility of their choice and to insert a copy in their will. The potential body donor should be made aware that, although a consent form does not have to be used in their will, to avoid confusion the wording of their consent should resemble the wording on the consent form provided by the establishment to which they wish to donate their body.

## 20.2.2   Other purposes

Consent for other purposes, for example organ donation, does not have to be in writing. Written consent is, of course, advisable for the avoidance of doubt.

Although such consent can be included in the will, speed is essential for transplants. It is, therefore, important to have some way of making doctors aware of the donor's wishes. Donor cards are useful but the most effective method is registration on the NHS Organ Donor Register (see www.organdonation.nhs.uk/register-to-donate/register-your-details/).

It is possible to appoint a representative under section 4 of the HTA 2004 to deal after death with the issue of consent. Such an appointment may be made orally in the presence of at least two witnesses present at the same time (section 4(4)) or in writing, in which case section 4(5) provides that it is valid only if it is:

(a)     signed by the person making it in the presence of at least one witness who attests the signature;

(b)     signed at the direction of the person making it, in his presence and in the presence of at least one witness who attests the signature; or

(c)     contained in a will made in accordance with the requirements of section 9 of the WA 1837, or Article 5 of the Wills and

Administration Proceedings (Northern Ireland) Order 1994 (SI 1994/ 1899 (NI 13)).

The decision of the representative will override decisions of other individuals, including family members. If the person appointed is incapable of giving consent, the appointment is disregarded (section 3(7) of the HTA 2004). If it is not reasonably practicable to communicate with the person appointed within the time available, the person will be treated as incapable of giving consent.

Where the deceased neither gave consent nor appointed a representative, a person who stood in a qualifying relationship to the deceased immediately before death can give consent on the deceased's behalf after the death (section 3(4) of the HTA 2004). Section 54 of the HTA 2004 defines qualifying relationships as follows:

(a)    spouse or civil partner;

(b)    partner;

(c)    parent;

(d)    child;

(e)    brother or sister;

(f)    grandparent;

(g)    grandchild;

(h)    child of a brother or sister;

(i)    step-parent;

(j)    half-brother, half-sister;

(k)    friend of long standing.

## 20.2.3    Should the wishes be included in the will?

If the deceased's wishes are included in the will, they are legally effective and so, to this extent, it is sensible to include them. However, in the case of organ donation, it is much more important to register and to ensure that all family members, partners and friends are aware of the deceased's wishes.

# 21 Practical Issues when Taking Instructions and at Execution

This chapter is in the nature of a checklist of matters mainly covered already in previous chapters. It deals in turn with:

(a) preliminary matters;

(b) terms of the will;

(c) executing wills.

## 21.1 Preliminary matters

### 21.1.1 Time frame

The speed with which a will should be prepared varies according to circumstances. In *White v Jones* [1995] 3 FCR 51, a testator gave instructions for a will in mid-July and died on 14 September. The firm instructed had not prepared the will and was held liable in negligence to the disappointed beneficiaries.

In *X (A Child) v Woollcombe-Yonge* [2001] WTLR 301, a solicitor was alleged to have been negligent on the basis that the testatrix, whom he knew to be suffering from terminal cancer, died before he had prepared the will. It would have been ready for execution 8 days after taking instructions. Neuberger J held that, on the facts, the amount of time taken was not unreasonable. It was significant that the testatrix was not expected to die in the near future and that she had suggested contacting the solicitor early in the following week to give him new contact details. Neuberger J went on to say:

> Where there is a plain and substantial risk of the client's imminent death, anything other than a handwritten rough codicil prepared on the spot for signature may be negligent. It is a question of the solicitor's judgment based on his assessment of the client's age and state of health.

An adviser who is preparing a will for a client should agree a time frame giving the client an opportunity to explain any time constraints such as approaching holidays or medical treatments. Provided the agreement is complied with, the adviser should be protected from liability. It goes without saying that advisers who break appointments for their own convenience will be exposed to a risk of negligence claims if the client dies before the will is prepared (see *Hooper v Fynemores (A Firm)* [2001] WTLR 1019).

### 21.1.2    Emergencies

As explained above, there may be occasions where a will is required urgently.

Professional advisers who are asked to prepare a will in a very short period need to consider whether they feel they can do a satisfactory job in the time allowed.

Obviously, complex tax planning is not something to be undertaken in such cases. The focus will be the dispositive provisions that the testator wants to make.

Remember though that what may be intended as a short-term will may, in fact, be the only will that the client ever makes. It is, therefore, important to make provision for survivorship periods and substitutional gifts and to describe property in such a way that the risk of ademption is minimised.

Where the major concern is to prevent the application of the intestacy rules and the testator is not certain what provisions to include, the most satisfactory solution may be to leave everything to a discretionary trust. The testator can leave a letter of wishes to guide the trustees. If the trustees appoint assets out of the trust within 2 years of death, the appointments will be read back into the will under section 144 of the IHTA 1984 (see para 17.2.1).

### 21.1.3    Cost

What is the fee for drafting the will? Advisers should be careful to leave no ambiguities. Does the fee extend to advice on related topics such as tax-efficient wills and the possibility of a challenge to the will after death under the I(PFD)A 1975? Does it cover overseeing execution of the will? Does it cover storage of the will?

### 21.1.4    Appointment of executors and trustees

There is no need to appoint a professional executor but there are circumstances, such as a divided family or a complicated estate, where having an expert is extremely helpful. An expert will charge and the basis of charging should be made clear to the client.

If a friend or family member is appointed, there may well be professional charges in any event if problems arise which are beyond the capability of the lay executor (see, further, Chapter 11).

On 6 May 2014, the SRA issued ethics guidance called, *Drafting and preparation of wills* (updated 11 July 2014), which dealt with the topic of appointment of the person preparing the will or the firm as executors. While stating that there was nothing inherently improper in such an appointment, it went on to set out the matters that those regulated by the SRA should consider and the steps that the will drafter should take as follows:

- You must not exploit your client's lack of knowledge for your own advantage by leading the client to believe that appointing a solicitor is essential or indeed the norm.

- You have a duty to act in your client's best interests. It would not therefore be proper to encourage the client to appoint you or your firm unless it is clearly in the client's best interests to do so. Whilst it may be beneficial to appoint a solicitor to act as an executor in certain circumstances (e.g. where the client's affairs are complex, or there are potential disputes in the family or all the beneficiaries are minors) there may be no advantage where, for example, the estate is small or straightforward. A professional executor is likely to be more expensive than a lay one and the client should be advised accordingly. Appointment of you or your firm should not be presented to clients as the default position either in on line or face to face services.

- Before drafting a will which appoints you or your firm as executor(s), you should be satisfied that the client has made the decision on a fully informed basis. You should therefore:

    - explain the options available to the client.

    - ensure the client understands that the executor(s) do not have to be professionals; that they may be a family member or a beneficiary under the will; and that lay executors can choose to instruct a solicitor to act for them if this proves necessary and will be indemnified out of the estate for the solicitors' fees.

    - document the advice given concerning appointment of executors and the client's decision on the file.

On 24 July 2018, the Law Society published a Practice Note, *Appointment of a professional executor*, which deals with the issues involved.

The Practice Note may be viewed at:

> www.lawsociety.org.uk/support-services/advice/practice-notes/appointment-of-a-professional-executor/

### 21.1.5    Is there any reason to doubt the testator's capacity or suspect undue influence?

If the testator is elderly or ill, the golden rule suggests obtaining a medical opinion as to capacity to make a will (see para 3.5.2). It is increasingly difficult to find a general practitioner (GP) who is willing to do this. Where a GP agrees to provide a report, the will drafter must provide a clear written explanation of the test of testamentary capacity. The test is set out in *Banks v Goodfellow* [1870] LR 5 QB 549 and requires the testator to understand:

(a)    the nature of the act and its effects;

(b)    the extent of the property of which he is disposing;

(c)    the claims he ought to consider.

In addition, the testator must not be suffering from a delusion which 'poisons his affections' (see, further, para 3.3).

There are several specialist organisations which exist to provide capacity reports for a variety of purposes, including the making of a will. Many practitioners find that using these organisations is preferable to using a GP because the report writers are experts and familiar with the various tests of capacity. In addition they will normally provide the report in a timely manner.

In the absence of medical evidence, the person taking instructions for the will should ask open questions designed to establish whether the test is satisfied and record the results in an attendance note.

Instructions should be taken, if possible, in the absence of anyone who stands to benefit from the will to avoid any later suggestion of undue pressure.

### 21.1.6    Does the testator have an earlier will?

If so, the terms should be considered and an explanation sought for any changes. Such a discussion will often reveal problems that would otherwise be unnoticed.

For example, a will may include a statement that it is a mutual will and is not to be revoked after the death of the other party. It may refer to persons whom the testator cannot remember, which may throw doubt on his testamentary capacity.

### 21.1.7    Family and marital status

The person preparing the will needs details of family and marital status to assess what, if any, tax planning needs to be done and the chances of a challenge to the will after death under the I(PFD)A 1975 (see para 2.2).

Single clients should be warned that the will is automatically revoked by marriage or the formation of a civil partnership.

When making wills for cohabitees some practitioners suggest including a statement that the couple are intending to marry or form a civil partnership and do not want the wills revoked by subsequent marriage or formation of a civil partnership, even though there is no immediate intention to do so. The wills remain valid even if the couple remain single but for the avoidance of doubt it is sensible to include a statement that the wills are not conditional on marriage or formation of a civil partnership.

If the client has young children, the question of guardians needs to be considered. Who will do it and what access will they have to the assets of the deceased? Guardians often need a bigger house to accommodate the extra numbers. Trustees will need powers to authorise them to use trust funds to buy a property with the guardians (see Chapter 12).

### 21.1.8    Extent of property owned or likely to be owned

The person preparing the will needs to know what assets the client has in order to form a view on whether inheritance tax is likely to be payable. A person's assets may be relatively modest at the date of the will but they may expect to inherit substantial amounts or they may own a business which is becoming increasingly successful.

There may be assets which present particular problems. A farmhouse is eligible for 100% agricultural property relief on its agricultural value but it is often difficult to predict whether HMRC will accept that a property is a farmhouse; the property must be of 'a character appropriate' to the agricultural land (see para 16.3 as regards agricultural property relief).

It is sensible to remind clients that they should consider how executors will identify and access online assets. For example, Bitcoin wallets cannot be accessed without the appropriate key, so potentially valuable assets may be lost to the family. Similarly, how will the family know about online bank accounts?

### 21.1.9    Are any assets owned jointly with another person?

If so, are they owned as beneficial joint tenants (in which case, they will pass to the survivor irrespective of the terms of the will) or are they owned as beneficial tenants in common (in which case, each co-owner is free to deal with his own share of the property by will)?

A beneficial joint tenancy can be severed, in which case it will become a beneficial tenancy in common. The easiest way to sever is to serve a notice on the other joint owner under section 36(2) of the LPA 1925. Serving notice is a unilateral act so it does not matter that the other joint tenant has lost capacity. Alternatively, notice can be served on a person appointed as a deputy or on an attorney acting under a lasting or enduring power of attorney (for a person who has lost capacity, see *Quigley v Masterson* [2011] EWHC 2529 (Ch)).

Serving notice is not the only way to sever a joint tenancy. The old equitable ways of severing were expressly preserved by section 36(2). These were set out in *Williams v Hensman* (1861) 1 J & Hem 546 as follows:

(a)    an act of any one of the persons interested acting upon his own share (e.g. charging the share as security for a debt);

(b)    mutual agreement; or

(c)    a course of dealing sufficient to indicate that the interests of all were mutually treated as constituting a tenancy in common.

(See also *Re Woolnough, Perkins v Borden* [2002] WTLR 595, *Carr v Isard* [2007] WTLR 409 and *Quigley v Masterson* [2011] EWHC 2529 (Ch).)

Severing a joint tenancy is often a necessary first step to allow a will to deal with the testator's share effectively. An adviser who allows a client to make a will without explaining the need for severance will be liable in negligence to the disappointed beneficiary (see, further, para 14.1).

Sometimes assets are in joint names purely as a matter of convenience. For example, an elderly person may put a bank account into joint names with an adult child so that the child can operate the account on behalf of the parent with no intention of transferring beneficial ownership to the child. It is advisable for the client to make sure that everyone involved understands the true position and to leave a written statement to avoid uncertainty and argument after death (see *Re Northall deceased* [2010] EWHC 1448 (Ch), where there was no intention to make a beneficial gift and *Aroso v Coutts* [2002] 1 All ER (Comm) 241, where there was).

## 21.1.10   Is there anyone who might assert a claim to assets of the client after death?

For example, where two people have cohabited in a property owned by one, the other often claims an interest in the property on the basis of an alleged contribution to the purchase price or money spent improving the property.

There used to be a presumption of a resulting trust which meant that the person contributing would be presumed to have an interest proportionate to the contribution.

Since the House of Lords' decision in *Stack v Dowden* [2007] UKHL 17, the presumption in a domestic consumer context is that beneficial title follows legal title. Hence, a person who claims that the beneficial ownership is in different hands from the legal ownership must produce evidence to prove this. So, in sole ownership cases the burden of proof falls upon the non-owner to show that he has any interest at all. In joint ownership cases, the burden falls upon the joint owner who claims to have something greater than a joint beneficial interest. See also the Supreme Court decision in *Jones v Kernott* [2011] UKSC 53, which explained some difficulties that had arisen in interpreting *Stack v Dowden*.

What does in 'the domestic consumer context' mean? In *Adekunle v Ritchie* [2007] WTLR 1505, the court held that it is not limited to cohabiting couples living together in a platonic or sexual relationship but can extend to a purchase by family members.

However, the purpose of the purchase may be significant. In *Laskar v Laskar* [2008] EWCA Civ 347, [2008] All ER (D) 104 (Feb), the Court of Appeal held that where property was purchased jointly as an investment, albeit by a mother and daughter, it was not appropriate to apply the presumption of joint beneficial ownership. Despite the familial relationship between the parties, it was clear that the purchase was nothing more than a business venture. Both parties led separate and distinct lives and maintained separate and distinct finances. The relationship was one between investors, and the presumption of joint beneficial ownership did not apply in such circumstances. Accordingly, there was nothing more than a resulting trust, and each party was entitled to the value of her own contribution.

The Privy Council took a more nuanced view in *Marr v Collie* [2017] UKPC 17 holding that where a property was bought in the joint names of a cohabiting couple as an investment, it did not follow inexorably that the 'resulting trust solution' provided the inevitable answer as to how its beneficial ownership was to be determined. It was entirely conceivable that partners in a relationship would buy, as an investment, property which was conveyed into their joint names with the intention that the beneficial ownership should be shared equally between them, even though they contributed in different shares to the purchase. Where there was evidence to support such a conclusion, it would be both illogical and wrong to impose the resulting trust solution on the subsequent distribution of the property. Depending on the parties' intention the correct result might be either a resulting trust or a division on the same basis as the legal title.

Ideally, the true position should be agreed and documented during the joint lifetime. However, often people are unwilling to 'stir up trouble' by discussing the matter. A statement of the client's view will at least ensure that both sides are presented in a later dispute.

### 21.1.11    Has the client made promises to leave property to anyone?

Testators are free to change their mind and renege on their promises. However, if the other party has relied on the promise to his detriment, the court may find that it would be unconscionable for the promise not to be kept even if there was not initially a legally binding contract. This is called proprietary estoppel.

If the elements of proprietary estoppel are established, the promisee will not necessarily get exactly what he has been promised. The court will order the minimum necessary to avoid an unconscionable result (see, further, para 2.5).

### 21.1.12    Inheritance tax considerations

Has the client made any gifts within the past 7 years or transferred any property on lifetime trusts? If so, the amount of tax payable on the death estate will be increased because the gifts and trusts will have used up some or all of the deceased's nil rate band. If the lifetime gifts or trusts exceed the nil rate band, inheritance tax will be payable on the excess if the client dies within 7 years.

Is the client a widow, widower or surviving civil partner? If so, he or she may benefit from a proportion of the nil rate band transferred from the first to die (section 8A–C of the IHTA 1984). This will mean that less of the client's estate will be chargeable to inheritance tax at 40%.

It may be appropriate to take into account the impact of inheritance tax when deciding what dispositions to make in the will. For example, leaving a residence or interest in a residence to a lineal descendant will normally obtain an additional nil rate band for the estate (see, further, Chapters 16 and 17).

### 21.1.13   Identifying beneficiaries

It is important to obtain correct names and addresses for individuals and institutions.

Where a testator wants to make charitable gifts, it is important to check the charity's registration number to ensure that: (a) it is a registered charity; and (b) it is accurately identified. Brightman J said in *Re Recher's Will Trust* [1972] Ch 526 that it was the draftsman's 'elementary duty' not only to get the name right, but also to ensure that the institution was in existence at the date of the will.

## 21.2   Terms of the will

### 21.2.1   Are the wills to be mutual?

If there is an agreement that property is to be left in a particular way and that the will is not to be revoked without the consent of the other party, the terms of the agreement should be set out in the will to make sure that there is no uncertainty after the first party's death (see *Charles v Fraser* [2010] EWHC Civ 2124, where the judge was very critical of a draftsman who had not recited the agreement in wills intended to be mutual).

Conversely, if parties are making 'mirror wills' which they do not intend to be mutual, it may be worth stating expressly that the wills are not intended to be mutual and that each party is free to change the disposition of his or her estate at any time. Again, this will make the position clear and avoid acrimonious argument after the death of the parties (see *Birch v Curtis* [2002] EWHC 1158 (Ch), [2002] 2 FLR 847, *Legg v Burton* [2017] EWHC 2088 (Ch) and see, further, para 2.3).

### 21.2.2   Are gifts to be free of tax or subject to inheritance tax?

Unless the will provides otherwise, the inheritance tax on legacies of UK property is paid from the residue of the estate (or property passing on intestacy). Testators need to appreciate this as the impact of inheritance tax may substantially reduce the amount available to the residuary beneficiary.

Inheritance tax on lifetime gifts, foreign property and property passing by survivorship is not normally payable from residue (or property passing on intestacy). Unless the will provides otherwise, the person taking the property will bear the burden of the tax. Again, the testator needs to consider whether this is satisfactory (see, also, para 22.3.1).

### 21.2.3    Are gifts of specific assets to be free of expenses?

Unless the will provides otherwise, a person who is left a specific legacy has to bear the costs of packing, transporting, etc the asset once the executor has assented the asset to the beneficiary. If the cost is likely to be significant, the testator may wish to direct that it is to be paid from residue (see para 15.3.4).

### 21.2.4    What is to happen to personal possessions?

Personal possessions are usually referred to as personal chattels, which is the expression used in the section 55(1)(x) of the AEA 1925 (see, further, para 13.5.1).

Dealing with personal chattels offers particular challenges. Personal chattels often include items of sentimental value, which may hold an importance disproportionate to their value for the testator and the beneficiaries. Testators often want to make gifts of particular items to a long list of individuals. It is rarely satisfactory to include the list in the will as every time the testator wants to make a change to the list, there will have to be a new will or codicil.

There are various options when it comes to dealing with personal chattels efficiently including:

(a)    to give named individuals the right to select one or more items;

(b)    to give the personal chattels to an individual (or the executors) with a request in the will that the individual gives effect to the testator's wishes as set out in an accompanying document. This allows the testator to change the wishes without having to execute a new will or codicil.

(See, further, paras 13.3.2, 13.3.3 and 13.3.4.) Whatever is decided, the effect of the provision must be clearly explained to the testator and careful drafting is essential to avoid any problems or misunderstandings.

### 21.2.5    Are pecuniary legacies to be contingent or absolute?

In the case of adults, legacies will normally be absolute but legacies to young children will normally be contingent on reaching a certain age, typically 18,

21 or 25. If the amounts are substantial it will normally be preferable to use a trust (see paras 21.2.6 and 21.2.7). If the subject matter is a residence or interest in a residence, it is important to consider whether the gift in its proposed form will attract the RNRB. See Chapters 16 and 17.

## 21.2.6    Are parents or guardians to have power to give the executors a receipt on behalf of minors?

Before the Children Act 1989, neither parents nor guardians had power to give a good receipt to executors on behalf of a minor beneficiary unless the will authorised it. Executors, therefore, had to hold the funds (or appoint separate trustees under section 42 of the AEA 1925) until the minor reached the age of 18 and could give a receipt.

The effect of sections 3 and 5 of the Children Act 1989 is to give parents and guardians that power.

In divided families, this may not be acceptable and so the will should state expressly that the executors must retain the funds until the minor reaches the age of 18 and can give a good receipt for the money. Alternatively, the legacy can be left on trust (see para 21.2.7).

## 21.2.7    Are assets to be left absolutely or on trust?

Many people dislike trusts, thinking them expensive and cumbersome, but they are an excellent way to protect assets.

EXAMPLE 1

> Fred, aged 65, has married Flossie, aged 67. They each have children from their previous marriages. They have bought a bungalow together and want to ensure that the survivor can live in it. They also want to pass their own assets on to their children.
>
> If they each leave their share of their assets on trust to the other for life, and then leave the capital to their children, they will achieve exactly what they want. The survivor will have the right to occupy the bungalow and to take the income from any invested capital but the capital will be preserved for the children. The assets of the first to die will also be protected from care home fees if the survivor has to go into residential care.

EXAMPLE 2

> Maude, a widow, has a substantial estate. She wants to leave the residue to her children but would like to leave each of her six grandchildren £50,000 contingent on them reaching the age of 25. If

she words the gifts as legacies, the executors will invest the money until each child reaches the age of 25 but unless the will makes express provision for the payment of income, the effect of section 175 of the LPA 1925 is that the grandchildren will not be entitled to the income earned by the funds. This will be paid to the residuary beneficiaries (see para 18.1) unless the will provides to the contrary.

Neither will the grandchildren be entitled to any capital growth; they will simply be entitled to £50,000 at the age of 25.

If Maude leaves £300,000 to trustees to hold on trust for her grandchildren contingent on reaching the age of 25, the rules are different. The grandchildren will benefit from the income produced which under section 31 of the Trustee Act 1925 can be applied for their benefit or accumulated. They will also share in any capital appreciation on the fund.

### 21.2.8     Need for review

It is important that testators are aware of the need to review wills. Pecuniary legacies may become derisory as a result of inflation. Conversely, they may become disproportionately large if the testator becomes less wealthy.

Beneficiaries may predecease. It is possible to provide for a substitutional beneficiary at the time the will is prepared, but it may be more satisfactory to recast the will if a major beneficiary predeceases.

Assets which have been specifically bequeathed may be sold leading to ademption. It is possible to provide in the will for a cash gift to be given to a beneficiary whose interest is adeemed but there are difficulties in fixing the value of the legacy. It is preferable to word the legacy to avoid ademption so far as possible.

For example, rather than giving 'the house in which I am currently living', give 'the house in which I am living at the date of my death'.

## 21.3     Executing wills

### 21.3.1     Supervised execution

As part of the will-making process, a person preparing a will for a client should offer to oversee execution, if the client wishes (see *Esterhuizen v Allied Dunbar Assurance plc* [1998] 2 FLR 668). This may involve a home visit or the client coming to the office.

If the person who prepared the will is overseeing execution, he should check the following matters:

(a)    The testator understands and is happy with the content of the will. If the will is complicated, it is better to explain the terms in 'bite sized chunks' rather than reading it out from beginning to end. In *Franks v Sinclair* [2006] EWHC 3365 (Ch), David Richards J commented that a complicated residuary gift was expressed in the 'customary technical language of wills, which most lay people will find impenetrable and many may consider to be gobbledegook'.

(b)    The testator signs or acknowledges an earlier signature in the presence of both witnesses present at the same time.

(c)    Each witness signs or acknowledges an earlier signature in the presence of the testator.

(d)    The witnesses must not be beneficiaries nor married to, or a civil partner of, a beneficiary.

(e)    Any 'last minute' alterations made on the face of the will are initialled by the testator and witnesses.

(f)    Where two people are making wills in virtually identical terms, make sure that each signs his or her own will and not the other person's.

## 21.3.2    Clear instructions for unsupervised execution

Testators are free to execute wills at home, but any professional who prepares a will which is to be executed at home should give clear instructions as to the order of events and as to who cannot be a witness.

## 21.3.3    Testator unable to sign

A testator who is unable to sign, because of either frailty or an injury, can make a mark which is intended to give effect to the will, or someone can sign on his behalf, but the signing must be in the testator's 'presence' and by his direction (see section 9(a) of the WA 1837 and *Barrett v Bem* [2011] EWHC 1247 (Ch)).

The attestation clause should state what has happened and include a statement that the testator knew and approved the contents of the will, as this is not presumed unless the testator actually signs the will (see, further, para 4.3.3).

## 21.3.4    Will returned for storage

Where a will that has been executed elsewhere is returned to a professional for storage, it should be inspected to check that everything appears to be in order (see *Humblestone v Martin Tolhurst Partnership* [2004] EWHC 151 (Ch)).

The preparation of a will for a client is normally 'an entire contract', i.e. a self-contained piece of work. Hence, when the work is completed and the final bill is submitted, there is no further obligation to the client unless the parties have agreed otherwise. This means that the person who prepared a will is normally under no obligation to inform the client of changes to the law which may affect the disposition of his estate – although, of course, the person may choose to do so. An agreement to store a will for a client does not of itself create any retainer, although the parties may agree otherwise.

Are family members to be told who is storing the will? If not, how will they know where the will is to be found? It is possible to register a will with professional organisations such as Certainty, the National Will Register. Alternatively, wills can be stored with the Probate Registry. See para 10.1.

On 6 May 2014, the SRA issued ethics guidance called *Drafting and preparation of wills* (updated 11 July 2014), which said that it may be in a client's best interests to use the low cost Probate Registry service rather than pay a firm or bank for storage. The guidance continues as follows:

> Other clients may prefer to have their will stored locally by you or their bank, where it can be retrieved readily and speedily by their executors or if they wish to alter their will. You should advise your client of the options available, but whatever your client decides, the key point is to ensure your client understands the importance of the executor(s) knowing where to find the will following the client's death. You should therefore advise your client to
>
> - ensure that the executors know where to find the will;
> - keep a copy of the will at home with the relevant details;
> - keep you informed of their new address if the client moves; and
> - keep the will under regular review.

# 22 Tips on Avoiding Drafting Pitfalls

Any number of mistakes can be made in a will but by and large they can be grouped under three headings:

(a)   failing to make provision for an event;

(b)   internal inconsistencies;

(c)   ignorance of a legal rule.

## 22.1    Failing to make provision for an event

Sometimes the failure is the result of not foreseeing that a particular event may occur; sometimes it is simply a careless error in the drafting.

### 22.1.1    Deaths occurring in 'wrong' order

People often assume that deaths will always occur in the 'right' order so that the older dies before the younger but this need not always be the case. Testators should always test out the will by considering what will happen if deaths occur in an unexpected order.

In the interests of certainty it is usually desirable to include a survivorship clause requiring a beneficiary to survive the testator by a certain period with a gift over to someone else if they do not.

EXAMPLE

Morag is a widow. She has three children, Ann, Ben and Colin.

Ann is married to Don whom Morag dislikes; they have one daughter, Zena.

Ben is married to Eva and has no children.

Colin and Morag are estranged and she has not seen him for 20 years.

Morag is seriously ill in hospital. Ann and Ben are involved in a car accident on the way to the hospital. Ben dies immediately. Morag dies later the same day. Ann dies on the following day.

Morag's will leaves everything to Ann and Ben in equal shares; there is no survivorship or substitutional gift.

Ann and Ben have wills which leave everything to their spouses.

Ann survives Morag so her half of the residue forms part of her estate. It will, therefore, pass under the terms of her will or under the intestacy rules if she has no will. Either way, it is likely to pass to her husband, Don.

Ben predeceased Morag and so his half share lapses. The residue was left in equal shares, which means that Ann and Ben were each entitled to one half. Ben's share does not pass to Ann; it is undisposed of property and will pass to those entitled on Morag's intestacy. This will be those of her children who survive her and reach the age of 18 or marry earlier. The lapsed half share of residue will, therefore, be divided between Ann's estate and Colin.

If Morag had been asked what she would want to happen in this scenario, she would probably have said that she would want her estate to be held on trust for Zena.

This could have been achieved by drafting the will as follows:

(a)    any beneficiary who fails to survive by 28 days is deemed to have predeceased;

(b)    if Ann or Ben predecease, their share is to be held on trust for their children or remoter issue, if any;

(c)    if Ann or Ben die without issue, their share is to be added to the share of the other;

(d)    if all the above gifts fail, the property is to go to a default beneficiary.

Remember, though, that survivorship clauses can only affect the disposition of property passing by will. They will not affect the disposition of property passing by survivorship (see para 22.1.3). Also, there can be circumstances (usually as between spouses and civil partners) where a survivorship clause is unhelpful (see para 22.1.2).

## 22.1.2    Survivorship clause resulting in double payment of pecuniary legacies

As explained at para 15.5.5, a survivorship clause can sometimes produce adverse inheritance tax consequences for spouses or cohabitees who are leaving everything to the other with the same substitutional provisions if the other predeceases. It is common to exclude the effect of a general survivorship on gifts to the surviving spouse or civil partner.

However, there is another possible problem in relation to survivorship clauses.

Two testators (usually spouses or civil partners but sometimes cohabitees, siblings or close friends) may agree that the estate of the first to die is to pass to the survivor and that on the survivor's death a number of pecuniary legacies – to relatives, friends, charities, etc – should be paid.

Each will has to include the legacies as no one knows what the order of deaths should be but, unless the will is carefully drafted, the legacies may be paid both on the first death and on the second death.

*Jump v Lister* [2016] EWHC 2160 (Ch) is an example of the problem. An elderly couple died in circumstances where the order of deaths was uncertain. The wife was the elder. The husband's will left everything to his wife but if she predeceased him, he left a number of substantial pecuniary legacies and a gift of residue to two nieces. The wife's will left everything to her husband but if he predeceased her, she left the same pecuniary legacies and made the same residuary gift. Unfortunately, both wills included a general survivorship clause which provided that any beneficiary who failed to survive by 28 days should be deemed to have predeceased.

The inclusion of the general survivorship clause was unfortunate.

The husband's gift to the wife obviously failed because she was deemed to have died first under section 184 of the LPA 1925 so the pecuniary legacies were payable.

The wife's gift to the husband failed because the general survivorship clause meant that he was to be treated as having predeceased, so the pecuniary legacies were payable a second time.

The result was that the amount taken by the nieces was significantly reduced as a result of what they claimed was the will drafter's negligence.

Where testators want to make pecuniary legacies payable only on the survivor's death, there are two ways of drafting the will:

(a)  Include a general survivorship clause but state that the legacies are to be halved if both deaths occur within the survivorship period.

(b)  Provide that the general survivorship period is not to apply to the gift to the survivor.

## 22.1.3  Joint property

A survivorship clause in a will affects only property passing under the will and not assets held jointly. Such assets pass to the survivor irrespective of the terms of the will. For many married couples and civil partners their major asset is the house and this is frequently held as beneficial joint tenants.

EXAMPLE

Anne and Ben own a house worth £800,000 as beneficial joint tenants and have £50,000 of other assets each. They each make wills leaving everything to the other, subject to surviving 28 days, with a gift over to their respective parents if the other fails to survive. Anne dies, followed 2 days later by Ben.

Anne's interest in the house passes by survivorship to Ben. Her parents inherit only the £50,000 of other assets. Ben's parents inherit the whole house plus Ben's other assets of £50,000.

Before making the will, Anne and Ben should have severed the joint tenancy, so that they held as tenants in common. They could then each have left their own share by will.

Alternatively, they could each have included a clause in their will saying that anything acquired as a result of the death of the other in the 28 days before death is to pass to the other's parents. This would cover the proceeds of life assurance policies as well as property passing by survivorship.

## 22.1.4   Mirror wills and gifts to agreed beneficiary

Couples sometimes want to leave a legacy to a mutual friend or relative. For example, Sami and Saleena want to give £10,000 to their niece, Nepota. Apart from this they want to give everything to the other with a gift over to charity if the other has predeceased or failed to survive by 28 days.

If each will says £10,000 to Nepota, residue to my spouse, Nepota will take £20,000 which is not what the couple want.

The will should say 'everything to my spouse but if my spouse predeceases, I give £10,000 to Nepota and the residue to charity'.

## 22.1.5   Ademption

As set out at para 8.3, specific gifts fail if the testator does not own assets corresponding to the description at the date of death. So a gift of 'the house in which I am now living' is ademed if the testator is living in a different house at the date of death. It is possible to draft more widely 'the house in which I am living at the date of my death' but this will not assist if the testator has no house at the date of death, having sold up and moved into residential care.

Similar problems can arise with company shares; if the company merges with another, the resulting organisation may be so different from the original that it is regarded as a completely different entity. A gift of shares in the original company will be adeemed.

It is often more satisfactory to leave important beneficiaries shares of residue rather than specific items to ensure that they all get something.

Alternatively, the bulk of the estate can be left to a discretionary trust. The trustees can then divide the available assets amongst the beneficiaries, taking into account the wishes of the testator as expressed in an accompanying letter of wishes.

Provided the assets are appointed out of the trust within 2 years of death, the estate will be treated for inheritance tax purposes as if left by the deceased to the appointees (see section 144 of the IHTA 1984 and para 17.2.1).

### 22.1.6 Failing to provide for one of two alternatives

A will may set out two alternatives but only explain what happens in one of them.

In *Hobart v Hobart* [2006] EWHC 1784 (Ch), Mr Hobart's will provided that if his wife survived him for 30 days his estate was to be held for her for life. If she failed to survive him for 30 days it was to be held for such of A, B, C and D as survived him equally if more than one and, in default, for Barnardo's absolutely.

There was no provision for the remainder interest after Mrs Hobart's death if, as occurred, she survived to take the life interest.

There was abundant evidence that Mr Hobart had intended the residue would pass to such of A, B, C and D as should be living at the death of Mr and Mrs Hobart. The draftsman was able to obtain rectification of the will under section 20 of the AJA 1982.

### 22.1.7 Not recognising that testator has a foreign will

As explained at para 5.3, it is important not to use a general revocation clause if the testator has a will dealing with foreign assets which he wants to remain effective. The revocation clause should be limited to wills dealing with assets in England and Wales or the United Kingdom or expressed to cover worldwide assets except for those in the foreign jurisdiction.

If limiting the effect of the will to assets in a particular place, be careful that the limitation is appropriate. In *Robinson v Royal Society* [2015] EWHC 3442 (Ch) a testator had already made a will dealing only with his assets in Switzerland and wanted a will to deal with his remaining assets. He gave an English firm of solicitors a list of the assets. The firm prepared a will limited to assets in the United Kingdom. The testator's major assets were bank accounts in the Channel Islands and the Isle of Man. The term 'United Kingdom' is limited to England and Wales, Scotland and Northern Ireland so, as drawn, the will did not deal with the bank accounts (see para 7.2.2).

## 22.2  Internal inconsistencies

### 22.2.1  Terminology

Defined terms are often used inconsistently. This is usually because clauses in the will have been taken from a variety of different sources. Such inconsistency can cause ambiguity and confusion.

EXAMPLES

(a)  At the beginning of the will, a clause appoints two people as executors and trustees and defines them as 'my Executors'. Later the will states that 'my Trustees shall have the following powers'.

(b)  A will directs that the testator's house is to be held for Larry for life, remainder to Rosie. It defines the property by name as 'The Willows'. Later the will makes various directions in relation to 'the Property' or 'the Property Fund'.

(c)  The will refers to 'my Residuary Estate', without the term having been defined at all.

### Inconsistent survivorship clauses

It is possible to attach a specific survivorship requirement to an individual gift or to include a general declaration that any beneficiary who fails to survive by a stated period is to be deemed to have predeceased (see para 22.1.1 and Appendix 1, clause 8.1 of the Will of James Matthew Appleby).

It is poor drafting to include both and will produce confusion if the stated survivorship periods are different.

*Shares of residue not adding up*

Faulty arithmetic may lead to the testator giving away more or less than the whole of the residue. In *Clarke v Brothwood* [2006] EWHC 2939 (Ch), [2006] All ER (D) 207 (Nov), the testator's will left the residue:

> 1/10 to a charity
>
> 1/10 to a charity
>
> 1/20 to a godchild
>
> 1/20 to a godchild
>
> 1/20 to a godchild
>
> 1/20 to a godchild

The effect was to leave 6/10 of the residue undisposed of. It was agreed that the intention had been to dispose of the entire residue in the proportions 10%, 10%, 20%, 20%, 20%, 20% and the draftsman was able to have the will rectified by the court under section 20 of the AJA 1982 (see para 7.6).

## 22.2.2    Late alterations

When making a last minute alteration to a will, it is very easy to introduce errors. In *Price v Craig* [2006] EWHC 2561 (Ch), an adviser had correctly drafted a will making various pecuniary legacies, and leaving the residue which was defined as 'the Trust Fund' to the children of friends of the testator. The testator then gave instructions that his wife was to have the right to any income from his share of the matrimonial home should it be sold, that the pecuniary legacies were only to be paid after his wife's death and only from the proceeds of sale of his property, and any balance was to be held for the same children.

The professional adviser amended the will to give all the estate to trustees and defined this as 'the Trust Fund'. The trustees were to hold the part of 'the Trust Fund' attributable to the proceeds of sale of the testator's share of the matrimonial home for the wife for life and this portion was defined as 'the Property Fund'. The will then went on to direct that 'the Property Fund' was to be divided amongst the children but never explained what was to happen to the rest of 'the Trust Fund' which was, therefore, undisposed of.

## 22.2.3    Unconditional conditions

Sometimes a clause which starts 'If X dies before me, the following provisions shall have effect' will include provisions, for example a professional charging clause, which are not intended to be conditional on

X's death. The converse is also common: a clause which is intended only to apply if X predeceases, is expressed to take effect unconditionally.

### 22.2.4   Dead trustee

It is common for couples to leave property to the other absolutely and if the other fails to survive on trust for a class of beneficiaries. Hence, the trust can only come into effect if the spouse is dead but wills often appoint the spouse as sole executor and trustee.

## 22.3   Ignorance of a legal rule

### 22.3.1   Burden of inheritance tax

If the will is silent, section 211 of the IHTA 1984 provides that the burden of tax will be a testamentary expense and therefore payable from residue if it is attributable to UK property which vests in the PRs and which is not immediately before death comprised in a trust in which the deceased had a qualifying interest in possession.

In the following cases, therefore, inheritance tax is not a testamentary expense but will fall on the person taking the property, unless the will provides otherwise:

(a)   foreign property;

(b)   property passing by survivorship, *DMC* (see para 1.3.1, *Donatio mortis causa*) or nomination (that is, property which does not vest in the PRs);

(c)   property comprised in a trust with a qualifying interest in possession immediately before the testator's death;

(d)   additional inheritance tax on lifetime gifts chargeable as a result of the testator's death;

(e)   property treated as part of the testator's estate as a result of the reservation of benefit rules (as in (b) above, the property does not vest in the PRs);

(f)   works of art and the like, where tax becomes payable as a result of sale or breach of an undertaking.

Hence, if a will dealing with UK property is silent, the burden of tax on specific and pecuniary legacies will fall on residue but the burden of tax on property passing by survivorship will fall on the surviving joint tenant, as will tax payable on lifetime gifts.

The effect of the statutory rules may be to reduce the residue or joint property unacceptably. The testator can change the effect but it is important to word the change in a way that achieves what the testator wants.

For example, a direction that 'inheritance tax payable on property passing under my will' is to be paid from residue merely restates the statutory position, whereas a direction to pay 'all inheritance tax *resulting* from my death' is much wider and throws the burden of all inheritance tax on to residue.

It is common for wills to restate the statutory position for the avoidance of doubt, usually by adding the words 'free of tax' to specific gifts and then directing that inheritance tax is to be paid from residue. It is important to be consistent. If some specific gifts are expressed to be free of tax and some are not, this may suggest that the beneficiaries taking the gifts which are not expressed to be free of tax are intended to bear the burden of tax.

## 22.3.2   Effect of section 41 of the Inheritance Tax Act 1984

In the case of gifts by will, testators are generally free to allocate the burden of tax as they wish. The only exception is section 41 of the IHTA 1984 which provides that, notwithstanding the terms of any disposition:

> none of the tax attributable to the value of the property comprised in residue shall fall on any gift of a share of residue if or to the extent that the transfer is exempt with respect to the gift.

The residue must be divided into shares and the tax on the non-exempt shares must be borne by those beneficiaries.

EXAMPLE

> Ted leaves his £1 million estate to be divided equally between his son, Sam and his wife. Ted has made no lifetime chargeable transfers and has not been married before so has no transferred nil rate band. The nil rate band at the date of his death is £325,000.
>
> Ted's wife will take £500,000. Sam's share suffers tax at 40% on £175,000 which amounts to £70,000. So he will only receive £430,000.
>
> If this result is explained to Ted when he is making his will, he may object on the basis that he wants his wife and son to receive the same amount. A direction in the will that the tax is to be paid and the net amount is to be divided equally will be ineffective because of section 41 of the IHTA 1984.

It is, however, possible to direct that the residue is to be divided *unequally* between the beneficiaries in such proportions that they each end up with the same amount.

The following clause achieves an unequal division:

> I declare that the shares of my estate of any beneficiaries who do not qualify for exemption from inheritance tax shall be deemed to be of amounts such that the amounts received, after payment of inheritance tax due, shall be the same for all the beneficiaries named in clause XX.

(See *Re Benham's Will Trusts* [1995] STC 210 for an example of such a clause, although the wording used in the will was rather obscure.)

Most taxpayers will not want the complexity of such a result. *Re Ratcliffe* [1999] STC 262 confirmed that a gift which merely directs an 'equal' division between exempt and non-exempt beneficiaries will not be construed as requiring an unequal division into pre-tax shares unless there was clear evidence of such a wish.

To make it clear that a testator accepts that the non-exempt and exempt beneficiaries will receive different amounts after tax, the following clause may be used:

> I declare that if the share in my estate of any beneficiary named in clause XX does not qualify for exemption from inheritance tax, that share shall bear its own tax so that the amount received by each beneficiary named in that clause is the same before the payment of inheritance tax.

## 22.3.3    Class gifts

Wills often contain gifts to a class of beneficiaries in the form 'to the children of X' or 'to the children of X who reach the age of 21'.

With such gifts it is necessary to decide whether the class is to remain open until all possible members have been ascertained (in which case, it will not be possible to distribute until all members have been ascertained) or whether it should close early to allow distribution to take place.

Convenience is in favour of early distribution but fairness suggests keeping the class open as long as there are potential entrants to the class.

The law in England and Wales is in favour of closing the class early to allow distribution. Class-closing rules are implied into wills unless the will provides otherwise. They operate to close the class as soon as there is a member who is entitled to immediate distribution. This facilitates the administration of the estate but can operate harshly in excluding members from benefit and cause family disharmony (see, further, para 7.7).

Failure to explain the effect of the rules to a testator may lead family members to allege negligence on the part of advisers.

EXAMPLES

  (a)  Grandma leaves £100,000 to be divided amongst her grandchildren. There are two grandchildren living at her death. The effect of the class closing rules is to close the class at Grandma's death and any future grandchildren will not benefit.

  (b)  Grandma leaves £100,000 to be divided amongst such of her grandchildren as reach the age of 25. There are two grandchildren living at her death, aged 22 and 20. No one is yet entitled to claim a share so the effect of the implied rules is that the class will remain open until the first grandchild reaches the age of 25. It will include any child born in the intervening period. Any grandchildren born after the class closes will not benefit.

Clearly, postponing distribution until all possible class members are identified is not a viable option as it would delay distribution unacceptably.

There is an alternative which allows distribution to those already entitled, while allowing additional members to be added – the 'best of both worlds' option. This may fit better with a testator's wishes. Obviously, the effect of the different options should be explained to the testator.

EXAMPLE

A testator makes a gift to his grandchildren contingent on reaching the age of 18. Three grandchildren, A, B and C are living at the date of death. A subsequently reaches the age of 18. After that date D and E are born. There are no further grandchildren.

Normally, the class will close as soon as A reaches the age of 18 with the result that D and E are excluded.

However, if the following clause is included the class will remain open after A has become entitled to a share, although the shares of the other class members will be smaller than the share taken by A:

My trustees shall hold the trust fund on trust absolutely for such of my grandchildren living at my death or born afterwards at any time during their parents' lifetime as reach the age of 18 or marry under that age and if more than one in equal shares PROVIDED that the share in the Trust Fund of any grandchild who has attained a vested interest shall not be diminished by the birth or marriage of or the attainment of the age of 18 by any further grandchildren.

Hence:

(a)   A takes one-third of the fund immediately;

(b)   B, C, D and E take one-quarter of the remaining fund at the age of 18.

## 'Spouse' does not include civil partner

The words 'spouse', 'husband' and 'wife' do not include civil partners, although somewhat confusingly they do include same sex spouses. Similarly, the word 'marriage' does not include civil partnerships but does include same sex marriages. If civil partners are to be included in a class of beneficiaries, it is necessary to say so.

EXAMPLE

'Marriage' is to include civil partnership as defined in section 1 of the Civil Partnership Act 2004 as amended and 'husband', 'wife', 'widower', 'widow', 'spouse' are to be construed accordingly.

## Meaning of 'child'

Children are first generation descendants. Issue are any generation, so can include grandchildren, great grandchildren, etc.

The Adoption Act 1976 provides that for testators dying after 31 December 1975 'children' includes adopted children. The FLRA 1987 provides that in any will or codicil made after 4 April 1988 references to children will include children whose parents were not married (unless the will provides otherwise).

Many precedents for wills exclude these provisions, so it is important to consider whether this is appropriate.

Children born as a result of assisted reproduction will be included (Human Fertilisation and Embryology Acts 1990 and 2008) even though not genetically related to their parents, as will surrogate children who are the subject of parental responsibility orders (see sections 54–56 of the Human Fertilisation and Embryology Act 2008) (see, also, para 7.8).

The word 'issue' does not include stepchildren (see *Reading v Reading* [2015] EWHC 946 (Ch)) (see para 7.2.2). If the intention is to include step-children, the will should say so expressly. The court may be willing to infer from the context that the word is being used in an extended sense to include step-children but no one wants a trip to court if it can be avoided.

## 22.3.4   Income and interest

*Income*

Immediate specific and residuary gifts carry with them the right to income produced by the assets.

Contingent and deferred gifts are governed by section 175 of the LPA 1925 and probably carry the right to income apart from deferred or deferred contingent residuary gifts of personalty but the position is not entirely clear.

It is normally preferable to make express provision for what is to happen to income produced during the period of deferral or contingency.

*Interest on pecuniary legacies*

Pecuniary legatees are entitled to interest to compensate them for late payment. Unless the will provides otherwise payment is normally due one year from the date of death and is at the rate which the court would order in the event of a dispute. According to CPR, PD 40, para 15, this is the rate payable on funds in court. At the time of writing this is a derisory 0.1% (rates are available from a table on the Court Funds Office section of the Justice website, www.justice.gov.uk).

It will normally be preferable to make express provision for the rate and period.

Unless the will provides otherwise, contingent pecuniary legacies do not carry the right to any interest (with limited exceptions: see, further, para 18.1.1). Interest earned on the legacy fund will, therefore, be paid to the person entitled to the residue of the estate. This is not normally what a testator wants and has adverse inheritance tax consequences as the residuary beneficiary will have an immediate post-death interest.

# Appendix 1
# A Family Will

This is an example of a will of a married man which, after giving some legacies, provides for everything to go to his wife if she survives for 28 days but, if not, it benefits such of his children as reach the age of 25. The will includes appropriate substitution and administrative provisions.

Following the will is a commentary on each clause, which aims at explaining its effect, as well as serving as an introduction to some of the terminology used elsewhere in this text.

# WILL OF JAMES MATTHEW APPLEBY

## 1. Identification and revocation

I, James Matthew Appleby of 'Black Gate', 12 Hoole Road, Westbridge, Hampshire WA8 1BJ revoke all former wills and declare this to be my last will ('my Will').

## 2. Appointment of executors and trustees

2.1    I appoint as my Executors and Trustees my wife Jane Appleby and my solicitor Peter Andrews of Montague & Co, Abbey Chambers, Westbridge, Hampshire WA1 3ES.

2.2    In my Will the expression 'my Trustees' means my Executors and the Trustees of my Will and of any trust arising under it.

2.3    Any of my Trustees who is engaged in a profession may charge fees for work done by them or their firm (whether or not the work is of a professional nature) on the same basis as if they were not one of my Trustees but employed to carry out the work on their behalf.

## 3. Appointment of guardians

If my wife dies before me, I appoint my sister Charlotte Riddell and her husband Andrew John Riddell, both of 27 The Old Green, Monks Heath, Hampshire WA6 3NM as guardians of any of my children who are under the age of eighteen.

## 4. Specific gifts

4.1    I give to my sister's husband, Andrew John Riddell, the car which I own at my death.

4.2    I give to my brother, Henry Appleby, my collection of antique clocks.

## 5. Pecuniary gift

I give one thousand pounds (£1,000) to the Westbridge Animal Refuge, registered charity number 6479035, for its general charitable purposes and declare that the receipt of the person appearing to be its treasurer or other proper officer shall be a sufficient discharge to my Trustees.

## 6. Gift of residue

Subject to the above gifts and to payment of my debts, funeral and testamentary expenses, I give all my estate to my wife Jane Appleby absolutely.

## 7. Substitutional gifts of residue

7.1    If my wife does not survive me or if this gift fails for any reason, I give all my estate subject to the gifts in clauses 4 and 5 above to my Trustees on trust to pay my debts, funeral and testamentary expenses.

7.2    Subject to clause 7.1 above, my Trustees shall divide my estate equally between my daughters, Charlene and Esme, provided they attain the age of 25.

7.3    If either of my daughters dies before attaining a vested interest leaving children, whether living at my death or born after, such children shall take (equally if more than one) the share of my estate which their mother would have taken had she survived me to attain a vested interest.

7.4    If the trusts of one half of my estate fail, that half is to be added to the other half.

## 8.  Declarations

8.1    Survivorship

Any beneficiary who is not proved to have survived me by twenty-eight days shall be treated as having died before me.

8.2    Charity ceasing to exist

If before my Trustees have given effect to any gift, any beneficiary which is a charity has ceased to exist, has changed its name, amalgamated with another charity or transferred its assets to another body, my Trustees shall give effect to such gift as if it had been a gift to the body in its new name or amalgamated form or to the body to which the assets were transferred.

## 9.  Trustees' powers

My Trustees shall in addition to and without prejudice to all statutory powers have the following powers and immunities, provided that they shall not exercise any of their powers so as to conflict with the beneficial provisions of my Will.

9.1    Advancement of capital

To pay or apply capital for the benefit of any one or more of my children or grandchildren as they think fit, provided that the capital advanced shall not exceed the vested or presumptive share in my estate of the beneficiary to whom it is made and all advances shall be taken into account on final distribution of my estate.

9.2    Maintenance

To apply or accumulate income in accordance with section 31 of the Trustee Act 1925 but subject to the following variation namely that throughout the section the age of twenty-one shall be substituted for eighteen and infancy shall mean the period before the attainment of twenty-one.

9.3    Investment

To invest as freely as if they were beneficially entitled.

9.4    Purchase of land

To apply money in the purchase or improvement of land or an interest in land in the United Kingdom or elsewhere on such terms as they may impose in their absolute discretion.

**Attestation**

Dated this      **8th**      day of      **June 2010**

Signed by the testator    )
in our joint presence     )              *James M Appleby*
and then by us in his     )

**Witness 1**

Signature:        *David Stephens*

Full name:        David Henry Stephens

Address:          18 Harby Avenue, Westbridge WA3 8FG

Occupation:     Teacher

**Witness 2**

Signature:        Hannah Stephens

Full name:        Hannah Rachel Stephens

Address:          18 Harby Avenue, Westbridge WA3 8FG

Occupation:     Designer

## Commentary on Mr Appleby's will

The words in bold are key terms referred to elsewhere in the text.

| | |
|---|---|
| **Clause 1 –** Introduction and opening words | This identifies the **testator** and states his full name to avoid dispute later as to whose will it is. |
| | It also includes a **revocation clause** to show that this will takes the place of any previous will. Even if this is Mr Appleby's first will, the clause avoids doubt as to whether or not there was an earlier will. |
| **Clause 2 –** Appointment of Executors and Trustees | Although it does not have to, a will should appoint one or more **executors** to administer the estate and carry out its terms. The executors apply to the **probate registry** for a **grant of probate** after death to confirm their authority to deal with the testator's assets. Here, a trust could arise under the will in clause 7, so it is usual to appoint the executors as trustees, although different people could have been appointed. The problem referred to at para 22.2.4 above will not arise. Although the trust can only come into effect if the wife dies, there is a second trustee who can act. |
| | Clause 2.3 is a professional charging clause which gives the solicitor, who is an executor, power to charge for his time and services in administering the estate. Generally, an executor is not allowed to charge for his time, although **section 29 of the Trustee Act 2000** does make some provision for professional executors to charge. Even so, it is good practice if a professional executor or trustee is appointed to include an express power to charge along the lines of clause 2.3 so that the testator is aware of the position. |
| **Clause 3 –** Appointment of guardians | A will can appoint **guardians** to look after the testator's minor children, although, as here, the appointment is usually worded to take effect only if the testator's spouse predeceases. |
| **Clauses 4.1 and 4.2 –** Specific gifts | A **specific gift** (or **specific legacy**) is a gift of a particular item of property owned by the testator (as distinct from any other property of the same kind). The testator must actually own the item at his death, otherwise the gift is said to **adeem** – or in other words, it fails. In this case the testator is referring to the car which he owns at his death. As long as he has a car at that time, the gift will not adeem, even if it is not the same car as that owned at the time the will was made. |
| | The gift in clause 4.2 can increase or decrease according to the number of clocks owned by the testator when he dies – only if he has none at all does the gift adeem. |

| | |
|---|---|
| **Clause 5** – Pecuniary gift | A **pecuniary gift** (or **pecuniary legacy**) is a gift of money. It is sometimes called a **general legacy** because, unlike a specific gift, it is not dependent on the testator having the precise amount of cash when he dies. In this case, if the testator had only a few hundred pounds in the bank, the charity would still get £1,000. The executors would sell assets in the estate (other than the subject matter of the specific gifts in clause 4) to raise the necessary cash. It should be noted that if the particular charity mentioned in the will no longer exists or changes its name or amalgamates with another charity, the legacy will still take effect – see clause 8.2 and the related commentary below. |
| **Clause 6** – Gift of residue<br><br>**Clause 7** – Substitutional gifts of residue | Clause 6 tells the executors to pay **debts, funeral and testamentary expenses** and pay what is left of the estate at this stage (usually called the **residue**) to Mr Appleby's wife.<br><br>Clause 7 goes on to say what happens if his wife does not survive him or the gift fails for some other reason (but see, also, clause 8.1 and the commentary). If a beneficiary dies before the testator, the gift will **lapse**. In this case, he provides for a **substitutional gift** so that his children will take if they attain the age of 25 (presumably, he thinks it unwise to let them have their inheritance before then). Since the children's interest is conditional on reaching the age of 25, they have a **contingent interest** whilst under that age. Once they reach the age of 25, they obtain a **vested interest**.<br><br>In clause 7.3, Mr Appleby has also contemplated the death of either or both children before the age of 25. He provides for a further substitution so that if they die before the age of 25 leaving children of their own, then those children (i.e. his grandchildren) will take their parent's share equally, although in the case of the grandchildren becoming entitled there is no expressed contingency and so their interests are absolute. This is to allow the estate to benefit from the RNRB. Gifts to grandchildren will not attract the RNRB if the grandchildren have contingent interests in a trust at the date of the deceased's death. An absolute interest means that the grandchildren will be entitled to claim the assets at 18. A testator needs to balance this disadvantage against the benefit of obtaining the additional RNRB on their death if inheritance tax is an issue. |

| | Mr Appleby is trying to ensure that whatever happens, his residue passes to his immediate family on the terms he wants. If a will contains a gift of residue which lapses (or there is no gift of residue at all), any property that is not disposed of by the will passes under the **intestacy rules** on a **partial intestacy**. The result may not be what the testator would have wanted. |
|---|---|
| **Clause 8** – Declarations | Having said who gets the property, the latter part of a will often includes provisions to assist with the interpretation of the will. |
| | Clause 8.1 is a **survivorship clause** to deal with the situation where, say, Mr Appleby and his wife die together in a common accident. There is little point in a beneficiary taking the testator's property if he or she does not live long enough to enjoy it. |
| | Clause 8.2 says what happens if a named charity has amalgamated, changed its name, etc. This is useful as it is reasonably common for charities to change their names or merge. It is also, sadly, common for charities to be wound up for lack of funds. |
| **Clause 9** – Trustees' powers | This clause provides the executors and trustees with **modified or extended powers**. These help them to administer the estate and any trust that arises, for example if the principal gift to Mr Appleby's wife fails for any reason and the substitution provision for the children takes effect. In this will, the extended powers are focused on ensuring there are sufficient financial and investment provisions available to deal with the children's entitlement pending them attaining a vested interest in capital. |
| **Attestation** | This part of the will includes the date which is written in when the will is executed. The date is sometimes inserted in the opening words. A will is not invalid for having no date, but problems can arise later in establishing whether it was made before or after any other will that turns up at the time of death. |
| | The testator and two witnesses sign to comply with the execution requirements of **section 9 of the WA 1837** (see Chapter 4). The wording immediately to the left of the testator's signature is the **attestation clause**, which raises a presumption that the will was correctly executed. Without such wording, the probate registry would require an **affidavit of due execution** to prove the correct procedure was carried out. |

# Appendix 2
# Intestacy Rules

Reference is made in Chapter 1 to the fact that making a will can avoid the application of the intestacy rules.

The following is a mere outline of how the intestacy rules apply. They justify a place in this book because they represent the default position if there is no will dealing with property that is nonetheless capable of being disposed of by will. Consequently, some knowledge of them is important to anyone involved in advising on the benefits of making a will. For further information, the reader should refer to a more detailed work.

The intestacy rules are derived from the AEA 1925, as amended, and apply only to property which is capable of being left by will.

EXAMPLE

Leticia dies without a will leaving her husband, Malcolm, and their two children. Leticia and Malcolm owned their house as beneficial joint tenants and had a joint bank account. Leticia had taken out a life assurance policy for £200,000 which she wrote in trust for the two children. She owned various investments worth £350,000.

Leticia dies intestate but the intestacy rules do not affect Leticia's share of the house or bank account (which pass to Malcolm automatically by survivorship). Nor do the rules affect the life policy (which passes to the children under the trust). Only her investments pass under the intestacy rules.

## 1 Order of entitlement on intestacy

The intestacy rules first direct payment of the funeral, testamentary and administration expenses, and any debts of the deceased. Any balance (after paying any pecuniary legacies in the will if it was a partial intestacy) is called the 'residuary estate' and section 46 of the AEA 1925 sets out who inherits it and in what order. Those entitled are divided into classes in descending order of entitlement as follows:

(a)    surviving spouse or civil partner, but if none,

(b)    issue on the 'statutory trusts', but if none,

(c)    parents, equally if both alive, but if none,

(d)    brothers and sisters of the whole blood on the 'statutory trusts', but if none,

(e)    brothers and sisters of the half blood on the 'statutory trusts', but if none,

(f)    grandparents, equally if more than one, but if none,

(g)    uncles and aunts of the whole blood on the 'statutory trusts', but if none,

(h)    uncles and aunts of the half blood on the 'statutory trusts', but if none,

(i)    the Crown, Duchy of Lancaster or Duke of Cornwall (as *bona vacantia*).

Some of the terms in this list require explanation.

A 'spouse' is the person of either sex married to the deceased at death, whether or not they were then living together. A divorced spouse is excluded (but only once the decree absolute is granted). A 'civil partner' means a party to a civil partnership registered by a same sex couple under the Civil Partnership Act 2004 as amended. In *Official Solicitor to the Senior Courts v Yemoh & others* [2010] EWHC 3727 (Ch), [2010] All ER (D) 213 (Dec), the court held that two or more persons could fall within the category of 'surviving spouse' for the purpose of section 46 of the AEA 1925 so that the surviving wives of a valid polygamous marriage could succeed to the husband's property on his death intestate.

The entitlement of the intestate's spouse or civil partner (but not other relatives) is in all cases conditional on that person surviving the intestate for 28 days. If he or she dies within 28 days, the estate is distributed as if he or she had not survived the intestate.

It is most important to note that a mere cohabitee, even if living with the intestate and no matter how long the relationship, has no *rights* under the intestacy rules. (However, such a person may have eligibility as an applicant for reasonable financial provision under the I(PFD)A 1975, or his or her circumstances may allow a claim against the estate on other grounds such as proprietary estoppel – see Chapter 2.)

'Issue' means straight blood line descendants – children, grandchildren, great grandchildren, and so on.

Brothers and sisters of the 'whole blood' have the same parents; brothers and sisters of the 'half blood' have one parent in common. If one of those half blood brothers or sisters has a child, the others become uncles and aunts of the half blood to the child.

Through all relationships, adopted, illegitimate and legitimated children have the same inheritance rights on intestacy as children born to married parents. Also, a person is treated as 'living' if they were *en ventre sa mère* at the intestate's death.

Some classes take on 'the statutory trusts', meaning that the class members take only if they fulfil certain conditions which will be mentioned later.

If there is no relative in any class who takes, the residuary estate is said to be *bona vacantia* (meaning vacant goods or ownerless property). The Crown, Duchy of Lancaster or Duke of Cornwall has discretion to provide for dependants, or for anyone for whom the intestate might reasonably have been expected to make provision. It is rare for an estate to be truly *bona vacantia* because genealogists can usually trace some relatives if the estate is large enough to meet the cost.

Subject to what is said below about a spouse or civil partner, classes are mutually exclusive and so as long as there is at least one person in a higher class, that person takes everything to the exclusion of those in lower classes.

EXAMPLE

> Iris has died intestate. She never married and had no children. Her father died before her. Her surviving relatives are her mother, her brother and her sister.
>
> Everything passes to her mother. Her brother and sister get nothing because they are in a lower class.
>
> If Iris's mother had also died before her, then in that case everything would be shared equally between her brother and sister on the statutory trusts.

The position is different if there is a surviving spouse or civil partner. Depending on the size of the estate, the spouse or civil partner may have to share the property if there are also issue in class (b) in the list above (see para 2 for an illustration).

# 2    Intestate dies on or after 1 October 2014 survived by spouse or civil partner and issue

This is a very common situation. If the intestate dies on or after 1 October 2014 survived by a spouse or civil partner *and issue*, the 'residuary estate' is distributed as follows:

(a)    The spouse or civil partner receives any 'personal chattels' absolutely. Personal chattels are defined in section 55(1)(x) of the AEA 1925 (as amended) (see main text, para 13.5.1) and may be summarised as movable tangible property being typically items of personal, household and ornamental use but not including cash or any items held solely as an investment nor items used solely or mainly for business purposes.

(b)    In addition, the spouse or civil partner receives a 'statutory legacy' of £250,000 free of inheritance tax and costs plus interest (at the Bank of England rate as at the date of death) from death until payment. If the residuary estate, apart from the personal chattels, is worth less than £250,000, the spouse or civil partner takes it all (and the issue will receive nothing).

(c)    If there is anything left of the residuary estate, it is divided into two equal Funds.

One Fund (A) is held on trust for the benefit of the spouse or civil partner absolutely while the other Fund (B) is held for the issue on the statutory trusts, the terms of which are as follows:

(a)    The main beneficiaries are the children of the intestate living at the intestate's death. Grandchildren (or other remoter issue) are not included, unless a child has died before the intestate (as to which, see (c) below).

(b)    The interests of the children are contingent on reaching the age of 18 (or marrying or forming a civil partnership under that age). Any child who already fulfils the condition at the intestate's death takes a vested interest. If a child dies *after* the intestate but without satisfying the condition, the child's interest fails and the estate is distributed as though that child had never existed. However, see (d) below.

(c)    If any child dies before the intestate, then any children of that deceased child living at the intestate's death take their parent's share equally between them, again on condition they reach the age of 18 or marry earlier or form a civil partnership. This form of substitution and division is known as a *per stirpes* distribution – meaning 'through the root'.

(d)    In the case of an intestate dying on or after 1 October 2014, a child who dies *after* the intestate but without having satisfied the contingency of reaching the age of 18 (or marrying or forming a civil partnership under that age) will be presumed to have died *immediately before* the intestate. The effect is that if the child so dying leaves any children, then those children can take their dead parent's share as in (c) above in the same way as if their parent had actually died before the intestate.

EXAMPLE

Joanne dies intestate survived by her husband, Kenneth, and their children, Mark aged 21 (who has a son, Quentin) and Nina aged 16. Their daughter, Lisa, died last year. Lisa's two children, Oliver and Paul (twins aged 3), are living at Joanne's death. Joanne had a house, held as joint tenants with Kenneth, and other property worth £565,000 after payment of debts, funeral and testamentary expenses. This figure includes personal chattels worth £15,000.

Joanne's share in the house passes to Kenneth automatically by survivorship. The rest of her estate passes under the intestacy rules as follows (assuming Kenneth survives by 28 days):

£15,000 personal chattels pass to Kenneth

£250,000 statutory legacy to Kenneth

£150,000 (Fund A) to Kenneth absolutely

£150,000 (Fund B) to issue on the statutory trusts

—————

£565,000

The statutory trusts apply to Fund B of £150,000 to determine the distribution between Joanne's issue and work this way.

Mark and Nina, Joanne's children, are living at her death and take one share each. The share Lisa would have taken had she survived is held for her children, Oliver and Paul, in equal shares. The interests of Nina, Oliver and Paul are contingent on attaining the age of 18 or earlier marriage or forming a civil partnership.

Mark has a vested interest in one-third of Fund B so is entitled to £50,000 on Joanne's death. If Mark should die shortly after Joanne, his share in Fund B forms part of his estate on death and so passes under his will if he left one.

Quentin has no direct entitlement under Joanne's intestacy because the substitution of grandchildren applies only if a child dies before the intestate, whereas Mark was alive at the date of Joanne's death having attained a bested interest. Nina has a contingent interest in one-third of Fund B which will vest when she reaches the age of 18 or if she marries or forms a civil partnership before the age of 18. If Nina should die under the age of 18 and without marrying or forming a civil partnership (and without leaving issue), her interest would fail. One half of Nina's share would pass to Mark and the other half would be held for Oliver and Paul equally.

Oliver and Paul have contingent interests in one-sixth of Fund B, which will vest when they reach the age of 18 or on earlier marriage or formation of a civil partnership. If Oliver should die under the age of 18 and without marrying or forming a civil partnership, his share would pass to Paul (and vice versa). If both Oliver and Paul were to die under the age of 18 and without marrying or forming a civil partnership, their shares would be divided equally between Mark and Nina. (Note, however, that if Oliver or Paul so died but left issue, then they would be treated as having died before Joanne (see (d) above) and so their respective shares would, instead, pass to their issue on the statutory trusts.)

# 3    Intestate dies on or after 1 October 2014 survived by spouse or civil partner but with no surviving issue

In this situation, if a person dies intestate on or after 1 October 2014 and there is a spouse or civil partner as before but no issue who survive (in the sense that they survive to acquire a vested interest under the statutory trust), then the spouse or civil partner takes the whole estate absolutely.

# 4    Intestate dies before 1 October 2014 survived by spouse or civil partner leaving either issue, or surviving parents or brothers and sisters of the whole blood or their issue

The rules of entitlement in paras 2 and 3 above were different for deaths before 1 October 2014. A surviving spouse or civil partner had more limited rights. For reasons of space we have not explained the old rules.

# 5 Distribution where there is no surviving spouse or civil partner

Where there is no surviving spouse or civil partner (or where the spouse or civil partner dies within 28 days of the intestate), the 'residuary estate' is divided between the relatives in the highest category in the list in section 46 of the AEA 1925 (see para 1 above).

EXAMPLE

> Tom dies intestate. He was not married to his partner, Penny, although the couple has a son, Simon, aged 13, Tom's only child. Tom's parents predeceased him but he is survived by his only sibling, his brother Bob, aged 40.
>
> Tom's estate is held on statutory trusts for Simon, contingently upon him attaining the age of 18 or marrying earlier. If Simon dies without leaving issue of his own before the contingency is fulfilled, Tom is treated as though he had died without issue and so Tom's estate passes to Bob absolutely.

It is worth noting by way of reminder that relatives in categories (c) to (h) of para 1 above can take only in a case where there is no surviving spouse or civil partner, and only then if there is no prior eligible issue in category (b) of para 1 above.

# Appendix 3
# Planning a Tax-efficient Will – Case Studies

## Case study A
## Providing for the family – Morva and Dan

Morva and Dan are married and have three children. They have a house worth £1 million which they own as beneficial joint tenants and other assets of about £800,000. They want the survivor to have the use of the combined assets and what is left is to go to the children.

They have these three main options:

(a)   *Option 1*: they can leave everything to the other absolutely, relying on the other to 'do the right thing' and leave the estate to the children.

(b)   *Option 2*: they can leave the estate to the other for life, and then to the children.

(c)   *Option 3*: they can leave assets equal to the available nil rate band to a discretionary trust created for the benefit of the surviving spouse, children and grandchildren with residue being left to the surviving spouse.

(d)   *Option 4*: this fourth option is really a variation on Option 3 in which the first to die leaves a residence or interest in a residence to the children.

## Option 1

They can leave everything to the other absolutely, relying on the other to 'do the right thing' and leave the estate to the children.

### Inheritance tax considerations

•   There will be no inheritance tax to pay on the first death as the spouse exemption will cover the entire estate.

- On the death of the survivor, there will be an inheritance tax charge on the combined assets. The survivor will benefit from a transferred nil rate band from the first to die. At 2019/20 rates this would cover £650,000. The assets of the estate may have increased and it is impossible to say whether or not the value of the nil rate band will have increased proportionally.

- The survivor will also benefit from an RNRB transferred from the first to die. In 2020/21 this will be £175,000 and thereafter it will rise in line with the Consumer Prices Index. If the assets have increased by the date of the second death to such an extent that the survivor's estate exceeds the taper threshold of £2 million, the double RNRB will be withdrawn at the rate of £1 for every £2 by which the threshold is exceeded.

- The survivor can, of course, make lifetime gifts to the extent that there are surplus assets. Such gifts are particularly worthwhile if the estate exceeds the RNRB taper threshold. Some of these gifts may be exempt from inheritance tax, for example, under the annual exemption (section 19 of the IHTA 1984) or the gifts in consideration of marriage exemption (section 22); those not exempt will cease to be cumulated after 7 years.

### Other considerations

- None of the combined capital is protected.

- The survivor may need care which is not funded by the state. None of the couple's assets are protected from fees.

- The survivor may disinherit the children, either deliberately, because of disagreement or inadvertently, because the spouse remarries, which revokes any existing will, and then dies intestate.

- The survivor may lose the capital in unwise investments.

## Option 2

They can leave the estate to the other for life, and then to the children.

### Inheritance tax considerations

- There will be no inheritance tax to pay on the first death as the spouse exemption will cover the entire estate.

- On the death of the survivor, there will be an inheritance tax charge on the combined assets. As in Option 1 the survivor will benefit from a transferred nil rate band and RNRB from the first to die. Again, the assets of the survivor's estate may have increased and may exceed the RNRB £2 million taper threshold in which case some or all of the RNRB will be lost.

- The survivor does not have immediate access to the capital to make lifetime gifts but this can be arranged. The terms of a trust usually include power for trustees to terminate the life interest in whole or in part. The trustees can use the power to accelerate the passing of capital to the children. Alternatively, the life tenant may surrender some or all of the life interest which will have the effect of advancing capital to the children. Transfers of capital from the life interest to the children will be transfers of value by the life tenant (potentially exempt if made as outright gifts). They will cease to be cumulated after 7 years.

- The terms of the trust usually give the trustees power to give capital to the life tenant in case of need. Such transfers have no inheritance tax implications as the life tenant is already deemed to own the capital for inheritance tax purposes.

## Other considerations

- The capital of the first to die is protected. Unless the trustees choose to advance all the capital to the life tenant, it is certain that property will pass under the terms of the trust to the children.

- Surviving spouses or civil partners may not be happy to have only a life interest in what they regard as their 'own' assets. It is not necessary, or advisable, to leave the whole of the estate of the first to die on life interest trusts. Personal chattels should always be excluded from the trust. Morva and Dan may decide to leave some of their assets to the other absolutely and only the balance on life interest trusts.

- It is possible for the survivor to be a trustee. This is reassuring as it means the survivor will retain some control over the assets; if appointing surviving spouses or civil partners as trustees, it is important to set out the extent to which they can exercise powers in their own favour.

## Option 3

They can leave assets equal to the available nil rate band to a discretionary trust created for the benefit of the surviving spouse, children and grandchildren, with the residue being left to the surviving spouse.

## Inheritance tax considerations

- There will be no inheritance tax to pay on the first death as the combination of nil rate band and spouse exemption will cover the entire estate.

- On the death of the survivor, there will be no transferred nil rate band available as this was used up on the first death. There will be transferred RNRB available (subject to the taper threshold) as the estate of the first to die will not have benefitted from the RNRB. The assets held in the trust are outside the estate of the survivor. They will only attract inheritance tax on anniversaries and exits to the extent that they exceed the nil rate band.

## Other considerations

- Some of the capital of the first to die is protected. Unless the trustees choose to appoint all the capital to the surviving spouse, there will be funds available for the children and grandchildren. The residue could also be protected if left to the surviving spouse as a life interest, as in Option 2.

- The survivor may not be happy to be one of a group of discretionary beneficiaries with no guarantee of receiving anything. However, it is only some of the estate of the first to die which is being left on discretionary trusts.

- As with Option 2, it is possible for the survivor to be a trustee; again, it is important to set out the extent to which he or she can exercise powers in his or her own favour.

- Capital and income can be made available to beneficiaries as required.

# Option 4

They may leave a residence or interest in a residence to the children and the residue to the survivor, either absolutely or on life interest trusts. This would use the RNRB of the first to die. The gift could be combined with a nil rate band discretionary trust as in Option 3.

## Inheritance tax considerations

- On the first death there will be no inheritance tax to pay on the residence, or share in the residence, to the extent that it is within the RNRB. The spouse exemption will cover the portion of the estate passing to the survivor.

- Leaving assets away from the survivor is useful in cases where the combined estates would exceed the taper threshold leading to loss of the combined RNRBs. As discussed under Option 1 and 2 above, the survivor can make lifetime gifts to reduce his or her estate but he or she may forget or lose capacity and be unable to make gifts.

## Other considerations

- Leaving an interest in the family's main residence to the children absolutely has the following drawbacks:
    - sharing the ownership of the matrimonial home between the survivor and the children is likely to lead to tensions and disagreements;
    - there is a risk that the home will have to be sold if one of the children is made bankrupt;
    - there may be problems if the house becomes unsuitable for the survivor. The value of their share may not be sufficient to allow them to purchase a suitable replacement property and the children may not be willing to allow their share of the sale proceeds to roll over into the replacement;
    - the children will acquire their share of the property at market value at the date of the first death. When they eventually dispose of the property, there may be a significant increase in value triggering a charge to capital gains tax;
    - giving the children an interest in the residence on first death is likely to be disadvantageous if they buy their own homes later. For stamp duty land tax they cannot benefit from any reduced rate otherwise available to 'first time buyers'; on the contrary, they will be liable to higher rate by buying what counts as a 'second home'.

- This option is more likely to appeal if the family has a second home or a former residence which is now let out as an investment.

- Where the family has only one residence but the first to die wants to leave an interest to the children, it is likely to be more satisfactory if the children are left an immediate post-death interest in the residence with a discretionary power for the trustees to appoint capital to them.

There is no 'best buy' and Morva and Dan may decide on a mixture. For example, they might leave personal chattels to the other absolutely, a nil rate band discretionary trust and the residue to the surviving spouse for life, with wide powers for the trustees to deal with capital.

## Case study B
## The remarrying widower – Ted

Ted was married to Dora who died leaving him everything. He is remarrying Wilma, a widow whose husband, Harry, died leaving her everything. Ted is planning to make a will and although he has children, he is minded to leave everything to Wilma.

Ted needs to rethink or the benefit of his transferred nil rate band and RNRB will be wasted.

Ted has a double nil rate band and RNRB (his own and Dora's) but he cannot pass any of them on to Wilma as no one can inherit more than one full nil rate band or RNRB. She already has the benefit of a transferred nil rate band and RNRB from Harry.

So far as the nil rate band is concerned, Ted should either leave assets to his children outright or, more likely, create a discretionary trust to which he transfers assets to the value of his enhanced nil rate band.

This will allow £650,000 (at current rates) to be transferred to the trust without any initial payment of inheritance tax.

However, once the trust is up and running, it has only the benefit of Ted's own nil rate band and so there will be 10-year anniversary charges and exit charges.

So far as the RNRB is concerned, his double RNRB will be wasted unless he leaves a residence or interest in a residence to his children. This has the disadvantages discussed in Option 4 of Case Study 1.

# Case study C
# Cohabitees – Catherine and Carl

Cohabitees suffer serious inheritance tax disadvantages when compared to married couples and civil partners:

(a)    There is no exemption from inheritance tax under section 18 of the IHTA 1984 where one cohabitee leaves property to the other. The exemption is limited to spouses and civil partners.

(b)    Unused nil rate band and RNRB of the first to die cannot be transferred to the survivor.

(c)    Children of one cohabitee are not step-children of the other so are not lineal descendants for the purposes of the RNRB.

From an inheritance tax point of view, it is clearly beneficial to formalise a cohabitation relationship.

Catherine and Carl are in their 70s and are happily cohabiting. They have each been married before (both divorced) and have children from their previous marriages. They are adamant that they do not wish to marry.

They have bought a house as beneficial tenants in common. Their respective estates are £1 million including their share of the house (£500,000 each).

They want to leave their half of the house to the other for life, remainder to their own children. Each will leave their other assets to their own children.

Let us assume that Catherine dies first, followed a year later by Carl.

## On Catherine's death

•    The assets passing immediately to Catherine's children will be tax free to the extent that they fall within her nil rate band. Any unused nil rate band cannot be passed to Carl as he is not married to her.

•    Catherine's RNRB is wasted. She has not left her interest in the residence to her children; she has left it to Carl. Like the ordinary nil rate band, her unused RNRB cannot be transferred to Carl.

## On Carl's death

•    The whole value of the home is included in Carl's estate for inheritance tax purposes. He has one nil rate band and one RNRB available.

- His RNRB will be capped at the value of his half of the residence. Where a person dies with an interest in possession in a residence held in trust, RNRB can only be set against the value of the trust property if lineal descendants of the beneficiary with an interest in possession are entitled to the residence held in trust. Because Catherine and Carl are not married, Catherine's children are not Carl's step-children and so are not lineal descendants of Carl. Whether Carl's estate benefits from a full RNRB therefore depends on the value of his half of the house.

## Alternatives

Catherine could leave her half of the family home:

(a)   *On discretionary trusts*: the value would not be included in Carl's inheritance tax estate (but there are likely to be anniversary and exit charges).

(b)   *To her children absolutely or on immediate post-death interest trusts*: this is unlikely to be popular with Carl. All the disadvantages of shared ownership discussed in Case Study A, Option 4 will arise.

(c)   *To her children absolutely with an option for Carl to purchase*: depending on family circumstances the option could be at an under value.

# Index

*References are to page numbers.*